OLD TESTAMENT MESSAGE

A Biblical-Theological Commentary

Carroll Stuhlmueller, C.P. and Martin McNamara, M.S.C.

EDITORS

Old Testament Message, Volume 6

1 - 2 SAMUEL, 1 - 2 KINGS

with an
Excursus on Davidic Dynasty
and
Holy City Zion

Charles Conroy, M.S.C.

 Michael Glazier, Inc.
Wilmington, Delaware

First published in 1983 by: MICHAEL GLAZIER, INC., 1723 Delaware Avenue, Wilmington, Delaware 19806
Distributed outside U.S., Canada & Philippines by: GILL & MACMILLAN, LTD., Goldenbridge, Inchicore, Dublin 8 Ireland

Library of Congress Catalog Card Number: 83-80109
International Standard Book Number
   Old Testament Message series: 0-89453-235-9
   SAMUEL - KINGS
      0-89453-241-3 (Michael Glazier, Inc.)
      7171-1170-9 (Gill & MacMillan, Ltd.)

Cover design by Lillian Brulc
Typography by Richard Reinsmith
Printed in the United States of America

Contents

The Books of Samuel: Commentary

The Book of Kings: Commentary

Editors' Preface

Old Testament Message brings into our life and religion today the ancient word of God to Israel. This word, according to the book of the prophet Isaiah, had soaked the earth like "rain and snow coming gently down from heaven" and had returned to God fruitfully in all forms of human life (Isa 55:10). The authors of this series remain true to this ancient Israelite heritage and draw us into the home, the temple and the marketplace of God's chosen people. Although they rely upon the tools of modern scholarship to uncover the distant places and culture of the biblical world, yet they also refocus these insights in a language clear and understandable for any interested reader today. They enable us, even if this be our first acquaintance with the Old Testament, to become sister and brother, or at least good neighbor, to our religious ancestors. In this way we begin to hear God's word ever more forcefully in our own times and across our world, within our prayer and worship, in our secular needs and perplexing problems.

Because life is complex and our world includes, at times in a single large city, vastly different styles of living, we have much to learn from the Israelite Scriptures. The Old Testament spans forty-six biblical books and almost nineteen hundred years of life. It extends through desert, agricultural and urban ways of human existence. The literary style embraces a world of literature and human emotions. Its history began with Moses and the birth-pangs of a new people, it came of age politically and economically under David and Solomon, it reeled under the fiery threats of prophets like Amos and Jeremiah. The people despaired and yet were re-created with new hope during the Babylonian exile. Later reconstruction in the homeland and then the trauma of apocalyptic movements prepared for the revelation of "the mystery hidden for ages in God who created all things" (Eph 3:9).

While the Old Testament telescopes twelve to nineteen hundred years of human existence within the small country of Israel, any single moment of time today witnesses to the reenactment of this entire history across the wide expanse of planet earth. Each verse of the Old Testament is being relived somewhere in our world today. We need, therefore, the *entire* Old Testament and all twenty-three volumes of this new set, in order to be totally a "Bible person" within today's widely diverse society.

The subtitle of this series—"A Biblical-Theological Commentary"—clarifies what these twenty-three volumes intend to do.

Their *purpose* is theological: to feel the pulse of God's word for its *religious* impact and direction.

Their *method* is biblical: to establish the scriptural word firmly within the life and culture of ancient Israel.

Their *style* is commentary: not to explain verse by verse but to follow a presentation of the message that is easily understandable to any serious reader, even if this person is untrained in ancient history and biblical languages.

Old Testament Message—like its predecessor, *New Testament Message*—is aimed at the entire English-speaking world and so is a collaborative effort of an international team. The twenty-one contributors are women and men drawn from North America, Ireland, Britain and Australia. They are scholars who have published in scientific journals, but they have been chosen equally as well for their proven ability to communicate on a popular level. This twenty-three book set comes from Roman Catholic writers, yet, like the Bible itself, it reaches beyond interpretations restricted to an individual church and so enables men and women rooted in biblical faith to unite and so to appreciate their own traditions more fully and more adequately.

Most of all, through the word of God, we seek the blessedness and joy of those
who walk in the law of the Lord!...
who seek God with their whole heart (Ps. 119:1-2).

Carroll Stuhlmueller, C.P.   Martin McNamara, M.S.C.

FOREWORD

The amount of material contained in the Books of Samuel and Kings has made it quite impossible to quote the entire biblical text in the present volume. Some selected chapters (nineteen in all) have been quoted in full to satisfy the norms of the series; the commentary, however, covers all the one hundred and two biblical chapters.

For the most part, then, readers will have to use their own bibles side-by-side with the commentary. As in the other volumes of the series, the translation followed here is that of the Revised Standard Version, and it is useful to note that its system of verse numbering differs slightly in a few chapters (indicated below in the respective section headings) from that found in some other English bibles. However this should cause little trouble in the present case to readers who use a translation other than the RSV.

Finally it hardly needs saying that a commentary such as this owes a great deal to the work of many scholars in the international world of OT studies. Since the format of the series does not permit individual acknowledgement of sources, all that can be done here is to make grateful mention of the debt in general.

Charles Conroy, M.S.C.

INTRODUCTION TO SAMUEL AND KINGS

The first step towards a deeper understanding of Samuel and Kings is the realization that they are not simply "historical books". It is true, of course, that Samuel and Kings contain much material that can be used by the historian of ancient Israel, but their primary purpose is not to serve as a source-book for the historian. Samuel and Kings are essentially theological works in narrative form; they present a complex theological interpretation of the monarchical period in Israel's history. What is more, they originally formed part of a extensive theological synthesis, known as the Deuteronomistic history, which included the Books of Deuteronomy, Joshua, and Judges, as well as Samuel and Kings. The present commentary, then, will try to stress the theological dimension of the texts, while not forgetting that the theology comes to us, for the most part, in and through the narrative form. Readers who wish to examine in greater detail the specifically historical questions that are raised by Samuel and Kings will find ample material in the various Histories of Israel mentioned in the reading list at the end of the volume.

Two introductory topics will be discussed briefly here: first, a summary account of the sources underlying Samuel and Kings, and of the redactional work that produced the final form of the text; secondly, an outline of some important theological themes that provide a key for the reading of these books.

I. From Separate Traditions to Final Text

1. SOURCE-MATERIAL

The Books of Samuel and Kings reached their final form after several centuries of literary growth, whose history is still obscure in many respects. All that can be done here is to indicate some positions supported by many scholars.

a)   With regard to 1 and 2 Samuel (and 1 Kgs 1-2): It is widely accepted that three smaller literary compositions have been incorporated here. First, the Ark Narrative which is found now (according to the more common opinion) in 1 Sam 4-6 and 2 Sam 6. Then, the Story of David's Rise to the Throne, generally seen as comprising 1 Sam 16 — 2 Sam 5. Finally, the so-called Succession Narrative which begins at 2 Sam 10 (or possibly earlier), continues up to 2 Sam 20, and concludes with the accession of Solomon in 1 Kgs 1-2. Further discussion on these three works will be found in the special introductions in the body of the commentary. It can be noted too that it is often possible to detect the existence of separate traditions that have gone into the making of those three compositions.

b)   With regard to 1 Kgs 3 to 2 Kgs 25: Here the text itself mentions some of the sources used by the compilers and editors: the Acts of Solomon (1 Kgs 11:41), which we may presume to have provided the basis for much of 1 Kgs 3-11; the Acts of the Kings of Judah, and the Acts of the Kings of Israel, which are mentioned many times after 1 Kgs 12. It is likely that much of the political, military, and cultic material concerning the two kingdoms comes ultimately from these two works which may have been combined into a synchronic presentation of the various reigns of Israel and

Judah down to the fall of Samaria in 722 B.C. As well as that, mention must be made of a large number of prophetic traditions, in particular the Elijah cycle (1 Kgs 17-19; 21; 2 Kgs 1) and the Elisha cycle (comprising much of 2 Kgs 2-13).

2. COMPOSITION AND REDACTION

The various source-materials mentioned above (and others besides) were combined, edited, updated, and at times drastically reinterpreted before the text as we have it now finally emerged. It is probable that this process took place in several stages; much of 1 Samuel, for instance, appears to show the signs of an intermediate level of redaction by a prophetically influenced author. There is still much uncertainty, however, about such intermediate redactional levels, so it will be more useful to pass on directly to the final form of the text.

The Books of Samuel and Kings were produced, practically as we know them now, shortly after 561 B.C., the date of the release of King Jehoiachin of Judah from his Babylonian imprisonment (2 Kgs 25:27-30). The authors responsible for this edition (together with the practically final form of Deuteronomy, Joshua, and Judges) are known as the Deuteronomists because of the strong theological influence exercised on them by the central themes of Deuteronomy. Within Samuel and Kings the Deuteronomistic interpretation of Israel's history under the monarchy is seen at its clearest in a number of key passages such as 1 Sam 12, 1 Kgs 8, and 2 Kgs 17, large sections of which are original Deuteronomistic compositions, but it is also conveyed by a considerable number of shorter comments scattered throughout the text as well as by the selection and arrangement of the material that had reached the Deuteronomistic editors from earlier stages of composition or occasionally as independent traditions.

Opinions differ as to the precise nature of the Deuteronomistic edition of Samuel and Kings. The simplest theory sees it as essentially the work of one individual who, about 550 B.C., collected and arranged most of the material, adding where appropriate his own theological comments; a few additions would have been made later by various hands. A second theory prefers to envisage a double redaction of the Deuteronomistic history: the first edition, containing the bulk of the material, was produced during the reign of King Josiah of Judah (ca. 639-609) and expressed the prevailing mood of national optimism (cf. 2 Kgs 22-23); the second edition was published during the Exile (around 550 B.C.) and had a far more sombre outlook on Israel's past and future. Finally, a third theory distinguishes three levels of Deuteronomistic redaction: the first, the Deuteronomistic history proper, was composed in the early part of the exilic period and presented a theological interpretation of Israel's history up to the Exile; a prophetic Deuteronomistic redaction followed some years later, incorporating many prophetic traditions and insisting on the recurrence throughout Israel's history of patterns of prophetic prediction and fulfilment; the third redaction, the nomistic or law-centered Deuteronomist, stressed the supreme importance of obedience to the law of Yahweh written in the book of the law (that is, Deuteronomy). Since discussion among scholars still continues about these theories, the present commentary will usually speak rather vaguely of "the Deuteronomists" without intending to opt for one or other of the theories.

In any case, all agree that the final Deuteronomistic edition of Samuel and Kings was produced during the Exile and was meant for readers who had experienced the calamities of the fall of Jerusalem and the destruction of the Temple. This setting is of crucial importance when one wishes to examine the theological message of these Books.

II. Some Important Theological Themes in Samuel and Kings

1. CULTIC CENTRALIZATION

The demand, stated vigorously in Deut 12, that Yahweh be worshipped with sacrifices only in the place that he himself chose for that purpose, is applied throughout the Book of Kings as the basic criterion for judging the various kings of Israel and Judah. The chosen place is the Jerusalem Temple; the account of its construction and dedication by Solomon (1 Kgs 5-8) provides the Deuteronomists with the occasion to stress the centrality of this Temple in the whole history of Yahweh's dealings with Israel (1 Kgs 6:1), and to insert one of their main theological passages in the form of Solomon's prayer (8:14-61). In point of fact it was only several centuries after Solomon's time, in the reign of King Josiah (639-609) that the Jerusalem Temple was officially recognized as the only legitimate place for sacrificial worship. Previously the many local sanctuaries throughout the land (referred to often in Kings as "the high places") were accepted as genuine Yahwistic cultic centres in principle, though the danger of syncretistic contamination with Canaanite fertility rites was always present. The Deuteronomistic insistence on the cultic legitimacy of Jerusalem alone can be seen as a way of bringing the whole area of sacrificial worship more explicitly under the dominion of Yahweh's word.

2. ATTITUDE TOWARDS THE MONARCHY

The fact, mentioned above, that the Deuteronomists judge the religious fidelity of the kings by their behaviour in the matter of sacrificial worship, already implies a relativizing of political power. The kings are not autonomous despots who might manipulate religion as a convenient instrument of their policies, but they are subject to the supreme judgement of the word of the Lord as found in the book of the law (see the programmatic formulation concerning the kings in Deut 17:14-20). The Deuteronomists go further than this, however, in that they attribute to the kings the main responsibility for the disasters that befell the northern kingdom in 722 B.C. (the fall of Samaria) and the southern kingdom in 587/6 B.C. (the fall of Jerusalem). It is not surprising that the Deuteronomistic attitude has at times been decribed as thoroughly anti-monarchical. Closer study of the text, however, shows that a more nuanced statement is called for in this question. Just two observations can be made here. In the chapters that present the origin of the monarchy (1 Sam 8-12) the Deuteronomistic editors left untouched several passages that express quite a positive attitude to the emergence of Saul as King (as will be seen in the commentary). Furthermore, the importance of Nathan's oracle (2 Sam 7) in the whole structure of the Deuteronomistic history, together with the idealized portrait of David found in several texts (e.g. 1 Kgs 3:3; 9:4; 11:4; 2 Kgs 18:3; 22:2), shows that one cannot accurately describe the Deuteronomistic attitude as anti-monarchical in principle.

Though one may have to consider the possibility that the different Deuteronomistic redactors had different attitudes towards the monarchy, the overall impression given by Samuel and Kings is that the Lord's people could have prospered under the monarchy if only the supremely important factor of obedience to the Lord's word, above all in cultic matters, had been accepted by the kings as their rule of life. The attitude that emerges from the final form of the text can be described as a combination of critique directed at the specific infidelities of individual kings, and of acceptance of the monarchical institution represented by the Davidic dynasty as the bearer of the Lord's word of promise. The underlying conviction is that forms of government and the exercise of power stand under Yahweh's word, which is a word of future-creating promise but also (when necessary) a word of dire judgement.

3. THE WORD OF GOD PROCLAIMED IN HISTORY BY THE PROPHETS

The primacy of the Lord's word, already evident in the preceding themes, is stressed still more by the frequent occurrence of a narrative pattern consisting of a prophetic prediction made in the Lord's name and its fulfilment in the immediate or distant future. Some examples: the removal of the family of Eli from the priestly office (1 Sam 2:27-36 and 1 Kgs 2:26-27); the building of the Temple by Solomon (2 Sam 7:13 and 1 Kgs 8:20); the destruction of the unlawful sanctuary at Bethel (1 Kgs 13:2 and 2 Kgs 23:15-16); the rebuilding of Jericho (Josh 6:26 and 1 Kgs 16:34); the death of Queen Jezebel (1 Kgs 21:23 and 2 Kgs 9:36); the devastation of Judah by the Babylonians and their allies (2 Kgs 21:10-15 and 24:2). These texts, and others besides, show the prophets as heralds of the Lord of history whose all-powerful word moves irresistibly towards its fulfilment. History is neither a matter of chance nor the outcome of the inevitable dialectic of immanent processes; on the contrary, for the Deuteronomists it stands under the sway of Yahweh's word.

4. THE WORD OF GOD WRITTEN IN THE BOOK OF THE LAW

The official authority given to the Deuteronomic law during Josiah's reign (see the comment on 2 Kgs 22-23) marks a major theological change in Israel's conception of the word of God. Now the word is understood as taking written form, and Israel is on its way to becoming a people of the Book. The words of this book of the law become the concrete norm for Israel's conduct because they are the concrete expression of the primacy of the Lord's authoritative word. Many Deuteronomistic passages in Samuel and Kings refer to this norm in a typical rhetorical style that abounds in the use of synonyms for the law, in repetitions, and in clauses of motivation (e.g. 1 Kgs 2:2-4; 9:4-9; 11:33-38; 2 Kgs 17:34b-40; 21:7-9). It could even be said that, for all the emphasis laid by the Deuteronomists on the Jerusa-

lem Temple, it is surpassed as the central symbol of Yahweh's lordship by the book of the law. It was the finding of
this book within the Temple itself that is shown as setting in
motion the religious reform of King Josiah (2 Kgs 22:8ff),
and while the Temple was looted and burned by the Babylonians in 587/6 B.C. the book of the law survived and became
the vital centre of the people's hope (Deut 30:1-10). (Other
aspects of the Deuteronomists' outlook on the future are
discussed in the comment on 2 Kgs 25:27-30.)

THE BOOKS OF SAMUEL: COMMENTARY

I. 1 Sam 1:1 — 4:1a
The Call of Samuel and the Rejection of Eli's Family

While this division could be termed the Infancy Narrative of Samuel, it also contains elements that look far ahead to later texts in the Books of Samuel and Kings. The narrative moves from the restricted horizons of an ordinary Israelite family and its domestic problems to the wide perspectives of Samuel's prophetic mission to Israel. It is an unmistakably theological narrative, for the decisive factors that bring about the changes of fortune are shown to be (1) Yahweh's gracious choice and call (1:1 — 2:11; 3:1 — 4:1a), and (2) his judgement on the cultic offences of Eli's sons (2:12-36). Even in the latter part, however, we find words of promise (2:35) and examples of fidelity (2:18-21, 26), which relieve the gloom of the surrounding verses. The themes of Yahweh's gracious choice and motivated rejection are fundamental in Samuel and Kings, and the reader's attention is drawn to this duality right from the start. The dominant note in these opening chapters, however, is one of divine favour, which we find associated with prophet (chap. 3), priest (2:35), and king (2:10, 35).

A. 1:1-20
THE BIRTH OF SAMUEL

1. *Comment.* The section begins by introducing the personages, Elkanah and his two wives (vv 1-2a); one can note that there was no prohibition of polygamy in that period. Tension is set up by the contrast between Peninnah's motherhood and Hannah's infertility (v 2b). The action takes place in the sanctuary of Shiloh (v 3). Situated in the territory of Ephraim, some 20 miles north of Jerusalem, this was one of the more important places of worship in premonarchical Israel. The ark of God was the most honoured cultic symbol there (cf. 3:3 with the comment), and the divine title "Lord of hosts" (1:3, 11) was especially associated with it. This title (sometimes just transliterated in English as Yahweh Sabaoth) is variously explained: the "hosts" may refer to the armies of Israel, or else to the heavenly hosts (the stars or, in later OT times, the angels); an idiomatic plural of intensification equivalent to "most powerful (Lord)" is a further possibility.

The conflict mounts in vv 4-8 with Peninnah's taunts and Hannah's depression (cf. Gen 16:1-6; 30:1-6). Hannah's prayer and vow made from the depths of her distress (vv 9-11) constitute the turning-point of the story. Her promise that no razor shall touch the head of her child (v 11), together with her assurance to the priest Eli that she has not taken wine or strong drink (v 15), shows that Samuel is presented here as a Nazirite (cf. Judg 13:3-7 for the case of Samson). Originally the Nazirites institution was a sacral state of dedication to Yahweh for a particular mission or service; in later times it became more a matter of temporary personal devotion whose details were regulated by law (cf. Num 6; Acts 18:18).

Though Eli's misunderstanding (vv 12-16) delays the climax, it has the effect of adding a priestly prayer to Hannah's own. The divine answer to their prayers comes with the birth of the long desired child who is named Samuel (vv 19-20).

2. *Significance* It is not uncommon in the Bible that the future greatness of a person is shown to have been foreshadowed in the unusual circumstances of his birth from a mother who is old (Gen 18 and 21: Isaac) or barren (Judg 13: Samson). The touching story of 1 Sam 1:1-20 is not told, then, primarily for its emotional appeal but rather to signal to the reader that this child will play an important part in the divine drama of history. Samuel's very existence is a living proof of Yahweh's gracious answer to the heartfelt prayer of a woman in anguish and distress; his mission will be to relieve the distress of an entire people. The similarities to the story of Samson's birth (Judg 13) prepare the reader for the presentation of Samuel as the last and greatest of Israel's judges or deliverers (cf. 1 Sam 7) before the change to the monarchical form of government.

B. 1:21 — 2:11
THE DEDICATION OF SAMUEL: HANNAH'S THANKSGIVING

1. *Comment.* The fulfilment of Hannah's vow (v 11) is now reported (1:21-28 and 2:11). Her husband agrees that she wait until the child is weaned (this could take up to three years: cf. 2 Macc 7:27) before bringing him to Shiloh (vv 21-23). When the time arrives, they go to the Lord's house at Shiloh and make their ritual offerings (the "ephah" mentioned in v 24 is a measure of dry capacity). Having presented the young boy Samuel to Eli for life-long service of the Lord, Hannah returns home with her husband (vv 24-28 and 2:11). The narrative report has been interrupted here by the later insertion of Hannah's prayer of thanksgiving (2:1-10). While the tone of exultant praise fits Hannah's situation reasonably well, as does the reference to the barren woman who has borne children (v 5), it is clear from the anachronistic mention of the king (v 10) that the poem was originally a royal psalm independent of its present context.

2. *Significance.* The unselfish fidelity shown by Hannah and Elkanah in fulfilling their vow and their care about the ritual customs of worship (vv 24-25) form a bright contrast

to the next section, where we read of the cultic abuses committed by Eli's own sons (2:12ff). Hannah's psalm, which has influenced the Magnificat (Lk 1:46-55) in several places, has an importance that goes beyond its immediate literary context. The reference to the anointed king (2:10) already brings to the reader's notice the institution of the monarchy in Israel, with which Samuel will be closely connected (chaps 8-12). There is a significant stress on the theme of reversal of fortune in vv 4-8. Israel's God kills and gives life, brings low and also raises up. As we read on through the later history of the monarchy, in which failures and disasters become ever more prominent, these words of Hannah's psalm should not be forgotten. Even the depths of Sheol, the underworld (v 6), are subject to Yahweh's life-giving intervention, if he so wills. Unrelieved pessimism and muted resignation cannot be the final response to the story of Israel's weakness.

C.   2:12 — 26
CONTRAST BETWEEN ELI'S SONS AND SAMUEL

1.   *Comment.*   The contrast is expressed in two phases: vv 12-17/18-21, and vv 22-25/26. In the first unit concerning Eli's sons (vv 12-17) we find them selfishly abusing their position of authority at Shiloh. The custom was that the priests could take for themselves a portion of the meat being prepared for the sacrificial meal by dipping a fork at random into the pot and being satisfied with whatever piece they got in that way. Eli's sons, however, demanded under threat of violence that they be given the raw meat with the fat, which was the part that should have been burnt in sacrifice (vv 13ff). Their disrespect towards the Lord and abuse of their position with regard to the worshippers brought the whole sanctuary of Shiloh into disrepute.

Samuel, on the other hand, is presented in a most sympathetic light (vv 18-21). The "linen ephod" (v 18) was a short garment with cultic associations (cf. 2 Sam 6:14); the word has other senses too, as will be seen at v 28 below. The Lord is not to be outdone in generosity: Hannah gives birth to five more children in place of the one she had dedicated to the Lord (vv 20-21).

The scene shifts back to Eli's sons in vv 22-25. The note about their sexual misbehaviour (v 22b), missing in some textual witnesses, may be a late post-exilic addition as is suggested by the verbal contacts with Exod 38:8 (Priestly tradition, post-exilic). Eli rebukes his sons but they refuse to give heed to his words. Verse 25b adds "for it was the will of the Lord to slay them," an expression that attributes directly to God's will what we would rather describe in terms of human responsibility; what is meant is that the wilful perseverance in wrongdoing of Eli's sons was the real and just cause of their death recounted at 4:11 (cf. 2 Sam 17:14).

The section concludes with a note about Samuel's growth in age and favour with God and the whole people (v 26: cf. Lk 2:52).

2. *Significance.* As Yahweh's blessing granted to Samuel from the very beginning becomes more and more manifest in the boy's life, the doom of Eli's family becomes correspondingly clearer. This motif of descent/ascent will be seen again in the case of Saul and David. Cultic abuses bring about the Lord's decree of rejection; the fate of Eli's sons is paradigmatic for the future course of the kings of Israel and Judah as judged by the Deuteronomists.

D. 2:27-36
ORACLE ABOUT A CHANGE OF PRIESTHOOD

1. *Comment.* This complex oracle of judgement and promise is spoken by an unidentified "man of God" (v 27). The first part (vv 27b-29) is an accusation that refers to the preceding section; its force is heightened by an account of Yahweh's favour to Eli's ancestors right from the time of the Egyptian sojourn. In this connection it is interesting to note that the names borne by Eli's sons, Hophni and Phinehas (1:3; 2:34), are of Egyptian origin. The ancestors of Eli (v 27) are probably to be taken as the tribe of Levi in general. At v 28 the RSV phrase "to wear an ephod" would refer to a

priestly garment (as at v 18); however the verb could also mean "to carry", and in this case there would be a reference to the ephod as a cultic instrument used in connection with the seeking of oracles (cf. 23:6, 9-12). Also in v 28 it can be noted that the term rendered by the RSV as "offerings by fire" more probably means simply "food-offerings."

The second part of the oracle (vv 30-36) consists of Yahweh's decree. The initial "therefore" (v 30) shows the just proportion between the offence and the punishment, which is then announced in detail in vv 30-34: the line of Eli will be dishonoured and will suffer grievous distress, though it will not be wiped out completely; the two sinful sons will die on the same day. A note of promise is added in vv 35-36: Yahweh will raise up a faithful priest, and thanks to him and his line some of Eli's descendants will survive. Though the immediate context might suggest that the "faithful priest" is Samuel himself, and there are texts where Samuel appears as exercising priestly functions (7:9; 9:13; 10:8), it is more likely that v 35 looks ahead to the Zadokite priestly line of Jerusalem (cf. 2 Sam 8:17 and comment). In King Josiah's time (late seventh century) the various local sanctuaries were suppressed and their Levitical priests were admitted as inferior ministers to the service of the Jerusalem Temple (cf. 2 Kgs 23:8-9), where the Zadokite priestly line held sway. This probably explains the statements in v 36. The "anointed" of the Lord in v 35b refers to the Davidic king, and the association of king and Temple here foreshadows the key text of 2 Sam 7.

2. *Significance.*   This section has an important set of prospective functions within Samuel and Kings. It announces the death of Eli's sons (v 34: cf. chap. 4), but that is just the first of the disasters to befall his descendants. Reference to these can be found in 1 Sam 22 (the massacre of the Elide priests of Nob) and finally in 1 Kgs 2 where the last Elide priest, Abiathar, is deposed and the priestly office in Jerusalem falls to Zadok alone. These wide-ranging references point to the hand of a Deuteronomistic redactor here, at least in vv 34-36, if not throughout the oracle.

E. 3:1 — 4:1a
SAMUEL'S PROPHETIC INITIATION

1. *Comment.* The opening note about the rarity of prophetic oracles and visions at that time (v 1) prepares for the theme of the following verses. The scene is set in vv 2-3: night has fallen, the aged and half-blind Eli has gone to take his rest outside the main room of the sanctuary, while the boy Samuel sleeps inside close by the ark of God. The ark was a portable wooden chest, which may have had images of cherubim (mythological creatures, part-animal, part-human in form) on its lid (cf. 4:4). While older texts prefer the designation "ark of God," texts of the Deuteronomic school tend to use "ark of the covenant", a name that expressed the idea that the box contained the two tables of the Law given to Moses on Mount Horeb or Sinai (cf. Deut 10:1-5; 1 Kgs 8:9). What the ark actually contained, if anything, is not known for certain, however, and it could well be that it was regarded in the early period mainly as the throne or footstool of the invisible Lord of hosts whose active presence it symbolized in a quasi-sacramental way (cf. Num 10:35-36: a text which suggests that the ark's history may extend back into the period of the desert wanderings of Israelite groups).

The Lord's call to Samuel is then narrated: three unsuccessful attempts (vv 4-5, 6-7, 8-9) build up the suspense, which is broken at last by the successful communication (vv 10-14) where Samuel is instructed to convey to Eli a divine announcement of judgement. At first Samuel hesitates to tell Eli the terrible news but his resistance is overcome by Eli's noble insistence (vv 15-18). One can note the use of a conventional formula of imprecation in v 17: "May God do so to you and more also," where the nature of the divine punitive action was left unspecified or perhaps was indicated by a gesture. The announcement of judgement (vv 11-14) is quite similar in its main lines to that of 2:30ff and may in fact have been reworked by Deuteronomistic redactors.

The concluding notes of 3:19-21, to which 4:1a can be

added (though the text is uncertain here), summarize the point of the story and stress the national dimension of Samuel's prophetic role. The phrase "from Dan to Beersheba" (v 20) — important cultic centres at the northern and southern extremities of Israelite territory — is a strong way of saying "the whole of Israel".

2. *Significance.* There is a curious irony in the fact that the priest Eli, who enables Samuel to recognize the strange voice as that of the Lord, is also the addressee of the divine oracle of condemnation. It is impossible not to admire the calm resignation with which he accepts the sentence: "It is the Lord: let him do what seems good to him" (v 18: cf. Job 1:21; 2:10). Eli's attitude here could well have served as a model for later generations of Israelites who were to hear Yahweh's word of judgement from his prophets. To bow humbly beneath the hand of the Lord was undoubtedly one of the responses that the Deuteronomists wished to elicit from their readers after the fall of Jerusalem.

Samuel's public ministry begins at this point, though we do not hear of him again until chap. 7. The prophet who has just announced the Lord's sentence on the chief priestly family of Israel will then be shown as Israel's deliverer and will play an important part in the beginnings of the monarchy. The confrontation of prophets with priests and kings will be a recurrent feature in the life of Israel.

II.   1 Sam 4:1b — 7:1
The Defeat of Israel; The Triumph of The Ark of God

The protagonist in this division is no human person but the ark of God, the powerful symbol of Yahweh's sovereignly free lordship. The Israelites bring the ark to the battlefield but it does not magically guarantee their victory; their army is routed and the ark captured by the Philistines (chap. 4). It was commonly held in the ancient Near East that victory over an enemy implied victory over the enemy's god, but the Philistines painfully discover that this does not

apply here (chap. 5). The victors are obliged to acknowledge
their defeat and send the captured ark back with rich compensatory offerings (chap. 6). Even in Israelite territory,
however, the ark does not lose its awesome power, for an act
of disrespect at Beth-shemesh is punished severely (6:19).
The ark is not merely a national symbol; it stands for the
holy power of Yahweh which transcends national
boundaries.

Apart from a text-critically dubious mention at 1 Sam
14:18, the ark does not appear again until 2 Sam 6 where we
read of its transfer by David from Baale-judah (an alternative name for Kiriath-jearim: 1 Sam 6:21f) to Jerusalem.
The movements of the ark find their proper conclusion here,
and it is not surprising that most scholars take 1 Sam 4:1b
—7:1 and 2 Sam 6 to have once constituted an independent
Ark Story. This literary unit, it is held, was formed and
transmitted by the priests in charge of the ark sanctuary at
Jerusalem in David's time, and served as the cultic narrative
about the foundation of that sanctuary. Though various
points of this literary hypothesis have been questioned
recently (some would prefer to see 2 Sam 6 as separate from
the rest, others note the contacts between 1 Sam 4 and what
precedes), it is clear in any case that there are important
thematic connections between 1 Sam 4:1b — 7:1 and 2 Sam
6 in the present form of the text. In other words, King David
and Zion-Jerusalem are already on the horizon as our text
moves to and fro across the borders of Philistia and Israel.

Nor is that all. When these chapters are read in the light of
the shattering experience of the destruction of Jerusalem's
Temple in 587/6 and the Exile, they can be seen as offering
meaning and hope for those dark years. The loss of the most
important cultic symbol and the death of the nation's religious and civil leaders need not mean that Israel has no
future. The end of an era is not necessarily the end of
Yahweh's gracious dealings with Israel. Even in the depths
of exile the Lord who "kills and brings to life" (1 Sam 2:6)
can show his sovereign power and bring his people back to
Jerusalem. Ezekiel's theme of the glory of Yahweh (Ezek

1-3; 8-11; 43:1-5: cf. 1 Sam 4:21-22) and Second Isaiah's theme of the triumphant homeward procession of the exiles to Jerusalem (Isa 40-55) can be seen foreshadowed in the Ark Story. There is a difference, of course: what the Ark Story, read in the context of the Deuteronomistic history, implies as a possibility, the exilic prophets proclaim as a reality soon to be accomplished.

A.   4:1b-22
THE ARK OF GOD IS CAPTURED BY THE PHILISTINES

4   Now Israel went out to battle against the Philistines; they encamped at Ebenezer and the Philistines encamped at Aphek. ²The Philistines drew up in line against Israel, and when the battle spread, Israel was defeated by the Philistines, who slew about four thousand men on the field of battle. ³And when the troops came to the camp, the elders of Israel said, "Why has the Lord put us to rout today before the Philistines? Let us bring the ark of the covenant of the Lord here from Shiloh, that he may come among us and save us from the power of our enemies." ⁴So the people sent to Shiloh, and brought from there the ark of the covenant of the Lord of hosts, who is enthroned on the cherubim; and the two sons of Eli, Hophni and Phinehas, were there with the ark of the covenant of God.

5 When the Ark of the covenant of the Lord came into the camp, all Israel gave a mighty shout, so that the earth resounded. ⁶And when the Philistines heard the noise of the shouting, they said, "What does this great shouting in the camp of the Hebrews mean?" And when they learned that the ark of the Lord had come to the camp, ⁷the Philistines were afraid; for they said, "A god has come into the camp." And they said, "Woe to us! For nothing like this has happened before. ⁸Woe to us! Who can deliver us from the power of these mighty gods? These are the gods who smote the Egyptians with every sort of

plague in the wilderness. [9]Take courage, and acquit yourselves like men, O Philistines, lest you become slaves to the Hebrews as they have been to you; acquit yourselves like men and fight."

10 So the Philistines fought, and Israel was defeated, and they fled, every man to his home; and there was a very great slaughter, for there fell of Israel thirty thousand foot soldiers. [11]And the ark of God was captured; and the two sons of Eli, Hophni and Phinehas, were slain.

12 A man of Benjamin ran from the battle line, and came to Shiloh the same day, with his clothes rent and with earth upon his head. [13]When he arrived, Eli was sitting upon his seat by the road watching, for his heart trembled for the ark of God. And when the man came into the city and told the news, all the city cried out. [14]When Eli heard the sound of the outcry, he said, "What is this uproar?" Then the man hastened and came and told Eli. [15]Now Eli was ninety-eight years old and his eyes were set, so that he could not see. [16]And the man said to Eli, "I am he who has come from the battle; I fled from the battle today." And he said, "How did it go, my son?" [17]He who brought the tidings answered and said, "Israel has fled before the Philistines, and there has also been a great slaughter among the people; your two sons also, Hophni and Phinehas, are dead, and the ark of God has been captured." [18]When he mentioned the ark of God, Eli fell over backward from his seat by the side of the gate; and his neck was broken and he died, for he was an old man, and heavy. He had judged Israel forty years.

19 Now his daughter-in-law, the wife of Phinehas, was with child, about to give birth. And when she heard the tidings that the ark of God was captured, and that her father-in-law and her husband were dead, she bowed and gave birth; for her pains came upon her. [20]And about the time of her death the women attending her said to her, "Fear not, for you have borne a son." But she did not answer or give heed. [21]And she named the child Ichabod, saying, "The glory has departed from Israel!" because the

ark of God had been captured and because of her father-in-law and her husband. [22]And she said, "The glory has departed from Israel, for the ark of God has been captured."

1. *Comment.* The Philistines, who have already appeared as Israel's enemies in the Samson stories (Judg 13-16), were an Indo-European people who began to occupy the western part of Palestine (which gets its name from them) about the same time as Israelite groups entered the land from the desert. By the time of the present confrontation the Philistines were solidly entrenched on the coastal plain from Gaza to the area of present-day Tel Aviv and were expanding into other areas. The battle recounted in this section took place at Aphek (v 1), probably a few miles east of Tel Aviv, in the second half of the eleventh century. It probably formed part of a Philistine offensive against Israelite territory (as a Greek variant reading in v 1 states explicitly).

After an initial repulse (v 2) the Israelites call for the ark to be brought from Shiloh to the battlefield to aid them in their difficulties (v 3). When the ark arrives, borne by Eli's two sons (v 4), the Israelite forces exult (v 5), while the Philistines are thrown into dismay. One can note the almost comical tone of caricature in their outcry at vv 7-8. The narrator uses this to stress the religious problem of the text: the Philistines appeal not to their gods but to their own human courage (v 9) in order to resist the mighty god of the Israelites. And they win the battle decisively (vv 10-11)! Yahweh does not intervene on the side of his people (contrast Judg 4 and 7). On the contrary, they suffer great losses (though the figure of 30,000 casualties given in v 10 is surely an exaggeration), and worse still the ark of God falls into the hands of their foes. Eli's two sons are among the dead (v 11); the oracle of 2:34 has been fulfilled.

Two scenes follow showing how the news of the ark's loss had fatal consequences. The suspenseful narrative of vv 12-18 tells how the news was brought to Eli; when the messenger announces the capture of the ark after all the other misfortunes (v 17), the old priest collapses and dies. A later redactor added a note that Eli had "judged Israel forty years" (v 18b); this puts him in line with the leaders of Israel mentioned in the Book of Judges and with Samuel (cf. 1 Sam 7:15), though in fact Eli's priestly function set him on a different plane. The second scene (vv 19-22) is a report about Eli's daughter-in-law who died in premature child-birth due to the shock caused by the news about the ark and about the deaths of her husband and father-in-law. Her child's name Ichabod (v 21) means "Alas for the glory!" or "Where is the glory?", and it sums up the dominant theme here of Yahweh's apparent absence.

2. *Significance.*   The battle of Aphek had important his-torical consequences, for it gave the Philistines effective control over much of the central highland area of Israel (cf. 1 Sam 13-14). But the narrator is not concerned with such matters; it is the loss of the ark (mentioned five times in the chapter) that torments him. How could Yahweh have allowed this defeat? The text powerfully demolishes the idea of an automatic protection afforded by Yahweh; it can be seen as a corrective to an exaggerated insistence on Yahweh-war traditions. What follows in chaps 5-6 will clarify the theological statement.

In its present context, moreover, after the narratives of chaps 1-3, the disaster of chap. 4 can be explained as the outcome of the cultic sins of Eli's sons and their father's lack of energy in restraining them. Israel's defeat, in other words, fits into the theological schema of wickedness / retribu-tion. The failure of her leaders brings all Israel to disaster, as would happen again centuries later in the kingdoms of Israel and Judah. 1 Sam 7:3-4 and Ps 78(77):59-64 offer further reflections on the present episode.

B.   5:1-12
THE VICTORIOUS ARK

> **5** When the Philistines captured the ark of God, they car-
> ried it from Ebenezer to Ashdod; ²then the Philistines
> took the ark of God and brought it into the house of

Dagon and set it up beside Dagon. ³And when the people of Ashdod rose early the next day, behold, Dagon had fallen face downward on the ground before the ark of the Lord. So they took Dagon and put him back in his place. ⁴But when they rose early on the next morning, behold, Dagon had fallen face downward on the ground before the ark of the Lord, and the head of Dagon and both his hands were lying cut off upon the threshold; only the trunk of Dagon was left to him. ⁵This is why the priests of Dagon and all who enter the house of Dagon do not tread on the threshold of Dagon in Ashdod to this day.

6 The hand of the Lord was heavy upon the people of Ashdod, and he terrified and afflicted them with tumors, both Ashdod and its territory. ⁷And when the men of Ashdod saw how things were, they said, "the ark of the God of Israel must not remain with us; for his hand is heavy upon us and upon Dagon our god." ⁸So they sent and gathered together all the lords of the Philistines, and said, "What shall we do with the ark of the God of Israel?" They answered, "Let the ark of the God of Israel be brought around to Gath." So they brought the ark of the God of Israel there. ⁹But after they had brought it around, the hand of the Lord was against the city, causing a very great panic, and he afflicted the men of the city, both young and old, so that tumors broke out upon them. ¹⁰So they sent the ark of God to Ekron. But when the ark of God came to Ekron, the people of Ekron cried out, "They have brought around to us the ark of the God of Israel to slay us and our people." ¹¹They sent therefore and gathered together all the lords of the Philistines, and said, "Send away the ark of the God of Israel, and let it return to its own place, that it may not slay us and our people." For there was a deathly panic throughout the whole city. The hand of God was very heavy there; ¹²the men who did not die were stricken with tumors, and the cry of the city went up to heaven.

1.   *Comment.*   The first unit (vv 1-5) tells of the confrontation between the Philistine god Dagon and the ark of

Yahweh. Dagon was an old Semitic divinity whose cult can be traced back into the third millennium, as in the recently discovered texts of Ebla. His main function had to do with harvests and fertility, and he appears in Ugaritic mythology as the father of the better known god Baal (or Hadad) the storm-god whose name will appear often in Kings. The captured ark is set up beside Dagon (the text never says "Dagon's statue"!) in the Philistine temple at Ashod (v 2). But the two cannot be put on the same plane, and the lesson is put across in two ways. First (v 3) Dagon is found face downward in a position of abject submission before the ark; then (v 4) Dagon loses his head and his hands — he can neither hear nor see nor help his devotees — and his trunk falls prostrate before the ark. A well-known ritual custom of the Dagon temple is then explained with reference to these happenings (v 5).

In the second unit (vv 6-12) three Philistine cities feel the power of Yahweh's ark in a continual crescendo. The ark terrified the Ashdodites and afflicted them with tumours (v 6); in Gath there was a very great panic, and both young and old were afflicted with tumours (v 9); finally at Ekron there was a deathly panic (v 11), some died and the others were stricken with tumours (v 12). The term translated as "tumours" may refer to boils resulting from bubonic plague or to haemorrhoids; in any case, a painful and humiliating affliction. Some English translations follow a Greek reading in v 6 and mention also a plague of rats or mice; the RSV follows the Hebrew text in not speaking of the rodents until 6:4. As a result of all these afflictions the Philistine cities one after the other refuse to keep the ark, and eventually petition is made to the Philistine rulers to send it back to Israel (v 11).

2. *Significance.*   In the account of Dagon's downfall one can hear a tone of mockery and contempt that is characteristic of the biblical attitude to idolatry (see the later polemical texts such as Isa 44:9-20 and Wis 13:10 — 14:31). The idolatrous abuses often denounced in Kings receive here an anticipatory judgement in the fate of Dagon father of Baal. There is a theo-political message too: if the god of the

Philistines is shown as subject to Yahweh, then the military supremacy of the Philistines can be overturned as soon as the Israelites remove the obstacles that cause Yahweh's displeasure.

C.   6:1 — 7:1
THE ARK RETURNS TO ISRAEL

6 The ark of the Lord was in the country of the Philistines seven months. ²And the Philistines called for the priests and the diviners and said, "What shall we do with the ark of the Lord? Tell us with what we shall send it to its place." ³They said, "If you send away the ark of the God of Israel, do not send it empty, but by all means return him a guilt offering. Then you will be healed, and it will be known to you why his hand does not turn away from you." ⁴And they said, "What is the guilt offering that we shall return to him?" They answered, "Five golden tumors and five golden mice, according to the number of the lords of the Philistines; for the same plague was upon all of you and upon your lords. ⁵So you must make images of your tumors and images of your mice that ravage the land, and give glory to the God of Israel; perhaps he will lighten his hand from off you and your gods and your land. ⁶Why should you harden your hearts as the Egyptians and Pharaoh hardened their hearts? After he had made sport of them, did not they let the people go, and they departed? ⁷Now then, take and prepare a new cart and two milch cows upon which there has never come a yoke, and yoke the cows to the cart, but take their calves home, away from them. ⁸And take the ark of the Lord and place it on the cart, and put in a box at its side the figures of gold, which you are returning to him as a guilt offering. Then send it off, and let it go its way. ⁹And watch; if it goes up on the way to its own land, to Beth-shemesh, then it is he who has done us this great harm; but if not, then we shall know that it is not his hand that struck us, it happened to us by chance."

¹⁰The men did so, and took two milch cows and yoked them to the cart and shut up their calves at home. ¹¹And they put the ark of the Lord on the cart, and the box with the golden mice and the images of their tumors. ¹²And the cows went straight in the direction of Beth-shemesh along one highway, lowing as they went; they turned neither to the right nor to the left, and the lords of the Philistines went after them as far as the border of Bethshemesh. ¹³Now the people of Bethshemesh were reaping their wheat harvest in the valley; and when they lifted up their eyes and saw the ark, they rejoiced to see it. ¹⁴The cart came into the field of Joshua of Beth-shemesh, and stopped there. A great stone was there; and they split up the wood of the cart and offered the cows as a burnt offering to the Lord. ¹⁵And the Levites took down the ark of the Lord and the box that was beside it, in which were the golden figures, and set them upon the great stone; and the men of Beth-shemesh offered burnt offerings and sacrificed sacrifices on that day to the Lord. ¹⁶And when the five lords of the Philistines saw it, they returned that day to Ekron.

¹⁷These are the golden tumors, which the Philistines returned as a guilt offering to the Lord: one for Ashdod, one for Gaza, one for Ashkelon, one for Gath, one for Ekron; ¹⁸also the golden mice, according to the number of all the cities of the Philistines belonging to the five lords, both fortified cities and unwalled villages. The great stone, beside which they set down the ark of the Lord, is a witness to this day in the field of Joshua of Beth-shemesh.

¹⁹And he slew some of the men of Beth-shemesh, because they looked into the ark of the Lord; he slew seventy men of them, and the people mourned because the Lord had made a great slaughter among the people. ²⁰Then the men of Beth-shemesh said, "Who is able to stand before the Lord, this holy God? And to whom shall he go up away from us?" ²¹So they sent messengers to the inhabitants of Kiriath-jearim, saying, "The Philistines

> have returned the ark of the Lord. Come down and take it
> up to you."
> 7 And the men of Kiriath-jearim came and took up the ark
> of the Lord, and brought it to the house of Abinadab on
> the hill; and they consecrated his son, Eleazar, to have
> charge of the ark of the Lord.

1.   *Comment.*   When the religious specialists of the Philistines are called in to advise on a course of action, they urge that the ark be sent back to Israel together with a compensatory guilt offering of golden tumours and golden mice (vv 1-6). Since the tumours undoubtedly refer to the afflictions suffered by the Philistine cities in chap. 5, one might expect that the golden mice (6:4, 5, 11, 18) would indicate a plague of mice. This, in fact, is mentioned by some Greek manuscripts at 5:6 and 6:1; should that be the original reading of the text, the reference might be to an invasion of fieldmice that ruined the crops (cf. 6:5). If, however, one prefers to follow the Hebrew text (as the RSV does), then the images of the mice could be taken with the images of the tumours as representing respectively the cause and the outward effect of the one real affliction of bubonic plague.

The Philistine priests and diviners also propose a test to see whether the disasters that have befallen them were really due to the wrath of Yahweh and not to mere chance (vv 7-9). The test consists in the use of milch cows to draw the cart with the ark and the golden offerings. The natural probability was that the cows would not bring the cart towards the Israelite town of Beth-shemesh: first, because they were not used to such work, having never been yoked before (v 7), and secondly, because they would tend to return to their calves who had been separated from them (v 7). When the cows act contrary to this probability, it is a clear sign that the hand of a divinity has intervened in the matter.

This in fact is what happens (vv 10-12). The ark is brought to Beth-shemesh where the inhabitants welcome it and offer sacrifices, while the Philistine lords return silently to Ekron (vv 13-16). One can note that the reference in v 15 to the

Levites as cultic personnel specialized in handling the ark may be a later redactional note (cf. Josh 3-4; 2 Sam 15:24). A summary note follows in vv 17-18.

In conclusion, two episodes contrast the disrespectful treatment of the ark by some inhabitants of Beth-shemesh (vv 19-20) with its reverent reception nearer to Jerusalem at Kiriath-jearim (6:21 — 7:1). Some translations have a longer reading based on the Greek text at v 19: "But the sons of Jeconiah did not rejoice with the rest of the men of Beth-shemesh when they welcomed the ark of the Lord, and he struck down seventy of them" (New English Bible); this refusal to share in the common joy might seem a better reason for the severe punishment than simply looking into the ark (but cf. 2 Sam 6:6-9).

2. *Significance.* A set of long-range word plays helps to highlight the meaning of this section. The glory (*kabod*) had departed from Israel (4:21-22); as a result the hand of Yahweh lay heavy (verb *kabed*) on the Philistines (5:6, 11); hence the priests and diviners urge the Philistines to give glory (*kabod*) to the God of Israel (6:5) in the hope that he will lighten his hand (6:5b) that had lain heavy upon them; the Philistines are advised not to harden their hearts (verb *kabed*, intensive form) as Pharaoh and the Egyptians had done long ago (6:6). This Egyptian reference, taken with 4:8, suggests that the departure of the ark from Philistia resembles a new Exodus; Yahweh leads his ark to the Promised Land and discomfits the hostile oppressors, despoiling them (the golden offerings) as the Egyptians had been despoiled (Exod 11:2-3; 12:35-36). The return of the ark, however, is not merely a matter of change of place; it must be a return to appropriate reverence (6:13-15 positively, and vv 19-20 negatively). The climax of the return wil be recounted in 2 Sam 6.

III. 1 Sam 7:2 — 15:35
Israel's First King, Saul

The monarchical form of government under which Israel lived for over four centuries (from before 1000 to 587/6) had an important, though mixed, impact on the life of the people. On the one hand, the influence it exercised was a negative one in many ways: political blunders and religious infidelity on the part of several of the kings led to the catastrophes of national defeat, deportation, and exile —for the northern Israelites in 722, for the Judaeans in 587/6; it is not surprising that we find many OT texts, especially in Kings and the prophets, that are sharply critical of the kings. On the other hand, however, the institution of monarchy, especially the line of David in Jerusalem, constituted the focal point for a whole range of splendid ideals and hopes —not least among them the expectation of an ideal "messianic" king — that were fully accepted into the religious life, worship, and writings of Israel, as we can see in many psalms and in some prophetic texts.

The chapters that concern us here, 1 Sam 7-15, present in miniature the main themes that emerged in that centuries-long debate about the monarchy in Israel. While indicating the importance of these chapters, this also hints at some of their problems. On the surface level the story-line is fairly simple: Samuel presides over the installation of Saul as first king, and later announces in the Lord's name that Saul has lost the Lord's favour which is transferred to a more worthy successor (David). On a deeper level, however, the attitudes that are implied, and occasionally expressed openly, in these chapters anticipate many of the principal themes that we find in the rest of Samuel and in Kings. The tension-filled relationships between prophets and kings, the triumphs and failures of the kings themselves, the enthusiasm and the rejection on the part of the people — all these appear between the lines of 1 Sam 7-15 and make these chapters crucial for the understanding of Samuel and Kings as a whole.

It has been customary, until recent years at least, to divide these chapters into two neat series of texts: the so-called pro-monarchical passages (e.g. 9:1 — 10:16 and 11:1-15) and the anti-monarchical ones (e.g. 8:1-22 and 12:1-25). The former series was usually seen as older and closer to historical reality, while the anti-monarchical texts were judged to be late (exilic or even post-exilic) and more theological than historical in purpose. One can suspect, however, that this division runs the risk of oversimplifying the complexities of the texts, both as regards their origin and their theological content. The comments that follow will try to indicate at least some of the various nuances and levels of meaning in these chapters that justify a more cautious position.

A. 7:2-17
VICTORY UNDER SAMUEL'S LEADERSHIP

1. *Comment.* Though the ark has returned to Israel, the Philistine domination continues and at length the people turn to the Lord in their distress (v 2). Samuel's first speech (v 3) insists that an effective break with idol-worship must be the sign of the people's sincerity in returning to Yahweh. One can notice here the names of the Canaanite deities Astarte and Baal. Astarte (or Ashtoreth) was a fertility goddess, and Baal the god of the thunderstorm (cf. v 10!) and of fertility; the plural forms of their names used here might refer to the several local variants of these deities or else to pagan divinities in general (cf. Judg 2:13; 10:6; 1 Sam 12:10). The Israelites pay heed to Samuel's words, and a public penitential rite is held at Mizpah (vv 5-6), about five miles north of Jerusalem, where the people openly acknowledge their sin. The libation ceremony mentioned in v 6 is unparalleled in the OT but its penitential significance is clear from the context.

At this point the text tells of another Philistine attack (vv 7-11). The first reaction of the Israelites is fear (v 7); they seek Yahweh's intervention through the cultic intercession of Samuel (vv 8-9) and amid divine thunderings the invaders are put to flight (vv 10-11). Yahweh's thundering is an image used elsewhere too for his intervention in human affairs (e.g. 1 Sam 2:10; 2 Sam 22:14). The image occurs here in the context of a "holy war" (perhaps better termed "Yahweh-war") description: prayer and sacrifice are the initial acts, then the Lord himself intervenes in the battle causing total confusion among the enemy (cf. Josh 10:10; Judg 4:15; 2 Sam 22:15). The main concern of such texts is to show that the people's deliverance in times of military crisis does not come from their own strength but only from Yahweh's free and powerful action.

Three consequences of the battle are then mentioned. A memorial stone is erected (v 12), bearing the same name, Ebenezer ("Stone of help"), as the locality where the Israelites encamped before the disastrous battle at Aphek (4:1). The Philistine menace was kept under control for the whole of Samuel's lifetime (v 13: but see chaps 13-14 below!), and Israel regained her lost territory (v 14). The concluding verses (15-17) report on Samuel's judicial activity in a number of well-known religious centres (v 16) as well as in his own town of Ramah (v 17).

In its present form the chapter is undoubtedly the work of Deuteronomistic authors. Older traditional material can be seen in vv 16-17 at least. It is debatable whether there was an old tradition behind the war-account in vv 5-12; even if there was, it must be noted that the Israelite victory cannot have been as complete and definitive as is depicted here (and in vv 13-14), since the Philistines were not defeated thoroughly until David's time (2 Sam 5:17-25; 8:1).

2. *Significance.*   This chapter presents roughly the same theological pattern that we find in several texts in the Book of Judges (e.g. 2:11ff): the Israelites suffer oppression as the just punishment for their infidelity to Yahweh; eventually they turn to him in repentance and beg his aid; Yahweh then raises up a deliverer to serve as his instrument in liberating his people. Though there are differences between 1 Sam 7 and the Judges texts, it is clear enough that Samuel is being presented here as in line with the great Deliverer-Judges of the past. (It will soon appear that he is the last of the line, and a new epoch is about to begin.)

On the one hand, then, chap. 7 faces backward, remotely to Judges and proximately to 1 Sam 2-6; the story of sin and defeat begun there under Eli and his sons reaches its positive climax here under Samuel's leadership. On the other hand, and more importantly, the chapter looks forward. In chap. 8 the Israelites will clamour for a king "to govern us and go out before us and fight our battles" (8:20); the verb for "govern" is the same in Hebrew as that translated "to judge" in 7:6, 15, 16, 17. The suggestion is that the people's request for a king at that point was uncalled for, since the functions of governing, judging, and fighting had been performed with complete success by Samuel (according to the Deuteronomistic authors of chap. 7).

B.   8:1-22
THE ISRAELITES ASK FOR A KING

8 When Samuel became old, he made his sons judges over Israel. ²The name of his first-born son was Joel, and the name of his second, Abijah; they were judges in Beersheba. ³Yet his sons did not walk in his ways, but turned aside after gain; they took bribes and perverted justice.

⁴Then all the elders of Israel gathered together and came to Samuel at Ramah, ⁵and said to him, "Behold, you are old and your sons do not walk in your ways; now appoint for us a king to govern us like all the nations." ⁶But the thing displeased Samuel when they said, "Give us a king to govern us." And Samuel prayed to the Lord. ⁷And the Lord said to Samuel, "Hearken to the voice of the people in all that they say to you; for they have not rejected you, but they have rejected me from being king over them. ⁸According to all the deeds which they have done to me, from the day I brought them up out of Egypt even to this day, forsaking me and serving other gods, so they are also doing to you. ⁹Now then, hearken to their voice; only, you shall solemnly warn them, and show them the ways of the king who shall reign over them."

¹⁰So Samuel told all the words of the Lord to the people who were asking a king from him. ¹¹He said, "These will be the ways of the king who will reign over

you: he will take your sons and appoint them to his chariots and to be his horsemen, and to run before his chariots; [12]and he will appoint for himself commanders of thousands and commanders of fifties, and some to plow his ground and to reap his harvest, and to make his implements of war and the equipment of his chariots. [13]He will take your daughters to be perfumers and cooks and bakers. [14]He will take the best of your fields and vineyards and olive orchards and give them to his servants. [15]He will take the tenth of your grain and of your vineyards and give it to his officers and to his servants. [16]He will take your menservants and maidservants, and the best of your cattle and your asses, and put them to work. [17]He will take the tenth of your flocks, and you shall be his slaves. [18]And in that day you will cry out because of your king, whom you have chosen for yourselves; but the Lord will not answer you in that day."

[19]But the people refused to listen to the voice of Samuel; and they said, "No! but we will have a king over us, [20]that we also may be like all the nations, and that our king may govern us and go out before us and fight our battles." [21]And when Samuel had heard all the words of the people, he repeated them in the ears of the Lord. [22]And the Lord said to Samuel, "Hearken to their voice, and make them a king." Samuel then said to the men of Israel, "Go every man to his city."

1. *Comment.*   Samuel, like Eli, finds himself with sons who are unworthy of him; Eli's sons had acted badly in cultic matters, Samuel's sons turn out to be corrupt judges; once again the problem of a succession in leadership is posed (vv 1-3). A solution is proposed by the elders of Israel in what appear to be quite reasonable terms (vv 4-5): they ask for a king, such as all the nations have, to rule over them in place of Samuel's unworthy sons. One can note that the phrase "like all the nations" (vv 5, 20) occurs elsewhere only at Deut 17:14 (part of the so-called law of the king, 17:14-20); this latter text is not anti-monarchical in principle (see v

15), though its concern is to resist tendencies to absolutize royal power.

Samuel takes the request of the elders badly and turns to the Lord in prayer (v 6). Yahweh's reply (vv 7-9) makes it clear that the request of the elders contains grave implications, nothing less than a rejection of Yahweh's immediate saving leadership over the people by his free appointment of a deliverer in times of crisis. Nonetheless he accedes to their request. The important theme of Yahweh's kingship (v 7) is found in two forms in the OT: (a) with reference to the heavenly court and the whole cosmos — e.g. Isa 6:1-5; Ps 95(94):3-5; 97(96); (b) with reference to a people as here —cf. Exod 15:18; Num 23:21; Judg 8:23; Isa 33:22. Both forms are found in ancient Near Eastern religions (with reference to various deities) before the emergence of Israel; the Yahwistic community took over the concept, purged it of its originally polytheistic implications (especially in the first form), and used it to express Yahweh's incomparable lordship over the entire range of reality, heavenly, cosmic, and societal.

In obedience to Yahweh's instructions (v 9b) Samuel announces to the people the "ways of the king" (vv 11-17), that is, those demands in terms of personnel, labour, and goods that the monarchical regime will make on the people. Since most of the points listed here are practically inevitable consequences of a centralized authority, it is not surprising that many parallels can be noted to extra-biblical texts that refer to Canaanite feudal kingdoms of pre-Israelite times. It is likely enough, however, that the actual experience of Israelite monarchy, perhaps especially during Solomon's reign (1 Kgs 4-5; 12), has left its mark on the description. Nothing is said of any possible advantages that a permanent centralized authority might bring; the description is at least slanted, if not outright polemical. Samuel concludes on a very negative note (v 18): the people's sufferings under their future king will be so great that they will cry out to Yahweh for relief, as they cried out in the past against their foreign oppressors; then, in the days of the Judges, Yahweh heard his people's cry, but in the days of the king he will refuse to listen to them.

Verses 19-22 form an inclusion with vv 4-9: there is a repetition of the people's request, of Samuel's prayer, and of Yahweh's reply. Finally Samuel sends the Israelites to their homes.

Chap. 8 has reached its present form after a complex process of literary growth whose details are not clear. One possible suggestion is that vv 1-5 and 21-22 belonged to a pre-Deuteronomistic prophetic redaction of the Saul and David traditions, while vv 6-20 were inserted (and in part directly authored) by Deuteronomistic editors.

2. *Significance.* As it stands the chapter undoubtedly paints a gloomy and unenthusiastic picture of kingly rule in Israel, but it can hardly be termed absolutely anti-monarchical. It is true that the people are blamed for requesting a king (v 7) and that the king's rule will cause them much distress (vv 11-17), yet the fact remains that Yahweh is presented as acceding to their request (vv 7, 9, 22). Their lack of trust in Yahweh's power to govern and save his people without the stable human institution of monarchy does not become a reason for his rejecting them. All the same, the monarchy is presented here as not an original part of the Lord's plan for his people. This implies that the absence of the monarchy, or its disappearance, will not make an essential difference in the relation between Yahweh and Israel. The message for exilic-period readers is clear.

It is historically likely that opposition to the monarchy in Israel was expressed right from the time of the earliest kings and perhaps even before that (cf. Judg 8:22-23; 9:7-15), though it is clear that the bitter experiences of the fall of the northern kingdom in 722, and of Judah in 587/6, would have increased anti-monarchical sentiment in some sectors of Israel. On the other hand, the monarchy certainly had its enthusiastic supporters from the very beginning, and we know that even after the disaster of 587/6 some Judaeans still pinned their hopes on a renewed form of the monarchy (cf. Jer 23:5-6; Ezek 37:15-28). This complex "yes" and "no" is reflected in the internal tensions of the present text of 1 Sam 8.

C. 9:1 — 10:16
SAUL, SEARCHING FOR HIS FATHER'S LOST ASSES, MEETS SAMUEL AND IS ANOINTED AS PRINCE OVER ISRAEL

9 There was a man of Benjamin whose name was Kish, the son of Abiel, son of Zeror, son of Becorath, son of Aphiah, a Benjaminite, a man of wealth; [2]and he had a son whose name was Saul, a handsome young man. There was not a man among the people of Israel more handsome than he; from his shoulders upward he was taller than any of the people.

[3]Now the asses of Kish, Saul's father, were lost. So Kish said to Saul his son, "Take one of the servants with you, and arise, go and look for the asses." [4]And they passed through the hill country of Ephraim and passed through the land of Shalishah, but they did not find them. And they passed through the land of Shaalim, but they were not there. Then they passed through the land of Benjamin, but did not find them.

[5]When they came to the land of Zuph, Saul said to his servant who was with him, "Come, let us go back, lest my father cease to care about the asses and become anxious about us." [6]But he said to him, "Behold, there is a man of God in this city, and he is a man that is held in honor; all that he says comes true. Let us go there; perhaps he can tell us about the journey on which we have set out." [7]Then Saul said to his servant, "But if we go, what can we bring the man? For the bread in our sacks is gone, and there is no present to bring to the man of God. What have we?" [8]The servant answered Saul again, "Here, I have with me the fourth part of a shekel of silver, and I will give it to the man of God, to tell us our way." [9](Formerly in Israel, when a man went to inquire of God, he said, "Come, let us

go to the seer"; for he who is now called a prophet was formerly called a seer.) [10]And Saul said to his servant, "Well said; come, let us go." So they went to the city where the man of God was.

[11]As they went up the hill to the city, they met young maidens coming out to draw water, and said to them, "Is the seer here?" [12]They answered, "He is; behold, he is just ahead of you. Make haste; he has come just now to the city, because the people have a sacrifice today on the high place. [13]As soon as you enter the city, you will find him, before he goes up to the high place to eat; for the people will not eat till he comes, since he must bless the sacrifice; afterward those eat who are invited. Now go up, for you will meet him immediately." [14]So they went up to the city. As they were entering the city, they saw Samuel coming out toward them on his way up to the high place.

[15]Now the day before Saul came, the Lord had revealed to Samuel: [16]"Tomorrow about this time I will send to you a man from the land of Benjamin, and you shall anoint him to be prince over my people Israel. He shall save my people from the hand of the Philistines; for I have seen the affliction of my people, because their cry has come to me." [17]When Samuel saw Saul, the Lord told him, "Here is the man of whom I spoke to you! He it is who shall rule over my people." [18]Then Saul approached Samuel in the gate, and said, "Tell me where is the house of the seer?" [19]Samuel answered Saul, "I am the seer; go up before me to the high place, for today you shall eat with me, and in the morning I will let you go and will tell you all that is on your mind. [20]As for your asses that were lost three days ago, do not set your mind on them, for they have been found. And for whom is all that is desirable in Israel? Is it not for you and for all your father's house?" [21]Saul answered, "Am I not a Benjaminite, from the least of the tribes of Israel? And is not my family the humblest of all the families of the tribe of Benjamin? Why then have you spoken to me in this way?"

[22]Then Samuel took Saul and his servant and brought

them into the hall and gave them a place at the head of those who had been invited, who were about thirty persons. ²³And Samuel said to the cook, "Bring the portion I gave you, of which I said to you, 'Put it aside.' " ²⁴So the cook took up the leg and the upper portion and set them before Saul; and Samuel said, "See, what was kept is set before you. Eat; because it was kept for you until the hour appointed, that you might eat with the guests."

So Saul ate with Samuel that day. ²⁵And when they came down from the high place into the city, a bed was spread for Saul upon the roof, and he lay down to sleep. ²⁶Then at the break of dawn Samuel called to Saul upon the roof, "Up, that I may send you on your way." So Saul arose, and both he and Samuel went out into the street.

²⁷As they were going down to the outskirts of the city, Samuel said to Saul, "Tell the servant to pass on before us, and when he has passed on stop here yourself for a while, that I may make known to you the word of God."

10 Then Samuel took a vial of oil and poured it on his head, and kissed him and said, "Has not the Lord anointed you to be prince over his people Israel? And you shall reign over the people of the Lord and you will save them from the hand of their enemies round about. And this shall be the sign to you that the Lord has anointed you to be prince over his heritage. ²When you depart from me today you will meet two men by Rachel's tomb in the territory of Benjamin at Zelzah, and they will say to you, 'The asses which you went to seek are found, and now your father has ceased to care about the asses and is anxious about you, saying, "What shall I do about my son?" ' ³Then you shall go on from there further and come to the oak of Tabor; three men going up to God at Bethel will meet you there, one carrying three kids, another carrying three loaves of bread, and another carrying a skin of wine. ⁴And they will greet you and give you two loaves of bread, which you shall accept from their hand. ⁵After that you shall come to Gibeath-elohim, where there is a garrison of the Philistines; and there, as you come to the city, you will meet a band of prophets coming down from the high place with harp, tambourine, flute, and lyre before them, prophesying. [6]Then the spirit of the Lord will come mightily upon you, and you shall prophesy with them and be turned into another man. [7]Now when these signs meet you, do whatever your hand finds to do, for God is with you. [8]And you shall go down before me to Gilgal; and behold, I am coming to you to offer burnt offerings and to sacrifice peace offerings. Seven days you shall wait, until I come to you and show you what you shall do."

[9]When he turned his back to leave Samuel, God gave him another heart; and all these signs came to pass that day. [10]When they came to Gibeah, behold, a band of prophets met him; and the spirit of God came mightily upon him, and he prophesied among them. [11]And when all who knew him before saw how he prophesied with the prophets, the people said to one another, "What has come over the son of Kish? Is Saul also among the prophets?" [12]And a man of the place answered, "And who is their father?" Therefore it became a proverb, "Is Saul also among the prophets?" [13]When he had finished prophesying, he came to the high place.

[14]Saul's uncle said to him and to his servant, "Where did you go?" And he said, "To seek the asses; and when we saw they were not to be found, we went to Samuel." [15]And Saul's uncle said, "Pray, tell me what Samuel said to you." [16]And Saul said to his uncle, "He told us plainly that the asses had been found." But about the matter of the kingdom, of which Samuel had spoken, he did not tell him anything.

1.   *Comment.*   The narrator begins with an elaborate and wholly positive introduction of Saul (vv 1-2). He belonged to the small but important tribe of Benjamin whose territory lay between Judah in the south and the central Palestinian tribe of Ephraim. Sent off by his father to look for some lost asses, Saul accompanied by a servant searches in three

localities without success (vv 3-4); in the fourth locality they decide to ask help from a well-known "man of God" (vv 5-6). This designation (cf. 2:27) stands in general for any publicly recognized religious personage noted for powers of intercession, miracle-working, or oracular gifts. Here the latter aspect predominates, and the title is taken as equivalent to "seer" (vv 9, 11, 18f), which in most OT occurrences is a synonym for "prophet" (as the explanatory gloss of v 9 notes).

Making sure that they have a suitable interview fee for the seer, Saul and his servant enter the city (vv 7-10), where they learn that the seer is to preside that very day over a communal sacrifice at the "high place" (vv 11-13). The latter term stands for the local sanctuary (cf. 1 Kgs 3:3 with comment). Throughout Kings these high places are referred to in derogatory terms, which reflects the Deuteronomistic position that Jerusalem is the only legitimate place for sacrificial worship; in 1 Sam 9, on the contrary, worship at the high place is taken for granted as normal and good.

The seer turns out to be none other than Samuel (v 14). His appearance here as a prophetic figure (cf. chap. 3), in contrast to his judicial and leadership roles in chaps 7 and 8, suggests that the old folk-tale which lies at the base of the present section was transmitted and edited in prophetic circles. An author's aside (vv 15-16) informs the reader that Yahweh had already instructed Samuel to anoint this Benjaminite youth as ruler of his people. The term *melek* ("king") is not used here, but rather *nagid* (RSV: "prince"), a title that may have originally indicated a charismatic military leader; it is also used, however, for king-designate (1 Sam 25:30; 2 Sam 5:2; 6:21; 7:8) or crown prince (1 Kgs 1:35). The rite of anointing (9:16, and also 10:1 in the Greek text followed by the RSV) signifies a transfer of power and a certain quality of holiness and inviolability (cf. 1 Sam 24:10; 26:9). One can note in the last phrase of 9:16 a strong similarity with Exod 3:7 (the call of Moses).

At Yahweh's direction (v 17) Samuel invites Saul to the cultic celebration, tells him that the lost asses have already been found, and in veiled language hints at a great destiny in store for him (vv 18-20). Saul's protestation of unworthiness because of his humble origins (v 21) resembles the reaction of Gideon at his call (Judg 6:15) and also recalls the hesitations of Moses (Exod 3-4). Saul takes part in the feast (vv 22-25), and next morning Samuel accompanies him on his way out of the town and anoints him in secret as leader and saviour of Israel (9:26 — 10:1). He then announces three signs to guarantee the authenticity of the anointing (vv 2, 3-4, 5-6); the mention of a Philistine garrison at Gibeath-elohim (v 5) — which may be Saul's hometown of Gibeah (v 10) — indicates the critical situation in Israel at that time and suggests the urgent need for a leader to deliver the people from foreign oppression. Finally Samuel encourages Saul to act valiantly (v 7) and arranges an appointment later at the cultic centre of Gilgal (v 8: a redactional verse, see 13:7ff).

The three signs come about as announced, the third one alone being narrated in detail (vv 9-13). The mention of a "band of prophets" here (vv 5-6, 10-13) provides an interesting insight into the variety of the phenomenon of prophecy in ancient Israel. This prophetic group does not communicate a divine message (as do the great OT prophets); their "prophesying" consists in ecstatic behaviour or possession trance, which appears to have been stimulated by music and the excitement of a cultic celebration (v 5); the contagious nature of this abnormal state is attributed to an influx of divine energy which v 6 describes as the mighty coming of the Lord's spirit. One gets the impression from vv 11-12 that these groups of ecstatic prophets were not highly regarded by the people in general (cf. 19:18-24). A meeting with Saul's uncle (vv 14-16) provides the occasion for a summary of the main points of the story with stress on the secret nature of Saul's calling.

2. *Significance.* In this pre-Deuteronomistic text the first king, Saul, is described in a sympathetic way, and his designation is explicitly said to have been a divine decision operating through the apparently accidental happenings of

everyday life and manifested by the prophetic words of Samuel. The allusions to the call of Moses (9:16) and that of the deliverer-judge Gideon (9:21) set Saul's mission in continuity with Israel's old traditions of charismatic leadership; the onrush of the spirit (10:6, 10) expresses this in another way. Samuel's presence and obvious approval counterbalance the negative impression left by his speeches in chap. 8. One can note, however, that 9:1 — 10:16 concerns the person and mission of Saul; it does not discuss the general theme of monarchy and in fact the term "king" does not occur here.

D.   10:17-27
SAUL IS CHOSEN PUBLICLY AND ACCLAIMED AS KING

[17]Now Samuel called the people together to the Lord at Mizpah; [18]and he said to the people of Israel, "Thus says the Lord, the God of Israel, 'I brought up Israel out of Egypt, and I delivered you from the hand of the Egyptians and from the hand of all the kingdoms that were oppressing you.' [19]But you have this day rejected your God, who saves you from all your calamities and your distresses; and you have said, 'No! but set a king over us.' Now therefore present yourselves before the Lord by your tribes and by your thousands."

[20]Then Samuel brought all the tribes of Israel near, and the tribe of Benjamin was taken by lot. [21]He brought the tribe of Benjamin near by its families, and the family of the Matrites was taken by lot; finally he brought the family of the Matrites near man by man, and Saul the son of Kish was taken by lot. But when they sought him, he could not be found. [22]So they inquired again of the Lord, "Did the man come hither?" and the Lord said, "Behold, he has hidden himself among the baggage." [23]Then they ran and fetched him from there; and when he stood among the people, he was taller than any of the people from his shoulders upward. [24]And Samuel said to all the

people, "Do you see him whom the Lord has chosen? There is none like him among all the people." And all the people shouted, "Long live the king!"

[25]Then Samuel told the people the rights and duties of the kingship; and he wrote them in a book and laid it up before the Lord. Then Samuel sent all the people away, each one to his home. [26]Saul also went to his home at Gibeah, and with him went men of valor whose hearts God had touched. [27]But some worthless fellows said, "How can this man save us?" And they despised him, and brought him no present. But he held his peace.

1. *Comment.* Samuel, once again in the role of national leader as well as prophet, summons the people to the cultic centre of Mizpah (cf. 7:5ff) and repeats the Lord's message that the people's request for a king is equivalent to a rejection of God (vv 17-19a: cf. 8:7-8). However he then initiates a choice by lot which eventually designates Saul (vv 19b-21); for the procedure see also Josh 7:16-18 and 1 Sam 14:38-42. Saul has gone into hiding (v 21b); perhaps the text intends this to be taken as a sign of his modesty and reluctance (cf. 9:21), or it may be a literary device to highlight the dramatic effect of his presentation to the assembled people in v 23. His imposing physical appearance (v 23: cf. 9:2) adds conviction to the choice by lot, and he is hailed as the king chosen by the Lord (v 24).

Samuel writes the royal constitution and deposits the document in the sanctuary before dismissing the people (v 25). Saul too returns home, accompanied by some warriors, though others treat him with contempt and refuse to acknowledge his position (vv 26-27). The RSV rendering of v 27b ("But he held his peace") is textually uncertain; another possibility is to read "About a month later", which would then be the introduction to chap. 11.

2. *Significance.* While Samuel's speech in vv 18-19a (probably Deuteronomistic) is clearly antagonistic to the monarchy, it is equally clear that the older traditions in vv 19b-27 present Saul in a favourable light. Samuel describes

him as the man chosen by the Lord (v 24), and those who doubt his ability to save the Israelites are termed "worthless fellows" (v 27). Verses 18-19a, then, modify the positive attitude of vv 19b-27 (just as chap. 8 has modified the positive presentation of 9:1 — 10:16). The tensions between these texts express the essential ambivalence of all attempts to embody religious convictions in concrete political institutions.

E.   11:1-15
SAUL'S FIRST MILITARY VICTORY AND HIS CONFIRMATION IN KINGSHIP

11   Nahash the Ammonite went up and besieged Jabesh-gilead; and all the men of Jabesh said to Nahash, "Make a treaty with us, and we will serve you." ²But Nahash the Ammonite said to them, "On this condition I will make a treaty with you, that I gouge out all your right eyes, and thus put disgrace upon all Israel." ³The elders of Jabesh said to him, "Give us seven days respite that we may send messengers through all the territory of Israel. Then, if there is no one to save us, we will give ourselves up to you." ⁴When the messengers came to Gibeah of Saul, they reported the matter in the ears of the people; and all the people wept aloud.

⁵Now Saul was coming from the field behind the oxen; and Saul said, "What ails the people, that they are weeping?" So they told him the tidings of the men of Jabesh. ⁶And the spirit of God came mightily upon Saul when he heard these words, and his anger was greatly kindled. ⁷He took a yoke of oxen, and cut them in pieces and sent them throughout all the territory of Israel by the hand of messengers, saying, "Whoever does not come out after Saul and Samuel, so shall it be done to his oxen!" Then the dread of the Lord fell upon the people, and they came out as one man. ⁸When he mustered them at Bezek, the men of Israel were three hundred thousand, and the men of Judah thirty thousand. ⁹And they said to the mes-

sengers who had come, "Thus shall you say to the men of Jabesh-gilead: 'Tomorrow, by the time the sun is hot, you shall have deliverance.' " When the messengers came and told the men of Jabesh, they were glad. ¹⁰Therefore the men of Jabesh said, "Tomorrow we will give ourselves up to you, and you may do to us whatever seems good to you." ¹¹And on the morrow Saul put the people in three companies; and they came into the midst of the camp in the morning watch, and cut down the Ammonites until the heat of the day; and those who survived were scattered, so that no two of them were left together.

¹²Then the people said to Samuel, "Who is it that said, 'Shall Saul reign over us?' Bring the men, that we may put them to death." ¹³But Saul said, "Not a man shall be put to death this day, for today the Lord has wrought deliverance in Israel." ¹⁴Then Samuel said to the people, "Come, let us go to Gilgal and there renew the kingdom." ¹⁵So all the people went to Gilgal, and there they made Saul king before the Lord in Gilgal. There they sacrificed peace offerings before the Lord, and there Saul and all the men of Israel rejoiced greatly.

1.   *Comment.*   The inhabitants of Jabesh-gilead, in dire distress caused by an Ammonite attack, send messengers throughout Israel to seek aid (vv 1-4). Other texts too note a relationship between the town of Jabesh-gilead, in the most northern Israelite settlement east of the Jordan, and the tribe of Benjamin or Saul's family in particular (cf. Judg 21:8-15; 1 Sam 31:11-13; 2 Sam 2:4-7; 21:11-14). The Ammonites, a Transjordanian people whose capital was situated in what is now the city of Amman, had already shown hostility to Israel in the time of the Judges (cf. Judg 10-12). It can be noted in fact that the whole account of 1 Sam 11:1-15 bears many resemblances to the narratives about the charismatic saviours in Judges.

When Saul, busy with his farm work, hears the news about Jabesh, an onrush of divine power takes possession of him (vv 5-6). This use of the term "spirit of God" (v 6) to indicate the force that impels a person to undertake military leadership or to perform heroic feats can also be seen in Judg 6:34; 11:29; 14:6, 19; 15:14. Saul's first act as leader is to call out the Israelite forces (vv 7-8); the symbolic action of cutting up the oxen (v 7) signifies a threat to the lives of those Israelites who would refuse to answer the call to arms (cf. Gen 15:9ff; Judg 19:29; Jer 34:18-20). The campaign is successful; the Ammonites are utterly routed and Jabesh is delivered from its plight (vv 9-11).

The aftermath of the battle is then described. Saul magnanimously refuses to execute vengeance on those Israelites who had earlier (10:27) opposed his leadership (vv 12-13: cf. 2 Sam 19:16-23). Samuel then summons the Israelites to Gilgal to "renew the kingdom" (v 14); this odd phrase is a redactional attempt to harmonize two originally independent traditions — Saul's acclamation as king at Mizpah (10:24) and the king-making celebrations at Gilgal (11:15). Saul is made king "before the Lord" (no sign of criticism here!); the tears of the Israelites (vv 4-5) are turned into great rejoicing (v 15).

2. *Significance.* This pre-Deuteronomistic text presents Saul as a charismatic military leader like the heroes of Judges. The key word "to save" dominates the narrative (vv 3, 9, 13), and it is when Saul has proved himself Israel's saviour that the people (not Samuel!) make him king (v 15). It has been suggested that this is the most accurate historical picture of the origins of Saul's kingship; the question remains an open one, however, since many details of chap. 11 could be explained as literary imitations of the older traditions about the Saviour-Judges. In any case, the attitude towards Saul here is unquestionably a positive one; internal opposition is not concealed (vv 12-13) but it is of no account.

F. 12:1-25
SAMUEL'S DISCOURSE

12 And Samuel said to all Israel, "Behold, I have hearkened to your voice in all that you have said to me, and have

made a king over you. ²And now, behold, the king walks before you; and I am old and gray, and behold, my sons are with you; and I have walked before you from my youth until this day. ³Here I am; testify against me before the Lord and before his anointed. Whose ox have I taken? Or whose ass have I taken? Or whom have I defrauded? Whom have I oppressed? Or from whose hand have I taken a bribe to blind my eyes with it? Testify against me and I will restore it to you." ⁴They said, "You have not defrauded us or oppressed us or taken anything from any man's hand." ⁵And he said to them, "The Lord is witness against you, and his anointed is witness this day, that you have not found anything in my hand." And they said, "He is witness."

⁶And Samuel said to the people, "The Lord is witness, who appointed Moses and Aaron and brought your fathers up and out of the land of Egypt. ⁷Now therefore stand still, that I may plead with you before the Lord concerning all the saving deeds of the Lord which he performed for you and for your fathers. ⁸When Jacob went into Egypt and the Egyptians oppressed them, then your fathers cried to the Lord and the Lord sent Moses and Aaron, who brought forth your fathers out of Egypt, and made them dwell in this place. ⁹But they forgot the Lord their God; and he sold them into the hand of Sisera, commander of the army of Jabin King of Hazor, and into the hand of the king of Moab; and they fought against them. ¹⁰And they cried to the Lord, and said, 'We have sinned, because we have forsaken the Lord, and have served the Baals and the Ashtaroth; but now deliver us out of the hand of our enemies, and we will serve thee.' ¹¹And the Lord sent Jerubbaal and Barak, and Jephthah, and Samuel and delivered you out of the hand of your enemies on every side; and you dwelt in safety. ¹²And when you saw that Nahash the king of the Ammonites came against you, you said to me, 'No, but a king shall reign over us,' when the Lord your God was your king. ¹³And now behold the king whom you have chosen, for

whom you have asked; behold, the Lord has set a king over you. [14]If you will fear the Lord and serve him and hearken to his voice and not rebel against the commandment of the Lord, and if both you and the king who reigns over you will follow the Lord your God, it will be well; [15]but if you will not hearken to the voice of the Lord, but rebel against the commandment of the Lord, then the hand of the Lord will be against you and your king. [16]Now therefore stand still and see this great thing, which the Lord will do before your eyes. [17]Is it not wheat harvest today? I will call upon the Lord, that he may send thunder and rain; and you shall know and see that your wickedness is great, which you have done in the sight of the Lord, in asking for yourselves a king." [18]So Samuel called upon the Lord, and the Lord sent thunder and rain that day; and all the people greatly feared the Lord and Samuel.

[19]And all the people said to Samuel, "Pray for your servants to the Lord your God, that we may not die; for we have added to all our sins this evil, to ask for ourselves a king." [20]And Samuel said to the people, "Fear not; you have done all this evil, yet do not turn aside from following the Lord, but serve the Lord with all your heart; [21]and do not turn aside after vain things which cannot profit or save, for they are vain. [22]For the Lord will not cast away his people, for his great name's sake, because it has pleased the Lord to make you a people for himself. [23]Moreover as for me, far be it from me that I should sin against the Lord by ceasing to pray for you; and I will instruct you in the good and the right way. [24]Only fear the Lord and serve him faithfully with all your heart; for consider what great things he has done for you. [25]But if you still do wickedly, you shall be swept away, both you and your king."

1. *Comment.*　As the text stands, the setting for this important chapter must still be the king-making ceremony

at Gilgal (11:15; note the words of presentation at 12:13). Samuel's time of public leadership has come to an end, and he begins his speech by insisting on the qualities of integrity and honesty that marked his service of the people (vv 1-5). The assembled people all agree. It is interesting to note that the reference to Samuel's sons in v 2 says nothing about their unworthy behaviour as corrupt judges (cf. 8:3, 5); not the slightest shadow is allowed to fall on the figure of Samuel in chap. 12.

The next part (vv 6-25) consists of a long discourse divided into several units and interrupted by a divine sign-action. First, Samuel recalls the Lord's earlier saving interventions in Israel's favour; he notes that Israel's response was often one of infidelity and abandonment of the Lord, and their present request for a king fits into this history of sin (vv 6-12). One can note that v 12 connects the request for a king with the Ammonite war (chap. 11), though the present arrangement of the text puts the request earlier in chap. 8.

Samuel then presents "the king" (Saul's name is never mentioned in chap. 12) and sets out the alternatives that are open to the people and their king: obedience to the Lord which will bring prosperity for people and king — or disobedience which will issue in the inevitable divine punishment (vv 13-15). At this point Samuel announces that the Lord will give the people a sign to prove that they have acted wickedly in asking for a king (vv 16-18); the sign — thunder and rain in the month of May (a most unusual occurrence in that area) — can be compared to Exod 4:1-9; Judg 6:36-40; 1 Kgs 18:21-40. The people then acknowledge their sin in having asked for a king and plead for Samuel's intercession; he assures them of this, urges them to renewed fidelity, warns against idolatry, and expresses again in a looser form the alternatives of service of Yahweh or rebellion (vv 19-25).

2. *Significance.*   Though there are pre-Deuteronomistic elements in the chapter (especially vv 1-5 and smaller parts within vv 6-25), the composition as a whole is the work of the Deuteronomists. It is in fact one of the key passages in

the structure of the Deuteronomistic history. The era of the Judges has come to an end and the monarchical era is beginning. The text looks back on the former period, noting the pattern that gave meaning to the events: the Lord's saving deeds, the people's abandonment of the Lord, oppression by foreigners as a punishment, after which the people acknowledge their sin and the Lord sends them a saviour (cf. Judg 2:6 — 3:6). Not an idyllic picture, indeed, but at least it began with the Lord's gracious initiatives. The monarchical period, however, has begun with the people's sin, a truly inauspicious start.

In spite of that, the attitude of the chapter can hardly be described as thoroughly anti-monarchical. Its main concern is to subordinate the institution of monarchy to the supreme obligation of total obedience to Yahweh's word in the covenant relationship. Israel will neither stand nor fall because of the monarchy as such; the criterion for her existence is obedience to the word. If that is accepted, then even the kings can experience prosperity (v 14); if obedience is refused, then disaster is sure to sweep down upon king and people. But the note of hope in v 22 is important: Israel's eventual disobedience cannot tie the Lord's hands, for ultimately it is "for his great name's sake" that he has acted in making Israel a people for himself; the same motive could lead him to raise sinful Israel from its ruins.

G. 13:1 — 14:52
SAUL AND JONATHAN DEFEAT THE PHILISTINES

1. *Comment.* The introductory note in 13:1 (which, as the RSV suggests, has reached us in a probably corrupted form) follows the pattern of the regnal formulas found many times in Kings; it is likely to be the work of a Deuteronomistic editor. The rest of the section is pre-Deuteronomistic.

The action begins with a report of an Israelite victory in a skirmish with a Philistine garrison that formed part of the occupying forces in the territory of Benjamin (vv 2-4). A large-scale confrontation follows, and at first things go badly for the Israelites; the Philistines approach with an enormous army (the figures of v 5 are surely hyperbolical!) and many of the Israelites fled (vv 5-7a).

At this point the battle report is interrupted by an account of a clash between Samuel and Saul (vv 7b-15a: probably the work of the prophetic redactor of the Saul and David material). Samuel had arranged to meet Saul at the sanctuary of Gilgal (10:8) but he fails to arrive within the appointed time of seven days. Seeing the critical situation of his troops (v 8b), Saul takes the initiative and offers a sacrifice at the sanctuary. When Samuel finally arrives, he rebukes Saul harshly for this action. Though the reader's sympathies may tend to be with Saul here, the text suggests that he failed to give proof of the total confidence in Yahweh and his representative Samuel that should have been the distinguishing mark of one who fights Yahweh's wars. One can note too that Samuel's announcement in vv 13-14 need not be taken as a rejection of Saul personally (as will be the case in chap. 15); what is meant is that Saul's successor will not be a son of his own but will be another man after the Lord's heart. The latter phrase, which indicates an attitude of complete loyalty to Yahweh, is the first allusion to David in 1 Sam. One can note that the past tense in v 14b means that the Lord has already made his choice of the prince (*nagid*: cf. 9:16) to come.

Verses 15b-22 return to the war narrative. Philistine raiding parties move about at will, and one reason for their success is the fact that they hold a monopoly of iron weapons. Iron-working was still a recent invention in that period, which archaeologists refer to as the Early Iron Age in Palestine.

The tables are turned, however, first by a heroic exploit performed by Saul's son Jonathan and his armour-bearer (13:23 — 14:15), and then by the follow-up attack on the Philistines made by Saul and the rest of the small Israelite army (14:16-23). In this account one can note that Saul's priest (14:3, 18-19, 36) is of the family of Eli of Shiloh (cf. 1

Sam 1-4). Where the RSV reads in 14:18 "the ark of God", many scholars prefer to follow the Greek text and read "the ephod", understanding it not as a garment (thus RSV at v 3) but rather as an instrument used in oracle-seeking. One can also note the presence of motifs and terms typical of the so-called holy war narratives in several places here (vv 6, 10, 12, 15, 23).

The hour of victory is darkened by tensions between Saul and Jonathan, and Saul and the people (vv 24-46). Jonathan unwittingly transgresses against a taboo laid upon the Israelites by Saul, and he criticizes his father for this (vv 24-30). The people too transgress by eating meat with the blood (cf. Gen 9:4; Lev 17:10-16; 19:26; Deut 12:20-27), but a satisfactory solution is quickly found for this (vv 31-35). Jonathan's transgression has more serious effects, and lots are cast to determine the identity of the culprit; Saul, in dogged fidelity to his oath, is ready to put his son Jonathan to death, but the people intervene to prevent this tragedy (vv 36-45). The incident has contacts with Gen 22 (Abraham and Isaac), Josh 7 (Achan's offence), and Judg 11:29-40 (Jephthah's daughter). One can note that the Urim and Thummim (14:41) were instruments used in oracle-seeking.

The section ends with some summary notes dealing with Saul's military campaigns (vv 47-48), his family (vv 49-51), and his creation of a small standing army (for the first time in Israel's history) as a defence against the continued Philistine attacks (v 52).

2. *Significance.* The struggle against overwhelmingly superior Philistine forces has been presented as the occasion for Saul's call to kingship (cf. 9:16) and is the explicit theme of the present section. The outcome of the struggle is twofold. On the one hand, Saul is shown as a brave and capable military leader under whose command the Israelites, inspired by Jonathan's exploit, won a spectacular victory that was due ultimately to Yahweh's favour. On the other hand, the struggle reveals negative aspects in Saul's behaviour: these emerge especially in the theological narrative of his clash with Samuel (13:7b-15a), in the account of his rash

oath which prevented the Israelites from reaping the full fruits of victory (14:24-30), and in the episode where he is shown as ready to kill his own son in blind fidelity to another rash oath (vv 38-44). All these foreshadow the downward trajectory of Saul's career, which will be shown explicitly from chap. 15 on. David has already appeared on the horizon in the anonymous allusion of 13:14, and the theme of his rise to the throne as Saul's divinely chosen successor has been announced in passing (13:13-14).

H.   15:1-35
SAUL'S DISOBEDIENCE BRINGS ABOUT HIS REJECTION AS KING

1. *Comment.*   The main part of the chapter comes from the prophetically influenced redactor of the Saul and David traditions, though there may be some use of older material about a campaign against the Amalekites (cf. 14:48). Samuel reappears here in the role of a prophet; he conveys to Saul the Lord's command to exterminate the nomadic Amalekites in punishment for their attacks against the Exodus generation of Israel (vv 1-3: cf. Exod 17:8-16 and Deut 25:17-19). The war of extermination (v 3) can also be referred to as "putting under the ban." The ban (Hebrew *herem*) was an extreme form of the notion that war was in some way a sacral act (as was generally held all over the ancient Near East). The total destruction of the enemy population and their property was regarded as a means of acknowledging the deity's supreme control of the destinies of war. The whole concept is undoubtedly abhorrent to readers of the Bible today. One can note, however, that Israel's neighbours, specifically the Moabites in Transjordan, had a similar practice, so that the biblical instances of the war of extermination (some of which, in any case, may be more in the nature of a theoretical blueprint than a factual description) can be seen as the acceptance of a cultural practice which had not yet been modified by a more advanced revelation of God's demands.

Saul obeys the command transmitted by Samuel, except

that he takes the Amalekite king alive and reserves the best of the booty for sacrifice to the Lord (vv 4-9). The Kenites (v 6) were a nomadic group who, according to one tradition (Judg 1:16; 4:11), traced their descent to the father-in-law of Moses; they are shown as friendly to the Exodus generation (Exod 18; Num 10: 29-32).

Yahweh's word comes again to Samuel, this time announcing his regret at having made Saul king; Saul excuses his act of disobedience by pleading his pious intentions with regard to the booty (vv 10-15). The town of Carmel (v 12) was situated in southern Judah and is to be distinguished from northern Mount Carmel (cf. 1 Kgs 18). A prophetic speech by Samuel follows in vv 16-19, where he recalls the Lord's past benefits to Saul in order to heighten the impact of his accusing questions. Saul simply repeats his conviction that he has not been at fault and insists on the religious purpose of the spared booty (vv 20-21). Samuel's reply in lapidary poetic form (vv 22-23) uncovers Saul's error by stating that obedience must take precedence over sacrifices, and he announces Saul's punishment by proclaiming his rejection by the Lord.

Saul now acknowledges his sin and pleads in vain with Samuel to return with him to take part in the sacrifice (vv 24-26). As Samuel turns to go, Saul in desperation clutches suppliantly at his robe and accidentally tears it; at this Samuel announces that the kingdom of Israel will be torn from Saul and given to a better man than he (vv 27-28). This incident can be compared to 1 Kgs 11:29-39 (a Deuteronomistic text), where however the tearing of the garment is a deliberate symbolic action. Samuel's words in v 29 are probably due to a later redactor intent on stressing the divine transcendence (cf. Num 23:19) and countervailing an over-literal anthropomorphic understanding of vv 11 and 35b. Saul again acknowledges his sin and pleads with Samuel to return with him to the sacrifice; this time Samuel silently complies (vv 30-31).

At the sanctuary of Gilgal Samuel personally slays the Amalekite king in a ritual act (vv 32-33). The term in v 32 which the RSV renders as "came cheerfully" is of uncertain meaning in Hebrew; other possible translations are "struggling," "with faltering step," or "in fetters." One can note the symbolic force of the concluding verses where Samuel and Saul are shown as going their separate ways (vv 34-35).

2. *Significance.* Chap. 15 explains Saul's failure as king in terms of his disobedience to a prophet's command in the Lord's name. The self-willed behaviour of the conquering king is confronted with the powerless word of a prophet who in reality speaks for the all-powerful Lord. Israel would later experience other cases of this prophetic contestation of royal power. The conflict is heightened here by the sympathetic way in which Saul is presented. He is a tragic figure in this chapter, not a villain; his offence was a well-meaning one (cf. vv 13-15 and 20-21), and Samuel himself is shown as suffering under the Lord's decision to reject Saul (vv 11b, 35). But more is at stake than personal relations between Saul and Samuel, as vv 22-23 make clear. This text, alluded to in Mk 12:33, is a summary of the cultic critique of the classical prophets (e.g. Isa 1:10-17; Hos 6:6; Am 5:21-24; Mic 6:6-8).

Chap. 15 has a pivot function in its context. On the one hand, it looks back to the beginnings of Saul's career (v 1 and 9:16; 10:1; v 17 and 9:21), and shows how the Lord has now turned away from the man whom he had earlier chosen (10:20-25). The stress on the verb "reject" (15:23, 26), which recalls 8:7, and the concluding note of v 35 with its repeated assertion of the Lord's regret at having made Saul king (cf. v 11), mark the end of Saul's career under the Lord's favour and guidance. On the other hand, chap. 15 suggests that Saul's rejection opens the way for David's rise to kingship (cf. v 28, though David's name is not mentioned: cf. 13:14), which leads on to 16:1-13 and all that follows.

IV. 1 Sam 16:1 — 2 Sam 1:27
Saul's Decline and David's Rise

These chapters form the first part of the story of David's rise to kingship over Judah and Israel. In the opinion of many scholars this was once an independent literary unit; its extent is generally held to be 1 Sam 16 — 2 Sam 5, with the climax in David's capture of Jerusalem and his choice of that city as his centre of power. There is some difference of opinion, however, about the limits of the original story of David's rise: its beginning is put by some at 1 Sam 15, while its end is occasionally set at 2 Sam 1 or 2 Sam 8. In any case, the pro-Davidic stance of the author is quite evident in his concern to show that David was no usurper, much less a traitor, but was the divinely chosen successor of Saul. This thesis is developed throughout the various episodes (originally separate traditions in many cases) that make up the confrontation of Saul and David.

The story could well have had a polemical thrust in contemporary politics at the time of its composition. It may have been aimed at disqualifying opposition to David himself on the part of disaffected Benjaminites, supporters of Saul's family (cf. 2 Sam 16:1-13; 19:16-30; 20:1-22); or perhaps its purpose was to discourage northern Israelite opposition to Solomon (cf. 1 Kgs 11) or his successor Rehoboam (1 Kgs 12). In any event, the material has now been incorporated in a much larger theological narrative of the origins of monarchy in Israel, the combined history of Saul and David. The subsequent Deuteronomistic redaction did not intervene to a great extent in 1 Sam 16 — 2 Sam 1.

The text, as we have it now, presents an idealized portrait of David whose every step amid difficult and compromising historical circumstances was guided by the Lord. Saul, deprived of the Lord's spirit, relies on violence to hold his throne and dispose of his rival. His downfall works itself out in a deepening gloom of suspicion, envy, persecution, and superstition (chap. 28), until he falls in battle against the Philistines, recovering in the manner of his dying something of the heroic grandeur that marked his own rise to the throne. David is guided by Yahweh along the path of nonviolence in Saul's regard; his rise from obscure origins to kingship over Judah and Israel is the Lord's work, the new sign of his presence in the history of his people.

A.   16:1-13
SAMUEL ANOINTS DAVID

1. *Comment.*   Samuel is ordered by Yahweh to go south to Bethlehem and anoint there as king one of the sons of Jesse (v 1). Bethlehem, a small Judaean town about six miles south of Jerusalem, appears first in history in a pre-biblical fourteenth century text. Mentioned in Judg 17 and 19 and in Ruth, it is most prominent in the OT as the birthplace of David; from this Davidic association the town later entered the tradition of royal "messianic" hope (Mic 5:2). The allusion to Samuel's fear of Saul (v 2), which contrasts strikingly with the relation between the two men in chap. 15, is probably meant to suggest that Saul has already fallen victim to the morbid suspicions that characterize his downward path in the texts that follow.

In the context of a sacrificial celebration organized by Samuel at Bethlehem, David, the youngest of Jesse's eight sons, is indicated by Yahweh as the chosen one (vv 4 — 12). The common folktale motif of the choice of the most unlikely person for a task is used here to highlight the divine initiative in the choice of the shepherd boy David (compare the case of Jacob and Esau in Gen 27; Ephraim and Manasseh in Gen 48). While David's handsome appearance is stressed (v 12: cf. 1 Sam 9:2; 10:23; 2 Sam 14:25 — 26), this is not the decisive factor in his choice; what matters is that David's heart is completely loyal to Yahweh (16:7; cf. 13:14).

David is then anointed by Samuel and a mighty onrush of the spirit of Yahweh takes possession of him as a permanent gift ("from that day forward," v 13). The Judaean David, no less than the Israelite Saul, receives his call to kingship in a charismatic way; the divine choice is notified by a prophet and authenticated by the gift of the spirit.

2. *Significance.*   The whole text appears to be the work of the prophetic redactor who was responsible for most of chap. 15 too. It is unlikely that a historically reliable tradition underlies the episode (for historical data about David's

royal anointings see 2 Sam 2:4 and 5:3); the purpose of 16:1-13 is decidedly theological. In chap. 15 the rejection of Saul was described and explained and now the choice of David follows; one can note the links between 16:1 and 15:35, and 16:13b and 15:34a. Several contacts exist too with the early part of the Saul traditions, especially 9:1 —10:16. In both cases there is a public sacrificial celebration presided over by Samuel, to which the chosen man is invited in an unusual way: Saul had been looking for the lost asses, David has been keeping his father's sheep. In this way too 16:1-13 is shown to mark a new beginning, destined to replace the failure of Saul's reign. All the historical vicissitudes that follow from 16:14 to 2 Sam 5 are given a theological interpretation in advance by the present section.

B.   16:14-23
DAVID ENTERS SAUL'S SERVICE: THE FIRST ACCOUNT

1. *Comment.*   This short section presents the reader with a problem and its solution. The problem is Saul's state of mind (vv 14-15): the spirit of Yahweh has left him (v 14a: probably an insertion by the prophetic redactor responsible for the preceding passage, in order to contrast with v 13), and "an evil spirit from the Lord" is tormenting him (vv 14b-15). The text is not interested in specifying the nature of the psychological disturbance in question; what matters is that the illness is interpreted as part of the Lord's guidance of events. The "spirit" is said to be "evil" in its effects on Saul; there are no ethical implications here.

Saul's attendants propose music as a remedy, and David is summoned to Saul's house. This provides the solution to Saul's problem, for the moment at least, since David is able to soothe Saul's torment by his skilful playing of the lyre. He is accepted into the king's service as his armour-bearer, and enjoys his lord's favour (vv 16-23). One can note the difference between the presentation of David here and in the preceding section. The shepherd boy of 16:1-13 is reflected only in v 19b here (possibly an addition by the redactor), while the stress is on David as a skilled musician and well-known warrior endowed with the gifts of prudent speech and good presence that make for success in court life (v 18). It is likely that several levels of tradition have been fused into a composite picture of David in this section; many scholars are of the opinion that the basic level constituted the original beginning of the story of David's rise.

2. *Significance.* David's future career as warrior, courtier, and (initially) favourite of Saul is clearly foreshadowed in this section. More important than these human qualities, however, is the theological qualification expressed by one of Saul's attendants in v 18: "the Lord is with him" — a key phrase in the story of David's rise (see, with slight variations, 1 Sam 16:18; 17:37; 18:12, 14, 28; 20:13; 2 Sam 5:10). This is the decisive factor in David's career.

C. 17:1 — 18:5
DAVID KILLS GOLIATH: SECOND ACCOUNT OF HIS ENTRY INTO SAUL'S SERVICE

1. *Comment.* The first unit (vv 1-11) sets the scene: as the Philistine and Israelite armies stand in confrontation, a gigantic heavily armed Philistine warrior named Goliath challenges the Israelites to put forward a champion of their own and decide the issue by single combat; the Israelites are too terrified to respond. One can note the insistence on Goliath's armour here; this introduces a motif that will recur at 17:38-39, 54; 18:4.

An abrupt change of scene brings the shepherd boy David into the story (vv 12-23). His father Jesse sends him from Bethlehem to bring provisions to his three older brothers who are serving in Saul's army; David's role as armour-bearer at Saul's court (16:21) is completely ignored here. The next unit (vv 24-30) contains two typical folktale motifs: the reward offered by the king to whoever would kill the Philistine (v 25: great riches and the hand of his daughter in marriage; the meaning of the third reward is disputed), and the note in vv 28-29 about the jealousy of the elder brother. Indeed the whole theme of chap. 17 — the lightly armed but quick-witted youth confronting the heavily armed giant —is one that is found in many literary traditions.

The stage is thus set for David's two encounters: first with Saul (vv 31-39), for whom David is but a youth inexperienced in war (contrast 16:18, 21), and then with the Philistine champion in the well-known combat scene (vv 40-51). The centre of both scenes is a theological speech by David (vv 34-37, 45-47). After David's victory the Israelites pursue the demoralized Philistines (vv 52-53), while David takes the trophies of victory (v 54). The mention of Jerusalem in v 54 is an anachronism; the city was still in the hands of the non-Israelite Jebusites, and its capture (by David) is told only in 2 Sam 5.

The final unit (17:55 — 18:5) tells of David's meeting with Saul after the battle (Saul does not know who David is: contrast 16:18-23), of the friendship between Saul's son Jonathan and David, and of David's success as a military commander in Saul's service. The symbolic force of Jonathan's gift of his robe and armour to David (18:4) should be noted: seen in the light of what follows, this can be taken to signify that Jonathan, Saul's heir, voluntarily steps aside and gives David full rights to become Saul's successor (cf. 20:14-16).

2. *Special Problems. a) Textual criticism:* While the RSV follows the Hebrew text, we find a considerably shorter version of the story in some Greek manuscripts, which do not contain 17:12-31 and 17:55 — 18:5 (and a few other verses too). The result is that this Greek version of the story fits the context much better, since the parts omitted are precisely those that tell of David's meeting with Saul as if it were their first meeting (which clashes with 16:14-23, as noted several times above). It is not possible here to enter into the technicalities of the various explanations that have been offered for this situation, but it can at least be noted that the present text of the story is clearly the product of a

long and complicated history of tradition and is the work of more than one author.

b) Historicity: This problem is raised by a comparison with 2 Sam 21:19 which states that Goliath was slain by a certain Elhanan of Bethlehem; critical study of the context of that notice favours its antiquity and reliability. Two explanations are then possible for 1 Sam 17. (1) The original level of tradition here told of a combat between David and an anonymous Philistine warrior; as time went on, this tradition was expanded and magnified, and in the process the name Goliath (which occurs here only at 17:4, 23) was borrowed from the Elhanan notice of 2 Sam 21 together with the description of his spear-shaft (17:7; 2 Sam 21:19). (2) 1 Sam 17 could also be read as a free theological composition in narrative form that borrowed motifs from 2 Sam 21:19, the purpose of the story being to illustrate David's role as the Lord's instrument in delivering his people.

3. *Significance.* The question of historicity is of secondary importance in any case; it is the theological statements of 17:26b, 36b-37, 45-47 (all spoken by David) that spell out the meaning of this gripping narrative. Human military power defies the Lord of Israel at its own peril; Yahweh can rescue his people by the unlikely means of a shepherd boy with his sling and a few stones. A lesson in the theology of history, useful for later generations, is conveyed here, but there is a more particular significance too in that it is David who is shown as the Lord's instrument.

Clearly the Lord's favour is with this youth, even in the crucible of battle when the other Israelites tremble with fear (17:11, 24). Great things are obviously in store for him. Small wonder that both Saul (18:2) and Jonathan (18:1, 3-4) as well as Saul's courtiers and all the people (18:5) regard David so highly. Who better than he is qualified to be the future king?

D. 18:6 — 20:42 (HEBREW: 18:6 — 21:1)
THE BREAK BETWEEN SAUL AND DAVID

1. *Comment.* This long section, though composed of several smaller units some of which were originally independent traditions, can now be read as a thematic unity which traces the deterioration in relations between Saul and David.

In 18:6-30 we find two occurrences of a narrative pattern consisting of a pair of incidents followed by a summary notice concerned with David's success and popularity. The first occurrence of the pattern (vv 6-16) presents the emergence of Saul's suspicions that David may be a rival for the throne (vv 6-9), followed by Saul's first attempt to kill David in a moment of psychic unbalance (vv 10-11); the summary of vv 12-16 focuses on David's military success, Saul's growing fear of him, and his popularity with all the people. The second unit (vv 17-30) tells of Saul's refusal to carry out his promise to give his eldest daughter Merab to David as his wife (vv 17-19), of the heroic way in which David fulfilled Saul's malevolent conditions for marrying his younger daughter Michal (vv 20-27), and concludes with the summary note of vv 28-30.

Chap. 19 begins with a scene where Jonathan comes between his father's homicidal intentions and David (vv 1-7), and ends with a scene where Samuel comes between Saul and David (vv 18-24). The centre of the chapter is taken up by an account of David's escape from a second attack on his life by the ailing Saul (vv 9-10) and then from Saul's messengers who had come to arrest him in his home and kill him (vv 11-17). The "image" mentioned in the latter scene (vv 13, 16) as having been used by Michal to trick Saul's messengers, was probably a statue of a household divinity (cf. Gen 31:19; Judg 17:5). The detail affords an interesting glimpse of popular religious practices in Israel; though such idols later came to be severely condemned (cf. 2 Kgs 23:24), the early narrator apparently saw nothing particularly blameworthy here; later readers, it is true, could take the

incident as reflecting badly on Michal's religious fidelity to
Yahweh (see then 2 Sam 6:16, 20-23). The final scene of the
chapter (vv 18-24) contradicts the statement of 15:35 that
Samuel never saw Saul again until the day of his death (cf.
chap. 28!). This is one indication that 19:18-24 is a later
addition to the story; another sign of this is the fact that the
popular proverb of v 24 has already been explained in a
similar, though not identical, pericope at 10:10-12. It can
also be noted that the term "Naioth" (vv 18ff), which the
RSV takes to be a place name, could also be rendered as a
common noun meaning "camps" or "sheds" (cf. New American Bible); in this case the reference might be to the rudi-
mentary community buildings of the prophetical fraternity
(cf. 2 Kgs 6:1-2).

In chap. 20 Jonathan's friendship with David, sealed by
oath in a sacred covenant (v 8), is the occasion for the public
manifestation of Saul's intention to have David killed; Jonathan acknowledges David's future royal destiny and gains
a promise of loyal gracious treatment for his own descendants; David gets word of Saul's intentions, thanks to a
stratagem engineered by Jonathan, and is enabled to escape.

2. *Significance.*   The sequence of events shows that the
initiative in the break between Saul and David came solely
from the former. David takes the initiative only against the
Philistines (18:6, 13-14, 27, 30; 19:8); he reacts to Saul's
violence only by evasion and flight (18:11; 19:10, 12, 17, 18;
20:1, 42). In this way the text insists on David's blamelessness with regard to Saul (see explicitly 19:4-5; 20:1, 8).

In other ways too the section paints contrasting pictures
of Saul and David. Saul is subject to possession by an evil
spirit (18:10; 19:9) which has already been interpreted as an
indication that Yahweh's spirit has abandoned him (16:14;
see also 18:12 but without mention of the spirit). Corroded
by jealous suspicion of David's popularity (18:8-9), he fears
him (18:12, 15, 29) and tries to get rid of him indirectly by
means of the Philistines (18:17, 21, 25; using his daughters as
unwitting pawns in the plan) or directly by means of his son
Jonathan and his courtiers (19:1). Twice he himself attempts

physical attack (18:10-11; 19:9-10). He sends messengers to kill David (19:11ff) and then orders Jonathan to have David seized and brought to him for execution (20:31). On realizing the strong bond of friendship between David and Jonathan, Saul violently rebukes his son (20:30) and tries to kill him too with a spear throw (20:33). Violent, treacherous, and an oath-breaker (cf. 19:6), Saul is shown here in almost wholly negative terms (except for 19:6-7). His political instinct may be sharp enough (18:8-9; 20:31), but he is quite out of tune with the Lord's guidance of events and people.

David, on the other hand, enjoys the Lord's favour (18:12, 14, 28). This is recognized and applauded by Jonathan (20:13-16, 22) who, far from seeking to ensure his own succession to the throne, actively supports David and enters into a covenant with him. Saul's daughter Michal too, who has fallen in love with David (18:20) and becomes his wife, later helps to save him from her father (19:11-17). All Israel and Judah admire his valour and success (18:6-7, 16, 28), and the venerable figure of Samuel is shown to be on David's side as well (19:18ff). While Saul is exposed as ungrateful in David's regard (19:4-5), David's own gratitude to Saul's son Jonathan is mentioned with deep pathos (20:41); this will have its repercussions later (cf. 2 Sam 9).

At this point it is clear that Saul is an abandoned and doomed man, while David is the Lord's choice for the throne. The following chapters delay the outcome but they do not put it in doubt.

E.   21:1 — 22:23 (HEBREW: 21:2 — 22:23)
DAVID'S FLIGHT FROM SAUL BEGINS; SAUL MASSACRES THE PRIESTS OF NOB

1. *Comment.* The tragic story of the priests of Nob opens and closes the section (21:1-9 and 22:6-23). Enclosed in this framework we find two narratives about David's meeting with foreign kings (Achish of Gath at 21:10-15; the king of Moab at 22:3-5) which themselves have a centre-

piece in the account of the gathering of David's first followers (22:1-2). The section does not offer a straightforward
chronicle of events; if it did, then the Nob units should be
placed together, since the intervening material (21:10 —
22:5) necessarily implies the passage of a considerable
period of time. Clearly, then, the author of the story of
David's rise has collected various traditions here and structured them according to literary criteria.

David's first stopping-place in his flight from Saul is at
the sanctuary of Nob (21:1-9). Situated a short distance
north of Jerusalem, Nob appears to have replaced Shiloh as
the centre of the Elide line of priests. David deceives the
priest Ahimelech into giving him food and a sword by telling
him a story about an urgent mission entrusted to him by
Saul. One can note David's assertion that his (non-existent)
followers have not had intercourse with women since the
start of their journey; this reflects the concept of "holy war"
which called for continence on the part of the soldiers (cf. 2
Sam 11:11). The scene has been witnessed by Doeg (v 7),
who was "detained before the Lord," that is, under some
religious obligation to be present in the sanctuary. Doeg, an
Edomite (a people related to the Israelites, living originally
in Transjordan to the east and south of the Dead Sea), is
described as the chief of Saul's herdsmen (thus RSV with the
Hebrew); a slight emendation would give the reading "chief
of Saul's runners (or, guard)" (cf. 22:17).

The scene shifts to the Philistine city of Gath (vv 10-15).
David seeks refuge there but he is obliged to escape by
another act of deception, this time by feigning madness,
when the Philistines begin to recall his victories over them in
the past. There is a surprising reference to David as "king of
the land" in v 11: in the mouth of the Philistines the phrase
apparently means that David is a local chieftain, but the
reader who knows the outcome of the story in its final form
can see here an unconscious prophecy. The Hebrew narrator takes delight in describing David's antics as he plays the
madman (v 13); the laugh is against the Philistines, natu-
rally, as their king lets it be understood that he has quite

enough lunatics in his kingdom already without needing an extra one (v 14). The whole scene (of dubious historicity) may have been inserted here in order to provide in advance a corrective to the rather more compromising presentation of chap. 27 where David appears as a willing vassal of the Philistine king, one of Israel's arch-enemies.

An interesting description of David's first followers is given in 22:1-2. They include not only people from his own clan but also those who, for one reason or another, were at odds with the existing social and economic order. One can recall the ancient Near Eastern (and OT) view that one of the main functions of a king was to ensure justice for his people. A friendly act in David's regard by the king of Moab is noted in vv 3-5; the Book of Ruth suggests there was a Moabite strain in David's own ancestry. The prophet Gad, mentioned for the first time in v 5, will reappear in 2 Sam 24.

The second part of the narrative about the priests of Nob follows in 22:6-23. The scene opens with Saul's address to his followers. He is sitting under a tamarisk tree with his spear in his hand (v 6). The spear reminds the reader of Saul's attempts on the lives of David (18:10-11; 19:9-10) and Jonathan (20:33) and thus provides a skilful introduction to the account of another scene of violence. The mention of the tamarisk tree acquires further resonance on a second reading of the story, once the reader knows that it is under a tamarisk tree that Saul is to be buried (31:13); already here in chap. 22, then, he is in the shadow of death. As Saul accuses his Benjaminite kinsmen of siding with David, he is informed by Doeg the Edomite (cf. 21:7) of the help given to David by Ahimelech the priest of Nob (vv 7-10). Ahimelech and all his family are summoned and accused of treason by Saul who refuses to listen to the priest's perfectly reasonable explanations and orders that he and his family be executed (vv 11-16). Saul's own bodyguard refuse to obey this impious command but Doeg has no such scruples; he kills eighty-five priests and goes on the massacre every living being in the town of Nob (vv 17-19). Only one of the priestly family, Abiathar, managed to ecape and he seeks refuge with David who admits his responsibility for what has happened (vv 20-23).

2. *Significance.* Saul continues to be depicted in a bad light. He is morbidly suspicious, even of his own tribesmen (22:7-8); he makes wild accusations against his son Jonathan (22:8b); he turns a deaf ear to Ahimelech's explanations (22:14-15). The only man who obeys his cruel command is an Edomite (a people whom later Israelites will hold in particular abhorrence: cf. Isa 63:1ff; Jer 49:7ff; Am 1:11-12).

Though David's deception of Ahimelech had tragic consequences, he acknowledges his responsibility (22:22) and the text puts the real blame on Doeg. While David began his flight without provisions, without weapons, and without followers, the end of the section finds him at the head of four hundred followers and having the support of the only surviving member of the priestly family of Nob. It is clear that he is led by God's guidance (cf. 22:3b), as is shown explicitly by his obedience to the voice of a prophet (22:5).

In the wider perspective of the Deuteronomistic edition of Samuel and Kings, the massacre of the Elide priests of Nob can be seen as a fulfilment of the prophetic announcement of 1 Sam 2:31, 33b; Abiathar is the "man . . . spared to weep out his eyes and grieve his heart" (2:33a) until his removal from the priestly office by Solomon (1 Kgs 2:26-27).

F.   23:1-29 (HEBREW: 23:1 — 24:1)
DAVID TWICE ELUDES SAUL'S PURSUIT

1. *Comment.* The localities mentioned in the several, originally independent, traditions of chap. 23 are all situated within or near the borders of Judah. The town of Keilah, the setting for vv 1-13, has been saved by David from Philistine attack (vv 1-5), but the ungrateful notables of the town intend to betray him to Saul; warned of this by an oracle David and his followers move out of Keilah in time, and Saul gives up the expedition (vv 6-13). At v 6 the New American Bible follows the Greek version in its longer

reading: "Abiathar, son of Ahimelech, who had fled to David, went down with David to Keilah, taking the ephod with him"; this avoids the clash with 22:20-23 present in the Hebrew text and the RSV.

The more general note of vv 14-18 contrasts the behaviour of Saul and of Jonathan towards David: Saul continually seeks David's life, but Jonathan comes to David in his hiding-place and encourages him by assuring him of his future kingship and by renewing the solemn covenant of friendship (cf. 18:3; 20:8). The wider theological perspectives of vv 16-18 suggest that these verses were inserted by the redactor of the combined Saul and David story.

The second detailed account of a pursuit expedition by Saul follows in vv 19-29. This time too David is betrayed by the local inhabitants (vv 19-20), and his position seems hopeless when suddenly a message comes to Saul reporting a Philistine raid which calls for the king's immediate presence elsewhere. David and his men are thus saved unwittingly by the Philistines, the account of whose defeat by David began the chapter.

2. *Significance.* The most important aspect of David's outlaw life in Judah is the Lord's continual assistance — by oracles (vv 2-4, 9-12), by the unexpected visit and encouraging words of Jonathan (vv 16-18), and by the final providential escape from Saul (v 27: only that here readers are left to supply the theological interpretation for themselves). Saul's pursuit is doomed to failure, not simply because of David's superior ability and knowledge of the terrain, but above all because "God did not give him into his hand" (v 14). In the crucible of betrayal (unavenged!) and distress the future king of Israel is being prepared for his mission, as Jonathan's words (v 17) remind the reader.

G. 24:1-22 (HEBREW: 24:2-23)
DAVID SPARES SAUL'S LIFE: THE FIRST
ACCOUNT

1. *Comment.* The first unit (vv 1-7) tells of another expedition organized by Saul to hunt down David who is in the

wilderness of En-gedi overlooking the western shore of the
Dead Sea. During the pursuit, however, it is David who has
Saul at his mercy when the king retires into a cave to relieve
himself (vv 2-3). David refuses to follow his men's urging to
kill his persecutor, but he stealthily cuts off a piece of Saul's
garment and allows the king to depart (vv 4-7). The oracle to
which David's soldiers allude in v 4 has not been mentioned
previously in these precise terms; Jonathan's words at 20:15-
16 are perhaps the closest but they do not have the form of
an oracle. David's action of cutting off part of Saul's robe
may not be quite as innocent as it might appear to be. In the
ancient Near East clothes could have a strong symbolical
signification, expressing the wearer's social dignity and
rights. Though David did not harm Saul bodily, he did
perform a gravely offensive act towards the king (compare 2
Sam 10:4-5), as is suggested too by his subsequent feelings of
remorse (v 5). The rest of the narrative, however, glosses
over this aspect and concentrates on David's refusal to take
Saul's life.

David then defends himself in a strongly rhetorical
speech, in which he blames Saul for listening to slanderous
accusations against him (v 9), gives proof of his innocence
by pointing to his behaviour that day (vv 10-11), and
appeals to Yahweh to vindicate his innocence (vv 12-15).
One can note that the term in v 12 which the RSV renders as
"avenge" does not imply the exercise of vendetta; the reference is rather to an act of defensive vindication which the
Lord is asked to perform in David's favour.

Saul admits his guilt and David's innocence, acknowledges him as future king (cf. 23:17), and asks him to guarantee under oath the safety of Saul's descendants (vv 16-21).
The latter point recalls Jonathan's statements at 20:14-16
(with an oath in v 17, as here). David takes the oath as
requested and the two men part (v 22).

2. *Significance.* The text insists above all on David's
condition of total blamelessness with regard to Saul and his
respect for the latter's status as the anointed one of Yahweh
(vv 6, 10). The break between the two is here attributed to

slanderous accusations to which Saul had mistakenly given ear (v 9); one notes that Saul's own suspicions, jealousy, and violence (often mentioned in chaps 18ff) are not considered. Saul is characterized here by his personal submission to Yahweh's designs for David's future. Not only is he moved to tears of repentance (v 16), but he hails David as future king (v 20: in strident contrast to his attitude presented at 20:31; 22:7-8, 13). This sudden change surprises the reader, and one's feeling that the chapter is far from being a wholly realistic account of events and (especially) words is heightened when one finds Saul at the start of chap. 26 back at his old activity of pursuing David.

The theological justification of David's rise to kingship comes to its first climax in this chapter. David has been shown as having already won the favour of all the people, of Samuel, of the priest Abiathar, and of Saul's own son and daughter; now it is Saul himself who acknowledges David's royal destiny and joins Jonathan (cf. 20:42) in pleading for mercy for his descendants.

H.   25:1-44
NABAL, ABIGAIL, AND DAVID

1. *Comment.*   An isolated notice about Samuel's death and burial (v 1a) precedes the introduction to the Abigail and Nabal story (vv 1b-3). The action takes place in the same south Judaean area as the preceding chapters. Nabal, a rich sheep-farmer, belongs to the Calebite clan, a strong group centered on Hebron and incorporated into the tribe of Judah. As an adjective the term *nabal* means "foolish, boorish, brutish" and, as v 25 notes explicitly, in this case the name suits its bearer. In contrast to her husband, Abigail is both intelligent and beautiful (v 3).

The action begins (vv 4-13) with David's message to Nabal requesting a contribution on the joyful occasion of Nabal's shearing-feast (cf. 2 Sam 13:23ff). Nabal's refusal is contemptuously brusque; his description of David as a runaway servant (v 10) is harsh but, it must be admitted, externally exact (cf. 22:2). The admirably polite phraseology of David's message in vv 6-8 does not really disguise the fact that he and his men have been making their living from what amounted to a protection racket. Nabal refuses to pay his protection money, so David organizes a punitive expedition against him and his household (v 13: cf. vv 33-34).

It is only the intervention of the quick-witted Abigail that averts the threatened destruction of her household (vv 14-35). She brings gifts to David (vv 14-23), makes a long and eloquent plea (vv 24-31), and receives a favourable reply from David who accepts her gifts, praises her lavishly, and calls off his troops (vv 32-35).

The denouement comes in two phases. The negative relationship between Nabal and David, created by the former's boorishness, ends in his death brought about directly by the Lord (vv 36-38). The curious remark in v 37 that Nabal's "heart died within him" ten days before his actual death (v 38) might refer to a heart attack or stroke, but it can also be taken in a metaphorical sense as "his courage died within him" (New American Bible). The positive relationship between Abigail and David, created by the former's quick thinking, resolute action, and eloquent words, ends in their marriage (vv 39-42). A romantic ending, but also a very practical one, because it undoubtedly won for David the support of the powerful Calebite families in southern Judah.

The section concludes with a note about David's other wives (vv 43-44). Saul's daughter Michal had been given to another man after David's flight; the sequel to this will be found at 2 Sam 3:12-16.

2. *Significance.*   On a more external level the text shows us something of David's way of life in his outlaw days, but its real concern goes deeper. The theme of David's blamelessness is important here, as it was in chap. 24, but now the situation is more complex. David is shown here as having decided initially to secure redress by violent self-help (v 13); he was held back from this, proximately by Abigail's inter-

vention (v 33) but ultimately by Yahweh's guidance (vv 26, 34, 39). No longer is David portrayed as blameless by his own natural tendency, so to speak, as we might be inclined to infer from chaps 24 and 26; his freedom from blood-guilt in chap. 25 is effected by the Lord against David's initial intention. The theme of David's innocence, one of the major concerns of the whole story of David's rise, reaches a deeper theological dimension here.

Verses 28-31 contain material of considerable theological importance. David has been appointed prince (*nagid*) of Israel (v 30: cf. 9:16); his descendants too are promised the Lord's support (v 28: the theme and phraseology recall the dynastic oracle of 2 Sam 7); his wars are Yahweh's wars (v 28: is this meant to correct the image of the rapacious outlaw chieftain reflected in the earlier part of the chapter?); his enemies, present and future (one thinks of Saul and, later, of Absalom), will be defeated by the Lord (v 29). There is undoubtedly much redactional material in vv 28-31, perhaps from the pre-Deuteronomistic editor of the combined Saul and David story.

I. 26:1-25
DAVID SPARES SAUL'S LIFE: THE SECOND ACCOUNT

1. *Comment.* The remarkable similarity between the present section and chap. 24 (with 23:19ff) may indicate that both narratives go back to a common early tradition, which developed in different ways in the course of transmission. Chap. 26 may have been transmitted in military circles (one notes the mention of Abishai and Joab, well-known officers in David's army, and the details about Saul's encampment); chap. 24, interested less in realistic details than in theological evaluation, may have developed in a more reflective environment.

The introduction to the story (vv 1-4) sets the scene by describing yet another pursuit expedition organized by Saul on the basis of information received from the Judaean

Ziphites (cf. 23:19-20). Action predominates in the first act (vv 5-12): David accompanied by his nephew Abishai steals into Saul's camp at night. Abishai and Joab (v 6) were the sons of David's sister Zeruiah (1 Chr 2:16); singly or together, the brothers will appear often in the narratives of 2 Sam. Abishai wants to kill the sleeping Saul but David forbids him in the central dialogue of vv 8-11 (cf. 1 Sam 24:4-7; 2 Sam 16:9ff; 19:21ff). Instead, the two just take Saul's spear and a jar of water from beside the sleeping king (the equivalent of the garment-cutting motif in chap. 24) and make their way out of the camp again. They are undisturbed, because a "deep sleep from the Lord" had fallen on all in the camp (v 12). This signifies that it was the Lord's special providence that made possible David's daring action; for other mentions of the often preternatural "deep sleep" see Gen 2:21; 15:12; Isa 29:10; Job 4:13; 33:15; Prov 19:15.

In the second act (vv 13-25) dialogue predominates. David, shouting from a nearby hill, chides Saul's general Abner for the negligence of the guards (vv 13-16). Addressing Saul he insists on his innocence and complains about being driven out of Israel (vv 18-20). The alternatives stated by David in v 19 can be compared to 2 Sam 15:25-26; the connection implied by vv 19-20 between absence from Israel and separation from the worship of Yahweh reflects an archaic concept of different local spheres of influence for different divinities, which disappeared with the explicit awareness of radical monotheism in later OT times. Saul admits his sin in David's regard and invites him to return (v 21). Though David does not accept the invitation, he sends back the spear and prays for the Lord's favour and deliverance. Finally Saul blesses David (v 25a), and the two go their separate ways (v 25b). The text does not tell of any other meeting between Saul and David.

2. *Significance.* As in chap. 24, the main point here is David's complete blamelessness; the break with Saul was not his fault. It may have been the result of slanderous instigations by some of Saul's courtiers (v 19: cf. 24:10), or it

may have been a mysterious decision of Yahweh himself (v 19: no parallel to this in chap. 24, but see 2 Sam 15:26; 16:11; 24:1). Though there are some glances into David's future career (especially in vv 23-25 where the hand of a later redactor is likely), these are less explicit than in chap. 24, and echoes of 2 Sam 7 do not occur here. David's words to Abner in v 16 can be taken as prophetic by the reader who knows the rest of the story (cf. 2 Sam 3), and the same can be said for v 10b (cf. 29:4, 31).

The image of Saul that emerges from chap. 26 is much less abject than was the case in chap. 24. The camp setting is more consonant with a king's dignity than the cave situation of chap. 24, and it is by a combination of David's courage and the Lord's providence (v 12) that Saul comes into David's power here, not by a very banal chance as at 24:3. Though Saul admits his guilt and error (26:21), he does not weep (contrast 24:16) and his words throughout are more dignified and indeed more generous (cf. v 21) than in chap. 24.

J.   27:1 — 28:2
DAVID IN THE SERVICE OF A PHILISTINE KING

1. *Comment.* This section consists of three short reports in 27:1-12, followed by the introduction (28:1-2) to the narrative of 29:1ff which has been separated from it by the insertion of 28:3-25. The first report (vv 1-4) explains why David sought refuge with Achish, the Philistine king of Gath in the area west of Judah. Next (vv 5-7) Achish's concession of the town of Ziklag to David is reported; such quasi-feudal grants were common in the Syro-Palestinian kingdoms and often carried with them the obligation to perform military service for the overlord, as is the case here. The third report (vv 8-12) tells how David deceived Achish by claiming to have plundered Judaean territories while in fact he was operating against non-Israelite tribes in the southern desert; the term "Negeb" (v 10) was a general name for the southern regions of Judah, sub-divided according to tribal or clan units (cf. 30:14).

At the start of another Philistine campaign against Israel (28:1-2) David is appointed by Achish as his permanent bodyguard. The narrative breaks off here, due to the insertion of vv 3-25, and the reader is left in a state of suspense. Up to now David has succeeded in tricking Achish, but the planned war against Israel seems to put him in an impossible position. On a second reading of the David story the irony of David's reply in v 2a will be appreciated better. What David can do will indeed become known to Achish but it will go beyond Achish's plans! It will be seen that 1 Kgs 2:39ff suggests that Achish was a vassal of Solomon and it is quite likely that he had been David's vassal before that (cf. 2 Sam 8:1, 12).

2. *Significance.* The historical fact that David was in the service of a Philistine king at the very time when Saul and the Israelites were disastrously defeated by the Philistines (see chaps 29-31) must have caused much embarrassment for later generations. We have already met one attempt to deal with the problem (21:10-15), and the apologetic tone of the present section is another sign of the awkwardness of the situation. The thesis is, of course, that David is free from blame. He went over to the Philistines only as a last resort, because Saul's persecution was threatening his destruction (vv 1, 4); during his Philistine service he never harmed the Judaeans but plundered the desert tribes who were Judah's enemies (on Amalek see chaps 15 and 30). So Achish was deceived, the Judaeans were spared, their enemies were slaughtered, and David and his followers were safe.

Some readers may find it disturbing that David is shown as having no scruples about killing off all the inhabitants of the areas he raided in order to prevent news of his real activities from reaching Achish (vv 9, 11). Two remarks may be useful here: (1) such violence was part of the conditions of the time — wars and raids, then as now, were a cruel and bloody business; (2) the purpose of this story (and of many other OT texts) is not to present the protagonist as a model of sainthood but to show, explicitly or (as here) implicitly, that the miseries as well as the splendours of human behaviour and history could be used by the Lord to further his transcendently holy designs. To take scandal at biblical texts of this kind is to ignore the realities of the human situation and the meaning of divine grace.

K. 28:3-25
SAUL AND THE WITCH OF ENDOR

1. *Comment.* The introduction (vv 3-7) describes the circumstances that reduced Saul to seeking knowledge of the future from a medium. The situation is that of the eve of the battle between Israel and the Philistines (cf. chap. 31); the Philistines are encamped in the northern plain of Jezreel (v 4) and the Israelites on Mount Gilboa overlooking the plain. Saul's expulsion of the mediums and wizards (v 3) has not been mentioned previous to this, but it is fully in accord with the stern disapproval and prohibition of such practices expressed by Exod 22:18; Lev 19:31; 20:6, 27: Deut 18:9-14; 2 Kgs 17:17; 21:6; 23:24; Isa 2:6; 8:19. In spite of that, Saul's fear and Yahweh's silence (vv 5-6) lead the king to seek out a medium in the village of Endor, a few miles south of Mount Tabor.

The woman is persuaded by the disguised king to overcome her fears and exercise her forbidden art; in a night seance she summons up the shade of Samuel from the underworld (vv 8-14). The details of the scene are not clear: it may be that the woman's technique was to call up the shade of the dead person through a trench or hole dug in the ground for that purpose (cf. Isa 29:4) and used also as a receptacle for sacrificial offerings for the dead. It would appear from vv 13-14 that only the medium actually saw the shade; Saul only hears the words of Samuel (vv 15ff). What the woman sees is termed "a god" (v 13 RSV); the Hebrew term can indicate any sort of otherworldly being, in this case a shade from the underworld of Sheol.

Samuel's words (vv 15-19) form the climax of the story. In uncompromising terms he denounces once again Saul's infidelity to Yahweh and declares that the battle against the

Philistines will end in total defeat for Israel and the death of Saul and his sons. The closing scene (vv 20-25) shows Saul prostrate with exhaustion and fear; the woman persuades him to overcome his depression and take some food, after which Saul and his attendants leave. It is still night.

2.   *Significance.*   Just as chap. 25, whose main characters were David and a woman (Abigail), was framed by two accounts about David and Saul (chaps 24; 26), so too chap. 28, whose main characters are Saul and a woman (the medium), is framed by two accounts about David and the Philistine king Achish (chaps 27; 29). The compositional similarity serves to highlight the thematic contrast: in chap. 25 David's glorious destiny is announced in very explicit terms (espec. vv 28-31), while in chap. 28 Saul reaches the nadir of his career prostrate on the ground beside a divination pit, doomed to die in battle on the following day.

The spirit-filled hero of chap. 11 is now fearful and despairing (vv 5, 15, 20); the inner contradictions of his life come to a head when he violates his own prohibition against recourse to mediums (vv 3, 9-10). The Lord's dreadful silence in his regard now (vv 6, 15) can be explained from Samuel's words as the outcome of Saul's former refusal to listen to the voice of the Lord (v 18). When Saul now invokes Yahweh's name (v 10), it is to guarantee impunity to a woman exercising her anti-Yahwistic divinatory art. Samuel's words to Saul in 15:23 come to mind: "For rebellion is as the sin of divination"; one can also note several direct allusions to chap. 15 in 28:17-18.

Just as Saul was only a background figure in chap. 25, so too David receives only a brief mention here (v 17), but this is enough to underline once again the basic movement of the whole story from 1 Sam 16 on: Saul's descent, David's rise.

L.   29:1-11
THE PHILISTINES FORBID DAVID TO TAKE
PART IN THE BATTLE AGAINST ISRAEL

1.   *Comment.*   The Philistines are mustering their forces at Aphek on the coastal plain (v 1: cf. 4:1); the topographical

note shows that the present section is chronologically prior to 28:3-25 where the Philistines had already arrived in the northern plain. The first unit (vv 1-5) tells how David's overlord, King Achish, tried in vain to defend his vassal against charges of possible treachery in the imminent battle, which had been brought against him by the other Philistine leaders. The possibility that mercenaries would change sides in the heat of a battle (v 4) is quite realistic and has a precedent (also involving Hebrews fighting for the Philistines) at 14:21. The song quoted by the Philistines in v 5 is also found at 18:7 and 21:12.

In the second unit (vv 6-11) Achish breaks the news to David that he must return to Ziklag and not take part in the battle; still protesting his loyalty, David leads his men away from the confrontation with Saul and the Israelites and journeys south. The gleeful attitude of the pro-Davidic narrator can be observed in several flashes of ironical humour here. Achish, totally unaware (vv 3, 6, 9) of David's deception recounted in 27:8-12, earnestly defends David's loyalty and suffers evident embarrassment in communicating to him the decision of the leaders (vv 6-7, 9-10). Achish even uses the name of Yahweh (v 6: its only occurrence in the chapter!) in an oath to express his convictions, and then in v 9 he uses for the same purpose a hyperbolical simile "you are as blameless in my sight as an angel of God" (the comparison appears to have been current in Jerusalem court style: see 2 Sam 14:17, 20; 19:27). David responds to the order of dismissal in a tone of sad reproof (v 8), as if the ingratitude of the Philistines pained him greatly; one notes the ambiguity of his reference to "the enemies of my lord the king" (v 8), since his lord the king could be Achish or could be Saul (for the latter see vv 4, 10).

2. *Significance.* The point of the section is to show how David was released from the dangerous predicament he found himself in at 28:1-2. It is the Philistines themselves who refuse to let him fight against Israel and make him leave quickly (v 10), so that when the battle takes place David and his men are far away to the south. Consequently David is absolutely innocent of any part in the deaths of Saul and his

sons — deaths that in fact turned out to be enormously to David's advantage. The theme of David's blamelessness under the Lord's providential guidance dominates the section.

M.   30:1-31
DAVID DEFEATS THE AMALEKITES

1.   *Comment.*   The introduction to this section (vv 1-6) describes the disastrous situation found by David and his men when they reached their base: the nomadic Amalekites had raided Ziklag in his absence, burnt the town, and carried off the women and children together with much booty; David's men are so embittered that they think even of stoning their leader, but David's trust in Yahweh remains unshaken. The central part (vv 7-20) tells of David's reaction: in obedience to an oracle-decision he sets out with six hundred of his soldiers, two hundred of whom are left behind after a while to guard the baggage; the Amalekites are taken by surprise in the midst of their victory carousal and are routed; David and his men regain their families and their possessions, and take much booty from the Amalekites besides.

A dispute about the division of the booty is told in vv 21-25. David overrides the objections of some disgruntled followers and decrees that the men who had been left to guard the baggage had a right to a share in the booty together with those who had actually fought in the battle. The easily remembered rhythmic form of the decision (v 24), together with the formal statement of v 25 (cf. Exod 15:25; Josh 24:25), suggests that the whole episode is meant as an exemplary justification of a military custom in Israel. A much later treatment of the question of booty taken in war can be seen in Num 31:25-47.

The section concludes (vv 26-31) with a report of the gifts which David selected from the booty and sent to various localities in Judah and neighbouring southern areas.

2.   *Significance.*   Everything seemed to have gone well for David at the end of chap. 29: he had avoided fighting against

Israel while remaining in the favour of his overlord Achish. All the more sudden and impressive, then, is the change to loss, suffering and opposition at 30:1-6. The proposal to stone David (v 6) suggests a resemblance between his situation and that of Moses (Exod 17:4). Suffering was part of David's way to the throne, and it will accompany him as king too (2 Sam 13-20). Of decisive importance, however, is the fact that David finds his strength in Yahweh in this hour of loss and isolation (v 6). Though opposed by his own followers, David is not abandoned by the Lord: the oracle mediated by the priest Abiathar (vv 7-8) is the practical sign of the Lord's assistance and this is proved when the "rescue" promised by the oracle is amply realized in vv 17-20.

The political outcome of this incident, as shown in vv 26-31, was a further improvement in relations between David and the Judaeans (see already 23:1-5; 27:8-12); this will bear fruit in 2 Sam 2.

N. 31:1-13
ISRAEL IS DEFEATED BY THE PHILISTINES;
SAUL AND HIS SONS DIE ON MOUNT GILBOA

1. *Comment.* The first unit (vv 1-7) is a rather laconic report of the crushing Philistine victory over Israel. The battle took place at the south-eastern end of the Plain of Jezreel, and its outcome gave the Philistines control over the Israelite settlements near the Plain and across the Jordan (cf. v 7). The situation had practically returned to what it had been at the start of Saul's reign. Three of Saul's sons, including Jonathan, fell in the battle (v 2); nothing is said of the presence of another son, Ishbosheth, who was Saul's successor for a short period (2 Sam 2:8ff). The king himself, badly wounded, committed suicide (vv 3-5) — an action rarely mentioned in the OT (see 2 Sam 17:23; 1 Kgs 16:18; 2 Macc 10:13; 14:37-46) and apparently not regarded as blameworthy by the present text.

Verses 8-13 describe how the bodies of Saul and his sons were treated. The Philistines cut off Saul's head and exposed his body on the walls of Beth-shan (a town in the Jordan valley near the site of the battle), showing that they viewed him as an extremely dangerous enemy. The kindly action of the men of Jabesh-gilead (vv 11-13) recalls Saul's deliverance of their town at the start of his career (1 Sam 11). They make a lightning raid on Beth-shan to seize the bodies of Saul and his sons and bury them with due honour and solemnity; the particular burial rite mentioned in vv 12-13 (part-cremation, part-burial) is not attested elsewhere; for the detail of the tamarisk tree (v 13) see 1 Sam 22:6 with the comment.

2. *Significance.* The image of Saul presented here does not insist on the negative traits that have been so frequently emphasized since 1 Sam 15 (or even 1 Sam 13). From the depths of his abjection depicted in chap. 28, Saul rises here to something approaching heroic stature, and this note will recur even more strongly in David's lament in the next chapter. Furthermore, Saul's death is not explicitly said here to have been the fitting outcome of his faults (contrast the parallel text in 1 Chr 10:13-14). Instead the reader's sympathy is gained by the description of the brutal treatment meted out to his body by the Philistines and then by the grateful reaction of the inhabitants of Jabesh. The reminiscence of 1 Sam 11, however, brought up by the latter incident, introduces a note of regret. Saul had started so well as the faithful instrument of Yahweh, under the influence of his spirit (1 Sam 11); he could have continued in that spirit but matters turned out differently.

David's name is not mentioned in this chapter, but the reader does not need to be told that the death of Saul and three of his sons has brought the throne of Israel much nearer to David's grasp.

O. 2 SAM 1:1-27
DAVID LEARNS OF ISRAEL'S DEFEAT AND LAMENTS OVER SAUL AND JONATHAN

1. *Comment.* The narrative part of the chapter (vv 1-16) tells how an Amalekite fugitive arrives from the battlefield

of Mount Gilboa (1 Sam 31) with news of Israel's defeat and the death of Saul and his sons. There are some notable discrepancies between the Amalekite's version of events and what has been narrated in the preceding chapter. No mention is made here of Saul's request to his armour-bearer nor of his falling on his own sword; instead the Amalekite claims that Saul suffering from his wounds asked him to put him out of agony, and he complied with the king's request. The most likely explanation for these differences is that the narrator wanted to portray the Amalekite as deliberately lying in order to win David's favour and a rich reward; the reader already knows from 1 Sam 30 what a cowardly and rapacious people the Amalekites are (cf. also 1 Sam 15). David's reaction to the message is then told (vv 11-16): after the customary rites of mourning, he confronts the Amalekite with the crime of having done violence to the Lord's anointed one (cf. 1 Sam 24:6, 10; 26:9, 11, 16, 23) and orders his immediate execution. One can note that David accepts the Amalekite's story at face value, since he has no other source of information; the reader knows better.

David's lament for Saul and Jonathan follows (vv 17-27). There is a detailed introduction (vv 17-18), and the poem itself with its refrain "How are the mighty fallen" (vv 19, 25, 27) conveys a deep feeling of personal and national grief that the passage of almost thirty centuries has done little to attenuate. One can note that the poem contains no reference to Yahweh; it is not a religious lamentation but a form of heroic elegy. Unfortunately the text presents several philological difficulties (especially in vv 21-22), with the result that translations can vary rather considerably at times; however this does not seriously affect the impact of the poem. Verse 18, as it stands, states that the text was taken from "the Book of Jashar" (the latter term means "the upright, or valiant, one"); this seems to have been an old collection of national or heroic poems; material from it has been used also at Josh 10:12-13 (and possibly 1 Kgs 8:12-13, if one accepts an indication in the Greek version there).

2. *Significance.* The narrative part of the chapter contains a vigorous assertion of David's complete innocence

with regard to Saul's death, already stressed in 1 Sam 27-31. The execution of the Amalekite for having incurred blood-guilt by killing the Lord's anointed (according to the Amalekite's own version of events at least) is presented as a patent demonstration of David's non-involvement, even though he stood to gain much by Saul's death. One can note, however, that David is not said to have refused Saul's crown and armlet which the Amalekite brought him (v 10); from now on, in fact, the kingship that had been Saul's begins to pass over in stages to David (2 Sam 2-5).

David's lament (vv 19-27), read in its wider context, is remarkable for the complete lack of resentment against Saul for all his ill-treatment of David. The reader is given the impression of an extraordinary magnanimity and nobility of character on David's part, which strengthens all the more the thematic assertion of his non-involvement in the king's death.

V.   2 Sam 2:1 — 8:18
David Becomes King over Judah and Israel

These chapters contain the final part of the theological narrative about David's rise to the throne together with other material about his reign. (See the Introduction to Division IV for the debate about the limits of the Rise narrative.) Events move more quickly here than in 1 Sam 16 — 2 Sam 1. Already in chap. 2 David is anointed as king of Judah, and war breaks out with the northern kingdom of Israel now led by Ishbosheth, a weak and ineffectual son of Saul. After the murder of Ishbosheth (chap. 4) the northern kingdom too passes to David.

The second part of the division focuses on Jerusalem. David captures the city from its non-Israelite lords, the Jebusites, and makes it his capital; the Philistines, rightly sensing that their vassal was becoming dangerously powerful, try to crush him but are soundly defeated and beaten back (chap. 5). Now that Jerusalem's safety is assured,

David orders the ark of Yahweh to be brought there (chap. 6). His subsequent proposal to build a temple in Jerusalem meets with a refusal from Yahweh speaking by the prophet Nathan, but David receives the promise of a stable dynasty (Nathan's oracle: chap. 7), for which he gives thanks to the Lord.

Chap. 8 can be read with what precedes, at least in the present form of the book. It reports the destruction of David's foreign enemies and the definitive establishment of his kingdom (cf. 1 Sam 20:15-16). (Chap. 9, though taken with the next division in accordance with the common opinion, can also be seen as connected with chap. 8: see 1 Sam 20:16, 42; 24:20-21.) Up to this point David is presented as wholly docile to the Lord's guidance, both amid the vicissitudes of his years as an outlaw and exile, and then amid the sequence of successes that led to his establishment on the thrones of Judah and Israel. In chaps 10-12 the situation will change.

A. 2:1-32
DAVID KING OF JUDAH; WAR WITH THE SAULIDE FORCES

1. *Comment.* The first part of this section (vv 1-11) contains three short reports. In response to a divine oracle David leaves his Philistine fiefdom of Ziklag and moves to the Judaean centre of Hebron where he is anointed king of Judah (vv 1-4a). He then sends a friendly message to the inhabitants of Jabesh-gilead (vv 4b-7: cf. 1 Sam 31:11-13); one can see beneath the pious language the outlines of a political manoeuvre to win over elements of the northern kingdom. The third unit (vv 8-11) gives information about the northern kingdom and about the length of David's reign at Hebron. The chronological data in vv 10a and 11 may be an insertion by a Deuteronomistic redactor. Though the northern kingdom was ruled by a son of Saul, the real power behind the throne was Abner (v 8), Saul's first cousin (1 Sam 14:50) and army commander (cf. 1 Sam 26:5). The new king's name was probably Ishbaal (cf. 1 Chr 8:33; 9:39); the

element "-baal" was understood by later scribes to refer to the Canaanite god Baal and so they replaced it here (and in some other OT names) with the element "-bosheth" which means "shame"; originally, however, the element "-baal" in such names probably referred to Yahweh, for "baal" is also a common noun meaning "lord" and there is no reason to think that Saul would have given his son an idolatrous name. Ishbaal's residence was at Mahanaim, east of the Jordan (v 8b), and it is probable that he ruled from there as a Philistine vassal. Technically, as far as the Philistines were concerned at least, David was in the same position. One can understand that it was in the Philistines' interest to allow their vassals weaken one another by their rivalry.

The second part of the chapter (vv 12-32) tells of a battle between David's general Joab and the Saulide general Abner. A challenge involving twelve champions of either side ends in slaughter and generalized fighting between the two forces, with David's men gaining the upper hand (vv 12-17). A graphic description of Abner's flight follows (cf. 2 Sam 20): Abner is forced to kill Joab's impetuous brother, Asahel, who twice refused to listen to Abner's warnings (vv 18-23); the pursuit continues under Joab and his other brother Abishai (cf. 1 Sam 26) until the two forces confront one another again, but this time a truce is agreed upon (vv 24-28) and both return to their bases (vv 29-32), leaving the issue of the war undecided in spite of the overwhelming victory of David's forces.

2. *Significance.* The royal anointing of David as king of Judah is the first empirical realization of what had been anticipated in the theological narrative of 1 Sam 16:1-13. David does not act autonomously here. The text stresses that his decision to go up to Hebron was an act of obedience to an explicit divine oracle (v 1); it was not just a carefully planned move by a skilled politician — a judgement that a historian would be quite justified in making! That a theological interpretation can stand beside an account of pragmatic political measures is a characteristic of much of the David story in 1 Sam and still more in 2 Sam.

Though David now finds himself in open rivalry with Saul's son, Ishbaal, the text insists on his abiding respect for Saul himself (vv 5-6). This reflects the theme of David's blamelessness that has been so prominent in the preceding chapters.

B. 3:1-39
ABNER NEGOTIATES WITH DAVID BUT IS MURDERED BY JOAB

1. *Comment.* The list of David's sons in vv 2-5 presents some of the leading personages of later narratives (chaps 13-20 and 1 Kgs 1-2). It is significant that the mother of David's third son, Absalom, was an Aramaean princess from the kingdom of Geshur (v 3), which was situated north of Israelite Gilead in Transjordan. The fact suggests that David's aims were far-reaching even when his territory was limited to Judah.

The main part of the chapter (vv 6-39) tells of the ambitions, treachery, and death of Ishbaal's general Abner. The break between Abner and his king comes when Ishbaal rebukes him for having taken one of Saul's concubines (vv 6-11). Ishbaal's agitation may have a political basis; for there are texts that could suggest that taking possession of a former king's wives or concubines was equivalent to putting forward a claim to his throne (cf. 2 Sam 16:21-22; 1 Kgs 2:13-25). Whether or not Abner actually intended that, he takes violent umbrage at Ishbaal's rebuke. It is idle to ask what divine oath Abner is referring to in vv 9-10 (cf. v 18) and how he knew about it; the text is phrased from the perspective of the theological interpretation of the narrator (cf. 1 Sam 24:4).

Abner now opens secret negotiations with David to bring the kingdom of Ishbaal over to him, and he complies with David's demand for the restitution of his wife Michal (vv 12-16). David's insistence in this matter (cf. 1 Sam 25:44) is not simply a sign of his affection for Michal but has a precise political aim: by re-establishing his marriage relationship to

Saul's house, he strengthens his position as claimant for the throne of Israel in the eyes of the northern tribes. The pathos of v 16, telling of Paltiel's separation from Michal, is rare in biblical narrative. Abner then wins over the elders of Israel and finally Saul's own tribe of Benjamin (vv 17-19).

The way is now clear for a meeting between Abner and David at Hebron; Abner is received in a friendly way by David and sets out again for Israel to finalize the take-over plot (vv 20-21). At this point Joab, David's military chief, arrives back in Hebron after a successful raid for plunder (an interesting insight into the means used by David to finance his kingdom in the early years), and harshly criticizes the king for having let Abner go when his visit might have been just a ruse to spy out Hebron's defences (vv 22-25). On his own initiative Joab sends messengers after Abner to bring him back to Hebron, and there at the city gate Joab treacherously murders him (vv 26-27). It can be noted that Joab's brutal frankness towards David (vv 24-25) and his unscrupulous use of treachery and violence (vv 26-27) are characteristics that will recur in later narratives (especially 2 Sam 18-20).

David protests his innocence and lays the curse of blood-guilt on Joab and his family and descendants (vv 28-29). In v 29 the reference to "one who holds a spindle" means that David wishes upon Joab the presence of effeminate males among his descendants, since spinning was regarded as typically a woman's occupation (cf. Prov 31:19). David then orders an honourable burial for Abner, mourns his death, and fasts till sunset as a sign of his non-involvement in the killing (vv 31-39). His final words at v 39b will find their fulfilment in 1 Kgs 2:28-34. It can be noted that Joab's brother, Abishai, is associated with him in the murder (vv 30, 39), though the actual account in vv 26-27 has not mentioned his presence.

2. *Significance.* The circumstances of Abner's death — at the hands of David's nephew, in the gateway of David's capital — must have raised questions about the king's responsibility. The main concern of chap. 3 is to emphasize

David's innocence in this affair, whose outcome was much to his advantage. Hence the statements of vv 26b, 28, and 37; hence the triple assertion that he had sent Abner away in peace (vv 21, 22, 23); hence the formal conclusion of v 37 to the effect that not only the Judaeans but also the northern Israelites recognized David's lack of involvement in the crime.

C. 4:1-12
THE MURDER OF ISHBAAL AND DAVID'S TREATMENT OF THE CULPRITS

1. *Comment.* Introductory material is given in vv 1-4. The demoralizing effect of Abner's death on Ishbaal and on Israel is noted (v 1). The action of Ishbaal's murderers might be explicable in part by their origin (vv 2-3). They came from the town of Beeroth, one of the Canaanite enclaves in the territory of Benjamin; Saul had tried to eliminate the Gibeonites, another Canaanite town in that area (cf. 2 Sam 21:1-2), and he may also have taken violent measures against Beeroth (cf. v 3 here); if so, the murder of Saul's son by the two Beerothites might be seen as a vendetta. Verse 4 mentions a son of Jonathan who has no part in the narrative here but will reappear in chap. 9; the original form of his name was probably Meribbaal, the form Mephibosheth being a deliberate scribal corruption (see the comment on Ishbaal's name at 2:8 above).

The main part of the chapter (vv 5-12) tells of the treacherous killing of Ishbaal (vv 5-7a) and of David's reaction to the news which was brought to him personally by the murderers together with Ishbaal's head (vv 7b-12). They present their deed as if done in the Lord's name, but David reminds them of the fate of the Amalekite messenger (cf. chap. 1). He orders their immediate execution and gives honourable burial to Ishbaal's head.

2. *Significance.* The point here is the same as in the preceding chapter. David had no complicity in a murder which was objectively to his advantage. He terms the mur-

derers "wicked men" (v 11), and condemns them to a shameful death (v 12), while he shows his respect for Ishbaal by describing him as "righteous" (v 11), that is, innocent of any crime that could justify his assassination. At this point the Saulide dynasty is doomed; Ishbaal apparently had no sons (or none capable of ruling), and the only Saulide in sight (v 4) is a crippled boy who, according to the ideas of the time, is obviously unfitted for the royal office.

D.   5:1-25
DAVID KING OF ISRAEL; THE CAPTURE OF JERUSALEM AND THE DEFEAT OF THE PHILISTINES

5 Then all the tribes of Israel came to David at Hebron, and said, "Behold, we are your bone and flesh. ²In times past, when Saul was king over us, it was you that led out and brought in Israel; and the Lord said to you, 'You shall be shephrd of my people Israel, and you shall be prince over Israel.'" ³So all the elders of Israel came to the king at Hebron; and King David made a covenant with them at Hebron before the Lord, and they anointed David king over Israel. ⁴David was thirty years old when he began to reign, and he reigned forty years. ⁵At Hebron he reigned over Judah seven years and six months; and at Jerusalem he reigned over all Israel and Judah thirty-three years.

⁶And the king and his men went to Jerusalem against the Jebusites, the inhabitants of the land, who said to David, "You will not come in here, but the blind and the lame will ward you off" — thinking, "David cannot come in here." ⁷Nevertheless David took the stronghold of Zion, that is, the city of David. ⁸And David said on that day, "Whoever would smite the Jebusites, let him get up the water shaft to attack the lame and the blind, who are hated by David's soul." Therefore it is said, "The blind and the lame shall not come into the house." ⁹And David dwelt in the stronghold, and called it the city of David. And David built the city round about from the Millo

inward. [10]And David became greater and greater, for the Lord, the God of hosts, was with him.

[11]And Hiram King of Tyre sent messengers to David, and cedar trees, also carpenters and masons who built David a house. [12]And David perceived that the Lord had established him king over Israel, and that he had exalted his kingdom for the sake of his people Israel.

[13]And David took more concubines and wives from Jerusalem, after he came from Hebron; and more sons and daughters were born to David. [14]And these are the names of those who were born to him in Jerusalem: Shammua, Shobab, Nathan, Solomon, [15]Ibhar, Elishua, Nepheg, Japhia, [16]Elishama, Eliada, and Eliphelet.

[17]When the Philistines heard that David had been anointed king over Israel, all the Philistines went up in search of David; but David heard of it and went down to the stronghold. [18]Now the Philistines had come and spread out in the valley of Rephaim. [19]And David inquired of the Lord, "Shall I go up against the Philistines? Wilt thou give them into my hand?" And the Lord said to David, "Go up; for I will certainly give the Philistines into your hand." [20]And David came to Baalperazim, and David defeated them there; and he said, "The Lord has broken through my enemies before me, like a bursting flood." Therefore, the name of that place is called Baalperazim. [21]And the Philistines left their idols there, and David and his men carried them away.

[22]And the Philistines came up yet again, and spread out in the valley of Rephaim. [23]And when David inquired of the Lord, he said, "You shall not go up; go around to their rear, and come upon them opposite the balsam trees. [24]And when you hear the sound of marching in the tops of the balsam trees, then bestir yourself; for then the Lord has gone out before you to smite the army of the Philistines." [25]And David did as the Lord commanded him, and smote the Philistines from Geba to Gezer.

1. *Comment.* The chapter opens with a report about David's covenant commitment with the northern Israelites

and their anointing of him as their king (vv 1-3). David now unites in his person the kingdoms of Judah and Israel; the personal union of the two kingdoms will last until the reign of Solomon's son Rehoboam (1 Kgs 12), when the northern tribes secede and re-establish a separate kingdom. The Israelites' speech in vv 1-2 may be the work of a theological redactor interpreting the significance of the original narrative datum of v 3. A Deuteronomistic redactor then appended the chronological notes of vv 4-5.

The second unit (vv 6-16) focuses on Jerusalem. First there is a short, but difficult, account of David's capture of the city (vv 6-8). Up to then it had remained a foreign enclave between Israel and Judah. Its lords, the Jebusites (v 6), may have been of mixed ethnic composition — part Canaanite, part Hittite. Though the city is actually named "Jebus" in a few biblical texts (Judg 19:10; 1 Chr 11:4), this is probably just a literary archaism; earlier extra-biblical documents, in fact, use name-forms (Uru-salim, and the like) that are similar to the Hebrew "Jerusalem." When David and his forces appear before the walls, the Jebusites express their confidence in the city's invincibility by stating that "the blind and the lame will ward you off" (v 6). This phrase might be a way of saying that the city's defences were so strong that even the disabled would suffice to repel the assailants. The suggestion has also been made, on the basis of a Hittite text, that some kind of magical force was attributed to the blind and the lame; they made visible the curse that would fall on the invaders if they dared to enter the city. In spite of that, David captured the Jebusite city (v 7: Zion was situated on the south-eastern hill, to the south of the present-day "Temple area"). How exactly he managed to do this is not altogether certain.

The problem lies in the translation of part of v 8. As the RSV presents it, the city was taken by a stratagem: some of David's men climbed up a water shaft (which can still be seen) that led from the source of the city's water supplies outside the walls to a point inside the fortifications (cf. 1 Chr 11:6). A second interpretation replaces the phrase "get up the water shaft" by "use his grappling iron" (thus the New English Bible); this would mean that the city was taken by storm. A third interpretation would see David ordering his men to cut off the city's water supplies, thus making its surrender inevitable. In any case, the city became David's own possession by right of conquest. The final part of v 8 explains a later prohibition against the entry of the blind and lame into the Temple — possibly for priestly service (cf. Lev 21:18, — on the grounds of the present episode.

The rest of the second unit is taken up by short notes about David's building activities in Jerusalem (vv 9, 11), his divinely granted success (vv 10, 12), and the names of his sons born in Jerusalem (vv 13-16: among them Solomon).

The last unit (vv 17-25) consists of two reports about the victories gained by David over the Philistines thanks to Yahweh's decisive intervention on his behalf (vv 17-21 and 22-25). The Philistines are defeated twice (as they had twice defeated Israel: 1 Sam 4 and 31), and they abandon their religious images to the victors (v 21: "their idols") just as the Israelites had lost their sacred symbol, the ark, to the Philistines (1 Sam 4). David's leadership cancels the negativity of the past. One can note that the present position of vv 17-25 may not be the original one but rather the work of the Deuteronomistic redactor. The Philistines were more likely to have attacked David soon after his anointing as king of Israel than to have waited until he captured Jerusalem; there is an excellent literary connection, in fact, between v 17a and v 3 in the present chapter.

2. *Significance.* Many scholars see in this chapter the original climax of the story of David's rise. Two important theological statements (vv 10, 12) can be noted in this regard: the former ascribes David's continual increase in greatness to Yahweh's being "with him" (a phrase often used earlier: e.g. 1 Sam 16:18; 17:37; 18:14); the more elaborate statement of v 12 refers to the Lord's role in the establishment and exaltation of David's kingdom (cf. 1 Sam 13:13; 2 Sam 7:12, 13; 1 Kgs 2:24).

David, then, has reached the heights towards which the

Lord was guiding him for so many years: he is king over Judah and Israel, and Jerusalem is his capital. Jerusalem, in fact, stands at the centre of the chapter, and will be more and more at the centre of Israel's history as presented in the rest of Samuel and in Kings.

E.   6:1-23
DAVID BRINGS THE ARK TO JERUSALEM

6 David again gathered all the chosen men of Israel, thirty thousand. [2]And David arose and went with all the people who were with him from Baale-judah, to bring up from there the ark of God, which is called by the name of the Lord of hosts who sits enthroned on the cherubim. [3]And they carried the ark of God upon a new cart, and brought it out of the house of Abinadab which was on the hill; and Uzzah and Ahio, the sons of Abinadab, were driving the new cart [4]with the ark of God; and Ahio went before the ark. [5]And David and all the house of Israel were making merry before the Lord with all their might, with songs and lyres and harps and tambourines and castanets and cymbals.

[6]And when they came to the threshing floor of Nacon, Uzzah put out his hand to the ark of God and took hold of it, for the oxen stumbled. [7]And the anger of the Lord was kindled against Uzzah; and God smote him there because he put forth his hand to the ark; and he died there beside the ark of God. [8]And David was angry because the Lord had broken forth upon Uzzah; and that place is called Perez-uzzah, to this day. [9]And David was afraid of the Lord that day; and he said, "How can the ark of the Lord come to me?" [10]So David was not willing to take the ark of the Lord into the city of David; but David took it aside to the house of Obededom the Gittite. [11]And the ark of the Lord remained in the house of Obededom the Gittite three months; and the Lord blessed Obededom and all his household.

[12]And it was told King David, "The Lord has blessed

the household of Obededom and all that belongs to him, because of the ark of God." So David went and brought up the ark of God from the house of Obededom to the city of David with rejoicing; [13]and when those who bore the ark of the Lord had gone six paces, he sacrificed an ox and a fatling. [14]And David danced before the Lord with all his might; and David was girded with a linen ephod. [15]So David and all the house of Israel brought up the ark of the Lord with shouting, and with the sound of the horn.

[16]As the ark of the Lord came into the city of David, Michal the daughter of Saul looked out of the window, and saw King David leaping and dancing before the Lord; and she despised him in her heart. [17]And they brought in the ark of the Lord, and set it in its place, inside the tent which David had pitched for it; and David offered burnt offerings and peace offerings before the Lord. [18]And when David had finished offering the burnt offerings and the peace offerings, he blessed the people in the name of the Lord of hosts, [19]and distributed among all the people, the whole multitude of Israel, both men and women, to each a cake of bread, a portion of meat, and a cake of raisins. Then all the people departed, each to his house.

[20]And David returned to bless his household. But Michal the daughter of Saul came out to meet David, and said, "How the king of Israel honored himself today, uncovering himself today before the eyes of his servants' maids, as one of the vulgar fellows shamelessly uncovers himself!" [21]And David said to Michal, "It was before the Lord, who chose me above your father, and above all his house, to appoint me as prince over Israel, the people of the Lord — and I will make merry before the Lord. [22]I will make myself yet more contemptible than this, and I will be abased in your eyes; but by the maids of whom you have spoken, by them I shall be held in honor." [23]And Michal the daughter of Saul had no child to the day of her death.

1. *Comment.* Many scholars see this chapter (except for the Michal episode) as the conclusion of the Ark Narrative (cf. 1 Sam 4:1 — 7:1); some, however, prefer to treat it as a separate unit reflecting Jerusalem liturgical traditions (cf. Ps 132[131]). Verses 1-11 tell of David's unsuccessful first attempt to bring the ark to Jerusalem from Baale-judah (v 2), probably an alternative name for Kiriath-jearim (1 Sam 7:1), where it had remained in what appears to have been a state of benign neglect since its return from Philistia. The disconcerting fate of the well-meaning Uzzah (vv 6-8) is meant to illustrate the notion of an awesome objective sacrality that envelops the ark almost as a physical atmosphere; if an unauthorized person infringes on this, even for a good motive, an automatic reaction is forthcoming. This primitive idea of sacrality and of God's action will give place to an ever clearer moral concept of God's holiness in later biblical writings influenced by prophetical insights.

Verses 12-19 then describe the joyful processional entry of the ark to Jerusalem. David offers sacrifice and wears the linen ephod, a cultic garment (vv 13-14: cf. 1 Sam 2:18); only at a later stage in Israel's religious history were the priests regarded as the sole offerers of sacrifice (cf. Num 18:7; 2 Chr 26:16-20). The ark is placed in a special cultic tent constructed for it by David (v 17); there was as yet no Yahwistic cultic building in Jerusalem.

A sub-plot (vv 16, 20-23) deals with the reaction of David's wife Michal to her husband's uninhibited display of religious fervour. She speaks ironically of David's honour (v 20); as a result she herself is denied the honour of motherhood (v 23). It has been suggested that these verses formed the original start of the so-called Succession Narrative (2 Sam 9-20; 1 Kgs 1-2); they might better be seen, however, as the work (in part at least) of the redactor of the combined Saul and David story.

2. *Significance.* While chap. 5 focused on Jerusalem as the political centre, chap. 6 tells how it also became the religious centre of David's kingdom. David achieved this by bringing to the city the most venerable cultic symbol of the

northern tribes, the ark of God, thus winning the religious allegiance of Israel for the new capital. With the ark, no doubt, came also northern religious traditions, and Jerusalem was soon to become a unique centre of religious synthesis between Israelite and Judaean traditions together with a Yahwistic adaptation of the pre-Davidic Jebusite religion native to the city. A new era in Israel's religious history had begun.

The Michal episode takes up again the theme of the rejection of Saul's house which ran through the whole story of David's rise. David's words in v 21 with their heavy emphasis on the Lord's choice (cf. 1 Sam 10:24; 16:8-10) sum up again the theological key to understanding David's rise to his present position, and the childlessness of Michal means that Saul's family will have no further part in kingship over the Lord's people, no share in the dynastic promise.

F.   7:1-29
NATHAN'S DYNASTIC ORACLE; DAVID'S PRAYER

7 Now when the king dwelt in his house, and the Lord had given him rest from all his enemies round about, [2]the king said to Nathan the prophet, "See now, I dwell in a house of cedar, but the ark of God dwells in a tent." [3]And Nathan said to the king, "Go, do all that is in your heart; for the Lord is with you."

[4]But that same night the word of the Lord came to Nathan, [5]"Go and tell my servant David, 'Thus says the Lord: Would you build me a house to dwell in? [6]I have not dwelt in a house since the day I brought up the people of Israel from Egypt to this day, but I have been moving about in a tent for my dwelling. [7]In all places where I have moved with all the people of Israel, did I speak a word with any of the judges of Israel, whom I commanded to shepherd my people Israel, saying, "Why have you not built me a house of cedar?"' [8]Now therefore thus you shall say to my servant David, 'Thus says the Lord of

hosts, I took you from the pasture, from following the sheep, that you should be prince over my people Israel; [9]and I have been with you wherever you went, and have cut off all your enemies from before you; and I will make for you a great name, like the name of the great ones of the earth. [10]And I will appoint a place for my people Israel, and will plant them, that they may dwell in their own place, and be disturbed no more; and violent men shall afflict them no more, as formerly, [11]from the time that I appointed judges over my people Israel; and I will give you rest from all your enemies. Moreover the Lord declares to you that the Lord will make you a house. [12]When your days are fulfilled and you lie down with your fathers, I will raise up your offspring after you, who shall come forth from your body, and I will establish his kingdom. [13]He shall build a house for my name, and I will establish the throne of his kingdom for ever. [14]I will be his father, and he shall be my son. When he commits iniquity, I will chasten him with the rod of men, with the stripes of the sons of men; [15]but I will not take my steadfast love from him, as I took it from Saul, whom I put away from before you. [16]And your house and your kingdom shall be made sure for ever before me; your throne shall be established for ever.'" [17]In accordance with all these words, and in accordance with all this vision, Nathan spoke to David.

[18]Then King David went in and sat before the Lord, and said, "Who am I, O Lord God, and what is my house, that thou hast brought me thus far? [19]And yet this was a small thing in thy eyes, O Lord God; thou hast spoken also of thy servant's house for a great while to come, and hast shown me future generations, O Lord God! [20]And what more can David say to thee? For thou knowest thy servant, O Lord God! [21]Because of thy promise, and according to thy own heart, thou hast wrought all this greatness, to make thy servant know it. [22]Therefore thou art great, O Lord God; for there is none like thee, and there is no God besides thee, according to all that we have

heard with our ears. [23]What other nation on earth is like thy people Israel, whom God went to redeem to be his people, making himself a name, and doing for them great and terrible things, by driving out before his people a nation and its gods? [24]And thou didst establish for thyself thy people Israel to be thy people for ever; and thou, O Lord, didst become their God. [25]And now, O Lord God, confirm for ever the word whch thou hast spoken concerning thy servant and concerning his house, and do as thou hast spoken; [26]and thy name will be magnified for ever, saying, 'The Lord of hosts is God over Israel,' and the house of thy servant David will be established before thee. [27]For thou, O Lord of hosts, the God of Israel, hast made this revelation to thy servant, saying, 'I will build you a house'; therefore thy servant has found courage to pray this prayer to thee. [28]And now, O Lord God, thou art God, and thy words are true, and thou hast promised this good thing to thy servant; [29]now therefore may it please thee to bless the house of thy servant, that it may continue for ever before thee; for thou, O Lord God, hast spoken, and with thy blessing shall the house of thy servant be blessed for ever."

1. *Comment.* This chapter is of fundamental importance not only for the Books of Samuel and Kings in their Deuteronomistic context but also for the general biblical theme of the messianic promise. It can be divided into an introduction, a complex prophetic oracle, and a prayer of thanksgiving and petition.

The introduction (vv 1-3) connects with what has gone before. David contrasts his own fine cedarwood house (cf. 5:11) with the modest cultic tent that sheltered the ark of Yahweh (cf. 6:17). His implicit proposal to build a worthier home for the ark meets with the initial approval of the court prophet Nathan who appears here for the first time (cf. 2 Sam 12; 1 Kgs 1).

The prophetic oracle (vv 4-17: the first and last verses forming a narrative framework) is dominated by a double antithesis: (a) it is not David who will build a house (=Temple) for the Lord, rather it is the Lord who will make a house (=dynasty) for David; (b) it is not David who will build the Temple, it is Solomon his son who will have that honour. There is undoubtedly a polemical tone to vv 5-7 where Yahweh's formal rejection of David's plan to build the temple is communicated to the king by Nathan, but it is not easy to identify the precise point of the refusal. One possibility would be to see it as reflecting an opposition in principle to the idea of a stable localization of Yahweh's presence in Israel; there are some OT texts, from the exilic period and afterwards, that express this opposition (cf. 1 Kgs 8:27; Isa 66:1-2). One could appeal to the antithesis in v 6 to support this view: the point there is not that the Israelites never had a cultic building up to that moment (there had been a "house of the Lord" at Shiloh: 1 Sam 1:9, 24), but rather that Yahweh's presence was not attached in a stable way to the building as such; the verb "dwell" has a strong durative sense here, and could indeed imply "enthroned." If that is the case, then 2 Sam 7:5-7 seems to polemize with the concept found in the old poetic fragment of 1 Kgs 8:12-13 whose unproblematic localization of the divine presence in the Temple shows Canaanite influence. One can also note, however, a possible implication of v 7: the building of a temple can only proceed from the free decision of the Lord; the mere fact of David's successes does not authorize him to undertake this work on his own initiative; he has been authorized to shepherd the Lord's people, and for the moment that is all.

The dynastic promise is expressed in vv 11b, 12-16 with a brief mention of the building of a temple by David's son (Solomon) in v 13a. David's line will enjoy an altogether special relationship with the Lord, which v 14a expresses by means of a legal formula of adoption; the same concept of the divine adoptive sonship of the Davidic king can be seen at Ps 2:7; 89(88): 26-27. The possibility of infidelity on the part of a Davidic king is taken into account (vv 14b-15); this certainly refers to Solomon, but may also be intended for all of David's successors on the throne. It is a hopeful message; the unfaithful king will indeed be punished, but will not experience outright rejection (as had happened in Saul's case).

David's prayer (vv 18-29) responds to the dynastic aspect of the oracle. The king protests his unworthiness, praises the graciousness of Yahweh towards him and towards his people Israel from the beginning of their existence, and fervently asks the Lord to fulfil the dynastic promise and to bless David's descendants for ever. Though the term "covenant" does not occur in the chapter, one can note that in effect two kinds of covenantal relationship are referred to here. First, the relationship between Yahweh and Israel (vv 23-24) is expressed by the so-called covenant formula, in essence "I will be their God, and they will be my people"(cf. v 24). Then, with regard to the relationship between David and the Lord, we find terms such as "steadfast love" (v 15) and "this good thing" (v 28) that are commonly associated with covenant relationships in other texts; so it can be said that 2 Sam 7 certainly presupposes the idea of the Lord's covenant with the House of David, though for an explicit formulation of the concept we must go to texts such as 2 Sam 23:5; Ps 89(88):3, 28, 34, 39; 132(131):12.

2. *Significance.* 2 Sam 7 plays a key role in the theological structure of the Deuteronomistic history. On the one hand, it looks back over past history: to the Exodus (vv 6, 23), to the Judges (vv 7, 11), and to Saul (v 15). On the other hand, it offers an interpretation of what lies in the future with respect to David: Solomon's reign (vv 12-15) and his building of the Temple (v 13a: cf. 1 Kgs 5-8), and then the whole duration of David's royal line (vv 13, 16, 19, 29). One can compare the function of Samuel's speech in 1 Sam 12.

The chapter's contribution to the theological message of the Deuteronomistic history is also considerable. At first sight the disaster of the fall of Jerusalem and the end of Judaean independence in 587/6 would appear to contradict the promise of the Lord's lasting favour towards the line of David. But it must be noted that the last episode of Kings (2

Kgs 25:27-30) tells of the release of the exiled Davidic king from his Babylonian imprisonment; seen in the light of 2 Sam 7:14b-15, this could be interpreted as a sign of hope that the flickering lamp of David would one day, in God's good time and by his good grace, became again a bright light for the nations and the centre of Israel's growth and tranquility (cf. 2 Sam 7:10).

Finally it can be noted that the importance of the chapter is reflected in the complexity of its literary history. Scholarly opinion is far from unanimous in this matter, but it seems that at least three strata should be distinguished in the text: the nucleus of the original oracle in its narrative setting; then a pre-Deuteronomistic redaction, possibly from the redactor of the combined Saul and David story; then various Deuteronomistic additions. In any case, it is certain that the chapter contains a considerable amount of later theological reflection that goes beyond the original oracle whose extent is now difficult to determine with precision.

G.   8:1-18
DAVID'S VICTORIOUS WARS

1.*Comment.*   Most of the chapter is taken up with a concise account of David's foreign wars (vv 1-14). The Philistines were defeated so soundly (v 1: cf. 5:17-25) that they never again posed a serious threat to Israel. The cruel treatment meted out to the Moabite soldiers (v 2) is unexplained, and it contrasts with the aid given by the king of Moab to David in his days of need (1 Sam 22:3-4). The campaigns against Zobah and Damascus (vv 3-8) and the submission of Hamath (vv 9-10) had the effect of extending David's lordship over large areas of Syria as far as the upper Euphrates. The Transjordanian states of Edom, Moab, and Ammon were also reduced to vassalage (vv 2, 12-14).

The Davidic Empire — for so it can be called — owed its existence, from the historical point of view, not only to the energy of David but also to the fact that the surrounding powers (Egypt, Assyria, and the Hittite states) were either too weak or too taken up with problems elsewhere to be able to intervene in Syro-Palestinian affairs. The empire remained more or less intact during Solomon's reign, but with the separation of Israel from Judah after his death the vassal-states regained their independence for the most part, and Jerusalem was no longer the centre of an empire.

The closing unit (vv 15-18) consists of a general note about David's judicial activity followed by an archival list of his principal officials. The offices of "recorder" (v 16) and "secretary" (v 17) were probably modelled on the Egyptian administrative system. According to v 17a the two chief priests were Zadok and Ahimelech, but the text is probably corrupt; for one thing, 2 Sam 15:24, 29; 20:25; 1 Kgs 1:7-8 speak of Abiathar (not Ahimelech) as priest together with Zadok. Abiathar has been mentioned often since 1 Sam 22:20, but Zadok's origins are quite obscure. It has been suggested that he was the Jebusite priest of the Jerusalem sanctuary when the city was taken by David; Zadok was permitted by David to retain his office in order to foster union between the defeated Jebusites and their new lords, and so he undertook the functions of priest of Yahweh together with Abiathar. Another hypothesis, however, argues that Zadok belonged to an old Judaean priestly family based at Hebron and claiming descent from Aaron. What is certain, in any case, is that the line of Zadok controlled the post-exilic priesthood in Jerusalem, and probably had a prominent role there too throughout the monarchical period. Finally, the "Cherethites and Pelethites" mentioned in v 18 were mercenary soldiers, probably Philistines, who owed allegiance directly to David and their general Benaiah; Joab, on the other hand, commanded the native Judaean (and Israelite?) militia (v 16).

2. *Significance.* David's empire can be seen as the fulfilment of the promises to the Patriarchs (note especially Gen 15: 18-21 which was formulated probably in view of Davidic times). It is the natural outcome of the Lord's blessing reported in 2 Sam 7 (note the connective "And after this" at 8:1), and the theological interpretative notes of 8:6b, 14b stress this all the more.

As well as the military campaigns, the king's patronage of
the cult is noted (v 11) and his judicial activity is presented
too (v 15). The latter point takes up a widespread ancient
Near Eastern ideal of kingship as the exercise of justice and
equity on behalf of the people. David fulfills this ideal: he
has subdued all the enemies of his people and has established a just order within the kingdom. What the people
requested at 1 Sam 8:20 appears to have been granted to
them at last by the Lord.

VI.   2 Sam 9:1 — 20:26
David's Reign: Family Problems and Their National Repercussions

The opening chapter of this division has the double function of making a connection with the preceding chapters
about David's rise, and of presenting some of the personages who will reappear in chaps 15-20. Two main topics
occupy the rest of the material: (1) the circumstances of
Solomon's birth in the setting of David's war against the
Ammonites (chaps 10-12); (2) the story of Absalom's rebellion against his father David — its causes, progress, outcome, and aftermath (chaps 13-20). Both topics illustrate
the fundamental theme of the Lord's guidance of David:
neither the king's own grave sins (chap. 11) nor the tragic
events in his family (the murder of his son Amnon; the
rebellion and death of the fratricide Absalom) brought
about the rejection of David and his house.

Generally acclaimed as one of the finest examples of
Hebrew narrative art, these chapters are usually taken
together with 1 Kgs 1-2. This literary composition (the
so-called Succession Narrative) is often said to have been
written in Solomon's reign or shortly afterwards. If one
takes the question "Who will sit on David's throne after
him?" (cf. 1 Kgs 1:20, 27) as the theme of the work, it can be
seen that the climax comes in 1 Kgs 1-2 where Solomon is
finally singled out as David's successor, is anointed, and
consolidates his hold on the throne after David's death. The

earlier chapters have told how those sons of David who had a better title to the throne than Solomon had, were eliminated one-by-one: Amnon (2 Sam 13), Absalom (2 Sam 15-18), and finally Adonijah (1 Kgs 1-2). The chapters that introduce Solomon's mother Bathsheba and come to a climax in the birth of Solomon (2 Sam 10-12) can easily be seen as part of the same thematic unity. The beginning of the Succession Narrative is a matter of dispute. Most scholars include 2 Sam 9 in the story but acknowledge that 9:1 as it stands could not be the formal introduction to a major literary unit. Some have suggested that 6:16, 20-23 should be included too, as an explanation why there was no question of a Saulide claimant to succeed David, but (as noted above) the suggestion is debatable.

What has just been outlined is the more or less standard presentation of the Succession Narrative; several recent studies have urged, in various ways, that matters are more complicated. Though there is as yet no agreement on the details, it would appear that the present text of 2 Sam 9-20 and 1 Kgs 1-2 contains the theological narration and commentary of several different authors; the succession theme is present, but only as one of several themes, and possibly not the earliest one. A close reading of 2 Sam 15-20, for instance, would appear to show that the focus of the text is more on David's restoration to the throne than on Absalom's failure to become David's successor. In addition, there are several passages throughout these chapters that seem to have a wider horizon, going back to 2 Sam 2 and probably even to parts of 1 Sam. Consequently it seems preferable now not to treat 2 Sam 9-20 (and 1 Kgs 1-2) as the self-contained composition of a Solomonic writer but to be alert to connections with the whole story of Saul and David and, perhaps, other parts of the Deuteronomistic history as well.

A. 9:1-13
DAVID'S LOYALTY TO JONATHAN'S SON, MERIBBAAL

1. *Comment.* There are no special introductory formulas at 9:1 that would indicate a major division in the text, so

chap. 9 as it stands can perhaps be taken as containing a particularly important piece of information about David's court that supplements the archival material of 8:16-18.

Verses 1-5 tell of David's inquiry about survivors of Saul's family; this, taken together with his injunction to Meribbaal not to fear (v 7), may indicate that the killing of the Saulides told in 2 Sam 21:1-14 preceded the present scene, but it is hard to establish chronological relations with certainty in texts whose redactional history is quite complicated. Having learned that a lame son of Jonathan, Meribbaal (4:4: see the comment there for the name-form), is living in northern Transjordan, David has him brought to Jerusalem. The king magnanimously grants Meribbaal the family property of Saul, which had apparently become crown land, and gives him a permanent place at the royal table in Jerusalem (vv 6-8). Ziba, an old Saulide retainer, is instructed to work the land for Meribbaal who himself is to remain in Jerusalem (vv 9-11); one can note that the first occurrence of the phrase "your master's son" in v 10 might better be read, in accordance with Greek witnesses, "your master's house". The chapter ends (vv 12-13) with a mention of Meribbaal's young son Mica (cf. 1 Chr 8:34-35), and a second reference to his lameness (cf. v 3).

2. *Significance.*   David, established now as king, is faithful to the promise made to Jonathan (1 Sam 20:15-16, 42), whose name occurs four times here; the term, *hesed* ("kindness, loyalty") occurs three times. Chap. 9 looks back over the whole story of David's rise and can be seen as the ideal resolution of the tension between Saul and David that provided the dramatic energy for so many of the episodes narrated there. David's generous treatment of Meribbaal, however, also illustrates the king's political shrewdness in having the representative of the former royal family under his immediate supervision and hence lessening the possible danger of a Saulide restoration attempt centred on Meribbaal and his son. The chapter also looks forward since it provides useful information about personages who will reappear in the story of Absalom's rebellion (16:1-4; 19:

24-30). The significance of chap. 9, then, is both theological and structural: the former with reference to David's rise, the latter by linking the Rise story to the Absalom narratives.

B. 10:1 — 12:31
THE AMMONITE WAR; DAVID'S ADULTERY
WITH BATHSHEBA; THE BIRTH OF SOLOMON

1. *Comment.*   This long section begins and ends with an account of the war against Ammon (10:1 — 11:1; 12:26-31); its centre is taken up with the narrative of David's sins of adultery and murder and the divine judgement pronounced on these crimes by the prophet Nathan. There are clear signs of careful redactional composition here: the war account was once a separate narrative, and it is likely that part at least of Nathan's intervention at 12:1-15a belongs to a later theological redaction of the original David and Bathsheba story.

The war account in chap. 10 insists on the responsibility of the Ammonites themselves (vv 1-5); in this way David's imperialistic expansion is justified. In fact, the victory over the Transjordanian Ammonites and their Aramaean allies from Syria was an important step in the growth of David's empire. The definitive victory over the Aramaeans, reported in 8:3ff, may have followed the Ammonite war of chaps 10-12, though it is possible that the same events are referred to in the two texts. One can note the prominence of Joab in the narrative (10:7-14; 11:1); this foreshadows his importance in the chapters that follow.

The next unit (11:2-27a) presents a vivid narrative of David's adultery with Bathsheba and the subsequent murder of her husband Uriah the Hittite. There is no explicit comment in these verses on David's behaviour; none is needed, since the manner of narration is sufficient to let the reader know that the king's actions were inexcusable. Nothing is said either about Bathsheba's responsibility. It appears from 1 Kgs 1 that she lacked neither ambition nor resourcefulness, so perhaps it was not altogether a coincidence that she happened to be bathing (v 2) just when and where David could see her; be that as it may, the text certainly presents Solomon's mother as a person of unexemplary morals. Her husband Uriah, on the contrary, is the most admirable personage in the story; David has him called from the battlefield in the hope that he will sleep with his wife and so appear as the father of the child that has been conceived; Uriah's repeated refusal is motivated by his fidelity to the old religious custom of observing continence during military campaigns (cf. 1 Sam 21:4-5); it is a Hittite foreigner who observes the traditional standards of behaviour in Israel! David then resorts to murder, and Uriah unwittingly carries his own death warrant back to Joab (a narrative motif found in other literatures too). Joab has Uriah killed as instructed, and the text makes it clear that he is able to foresee and manipulate the king's reaction (vv 18-25). Verses 26-27a seem to close the incident: Bathsheba carefully observes the mourning proprieties for her husband, David then takes her officially as his wife, and their son is born. All seems well.

"But the thing that David had done displeased the Lord" (11:27b), and the following unit down to 12:23 describes the consequences of that statement. The Nathan scene in vv 1-15 has a dramatic force that makes it one of the most memorable of biblical texts. The use of a parable or similar text-type to bring about a self-condemnation on the part of the person addressed (vv 1-7a) is also found at 2 Sam 14 and 1 Kgs 20:35ff. David in his indignant reaction orders a fourfold restitution (v 6: cf. Exod 22:1); one can note that four of David's sons would subsequently die untimely deaths (the unnamed first child by Bathsheba; Amnon in chap. 13; Absalom in chap. 18; Adonijah in 1 Kgs 2). Nathan's blunt accusation "You are the man" (v 7a) leads on to a two-part oracle announcing the king's punishment (vv 7b-10, 11-12); the historical perspectives of the first part lead one to suspect the hand of a Deuteronomistic redactor there at least; the second part will be fulfilled in 16:21-22. When

David replies with a frank acknowledgement of his guilt (v 13a), Nathan announces his reprieve from the sentence of violent death but the child's death must take place as announced (vv 13b-14); this interpretation of the child's death as a punishment for the sin of its parents runs counter to the insistence on individual responsibility found in texts such as Deut 24:16; 2 Kgs 14:6; Jer 31:29-30; Ezek 18.

The rest of the unit is taken up with a detailed account of David's unconventional reaction to the death of the child (vv 15b-23: contrast 18:33 — 19:4). The conclusion in vv 24-25 reports briefly the birth of Solomon, Bathsheba's second child by David, and stresses the Lord's love for him. The name "Jedidiah" (v 25: meaning "beloved of the Lord") is not used elsewhere for Solomon.

The section concludes in 12:26-31 with the final part of the Ammonite war account. The capture of Rabbah, their capital, is narrated; rich booty is taken from the city; the population is set to forced labour, a detail that gives us an insight into the economic infrastructure of the Davidic Empire. David's return to Jerusalem (v 31) brings the whole section to a point of rest.

2. *Significance.* These chapters present us with a double image of David: in the public sphere, a successful king and conqueror; in his private life, a sinner exposed by the prophetic word of Nathan. It is a remarkable testimony to the objectivity of the final editors of Samuel and Kings that David, their ideal figure, is shown in this mixture of light and shade, with no attempt made to expurgate the unedifying aspects (as has been done quite thoroughly in Chronicles, on the contrary).

Up to this point David's career has been shown as an unbroken story of faithful response to the Lord's guidance, but from now on a dark shadow is cast over his life by sin and its consequences. At the height of his power David begins to act as a typical despot, dealing with life and death simply in accordance with his own desires and self-interest. His guilt is great; indeed Saul's offences, for which he and his sons lost the throne, might seem light in comparison.

Why then was David not immediately rejected as Saul had been? The only explanation is that of 2 Sam 7: David and his family were chosen as bearers of the Lord's promise. Unworthy though they may show themselves to be, a space for repentance is offered to them so that the promise may be fulfilled in the future (cf. 7:14-15). The mention of Yahweh's love for Solomon (12:24-25) is a hint in that direction.

The clash between prophet and king reflects a situation that repeated itself many times during the monarchical period in Israel and Judah. The kings often needed reminding that political power and reasons of state were subordinate in Israel to Yahweh's dominion and the imperious demands of ethical principles.

Chaps 11 and 12 also provide a key to interpret what follows in chaps 13-20 and 1 Kgs 1-2. There it will indeed be seen that "the sword shall never depart" from David's house (cf. 12:10) in punishment for his having had Uriah killed in battle, and the wrong done to Uriah's marriage will be met by Absalom's appropriation of David's concubines (16:21-22).

C.   13:1 — 14:33
THE MURDER OF AMNON; THE FLIGHT AND RETURN OF ABSALOM

1. *Comment.* This section opens a sequence of eight chapters which deal mainly with the relations between David and several of his children, particularly Absalom; political events are presented within the setting of this family narrative.

The first of the four units into which the present section can be divided (13:1-22) tells how disorder and hatred entered into David's family through the lustful behaviour of Amnon, David's eldest son, who raped Absalom's virginal sister Tamar, his own half-sister. (One can note a degree of correspondence with David's own actions in chap. 11.) The story is told with great skill and delicacy; the narrator passes no explicit moral judgements but Tamar's words in vv 12-13 clearly reflect his point of view. Amnon's act of violence goes against the most basic and traditional norms of conduct in Israel and is utterly inexcusable; all the more so, since a marriage with Tamar is seen here as possible (v 13: see Gen 20:12 for evidence in favour of this, in spite of Lev 18:9, 11; 20:17; Deut 27:22). The heavy stress on hatred in v 15 is both psychologically acute and thematically important. Here, in fact, deep hatred takes over from shallow love; Amnon's hatred will generate Absalom's hatred (v 22), and the consequences will prove fatal for the former (13:23ff). Meanwhile Tamar's life is ruined (vv 18-20). David's reaction is one of great anger but he takes no action against Amnon (v 21: RSV with the Hebrew); the Greek text has an addition at the end of v 21, partially attested in a Qumran Hebrew text also, which may be more original: "but he did not cause his son Amnon pain, because he loved him seeing that he was his first-born" (cf. 1 Kgs 1:6).

The second scene (13:23-37) describes Absalom's vengeance for the wrong done to his sister. Just as Amnon had used a stratagem involving food to get Tamar into his power (vv 5-11), so too Absalom uses the festive occasion of the sheep-shearing feast (cf. 1 Sam 25:8) to get Amnon into his power (vv 23-28). On both occasions the king is involved unwittingly in the scheme. The murder of Amnon is told laconically (v 29a), and most of what follows in vv 29b-36 is taken up by an account of how the news of the tragedy reached the court. One notes here the presence of the "wise" Jonadab whose craftiness had caused so much damage earlier (vv 3-5). David's mourning is loud and demonstrative (contrast 12:20-23), and the concluding note in v 37 stresses the intensity of his grief while also mentioning Absalom's flight to the north Transjordanian kingdom of Geshur which was his mother's homeland (cf. 3:3).

Absalom's return to Jerusalem, but not to the court, after three years of exile is told in the third scene (13:38 — 14:24). Once again a stratagem sets events in motion: David's grief over Amnon is beginning to yield place to a longing for the return of Absalom; this is noticed by Joab who instructs a "wise woman" from the Judaean town of Tekoa to act out a scene before the king's tribunal that will bring David to come to a decision about Absalom's return. The woman presents herself before the king in the guise of a widow seeking royal protection for her only son whose life is endangered by the custom of private blood-vengeance (14:5-7). Skilfully weaving her web of words around the king, she brings him to guarantee under oath her son's safety (vv 8-11). Then she begins to draw a parallel to David's own position with regard to Absalom (vv 12-14: the general sense is clear, though some of the details remain obscure), and closes her advocacy by returning to the fictitious case of her son and by complimenting the king on his discernment (vv 15-17). David has understood the woman's rather contorted allusions (the comparable scene at 12:1-7 is much clearer), and he suspects that Joab's hand is behind the whole performance; the woman confirms his suspicion with further flattering expressions (vv 18-20). The king sends Joab to bring Absalom back to Jerusalem but the reconciliation is not complete, for Absalom is forbidden to enter the king's presence (vv 21-24).

At this point the narrative is interrupted by a very positive description of Absalom (vv 25-27), which emphasizes his handsome appearance and lack of physical blemish — qualities that are most appropriate for a king (cf. 1 Sam 9:2; 16:12). One notes that his beautiful daughter Tamar (v 27) bears the same name as her unfortunate aunt (13:1-20).

The final scene (14:28-33) takes place two years later; the descriptive interlude of vv 25-27 has helped to suggest the passage of time. Absalom wants to be readmitted to the court; Joab refuses twice to act as mediator on his behalf, so Absalom resorts to a stratagem (cf. 13:5ff; 13:24ff; 14:2ff). He orders Joab's field to be set on fire; this brings Joab to Absalom at last and makes him listen to the latter's violent appeal (v 32). One can note that Absalom's impassioned words, "if there is guilt in me, let him kill me" (v 32: cf. 1 Sam 20:8) are heavy with dramatic irony for the reader who knows what is to come: soon, it is Absalom who will be seeking to kill the king (15:14), thus incurring terrible guilt which will lead to his own death at the hands of Joab (18:9ff). Joab goes to the king who receives Absalom, and a kiss of reconciliation appears to terminate the whole tragic sequence of events (14:33).

2. *Significance.* These chapters can be read as the prehistory of Absalom's revolt against David told in chaps 15-18. The story begins as a family drama: there is no indication that Absalom hated Amnon as a rival for the throne; his hatred and the subsequent fratricide were clearly motivated by a desire to avenge the wrong done to Tamar (13:22, 32). But the ever-increasing involvement of Joab suggests that political considerations were not absent, at least after Absalom's exclusion from the court. It is strange that the reconciliation scene of 14:33 is presented without any dialogue (though the narrator is clearly a master of dialogue!) and with the use of David's title "the king" rather than his personal name; the reader is left with a certain feeling of unease that the reconciliation is not a wholehearted one on Absalom's side or at least leaves something to be desired. What follows will make that suspicion a solid certainty.

D.   15:1 — 16:14
ABSALOM'S REVOLT; DAVID'S FLIGHT FROM JERUSALEM

1. *Comment.*   The first unit (15:1-12) describes Absalom's preparations. He builds up an impressive public image (v 1), undermines the countryfolk's trust in the administration of justice at David's court, and presents himself as a more concerned and accessible candidate for the office of judge and leader (vv 2-6). The anti-Absalom slant of the text here makes it questionable whether vv 3-6 can be used to show that there actually were serious shortcomings in the administration of justice at Jerusalem; however the fact that Absalom gained widespread support from both Israelites

and Judaeans (cf. 19:9-15) shows that there was much popular discontent with David's reign, probably for a whole variety of reasons. Empires generally take their toll internally. Having spent some time on these remote preparations (the "four years" of v 7 is textually uncertain), Absalom is ready to move openly. He employs a pious stratagem to absent himself from the capital and gather his forces at the old Judaean centre of Hebron (vv 7-12). Verse 11 is careful to exculpate the Jerusalemites who, like David himself, suspected nothing of Absalom's treasonable intentions. Ahithophel (v 12) will prove to be one of Absalom's most able supporters.

The next unit (15:13 — 16:14) begins with an account of David's hurried departure from Jerusalem (15:13-18). He is accompanied by his household and by the mercenary soldiers (v 18), while ten concubines are left behind as a living proof of his ownership of the palace and the city (v 16: cf. 16:21-22; 20:3). Five scenes follow, telling of David's meetings with various personages or groups. The first three scenes present David's faithful supporters: the Philistine (!) mercenary Ittai (15:19-22), the priests Zadok and Abiathar and their sons (15:24-29), and the old counsellor Hushai (15:32-36). After each of these scenes there is a brief descriptive or narrative passage (vv 23, 30-31, 37). One can note in particular 15:31 where David is shown as fully aware of the danger represented by Ahithophel; his prayer to the Lord here is followed immediately by the meeting with Hushai (15:32ff) who will be the means by which Yahweh will counteract Ahithophel's deadly advice to Absalom (cf. 17:1-14).

In the fourth and fifth scenes David meets persons associated with the house of Saul: Ziba the steward of Meribbaal (16:1-4: cf. chap. 9), and Shimei, a member of Saul's own Benjaminite clan (16:5-13). These meetings are less favourable to David than the first three. Ziba, it is true, professes loyalty, brings David provisions, and accuses his master Meribbaal of siding with the rebels in order to be proclaimed king. As a reward David grants Ziba all the property formerly assigned to Meribbaal (chap. 9). Meribbaal himself, however, offers quite a different version of events later (19:24ff), and it is not easy to decide whether it is he or Ziba who is telling the truth. The Shimei episode, in any case, is clear in its meaning. The infuriated Benjaminite refers to David as a "man of blood" (vv 7-8: possibly an allusion to what is recounted in 21:1-14), and heaps curses and insults on the king. Abishai's proposal to decapitate "this dead dog" (v 9) is rejected by David in an admirable speech (vv 10-12: cf. 1 Sam 26:8-11). The section ends with the arrival of David and his followers at the Jordan where they rested from their fatigue (v 14).

2. *Significance.* A theological understanding of the flight from Jerusalem is provided especially in David's words of 15:25-26 and 16:10-12. He sees Yahweh's hand behind his misfortunes and sufferings, but he is fully submissive to the Lord's dispositions both for the present (16:10-11) and for the future (15:25-26; 16:12). The eventual return to Jerusalem and restoration to the throne will be the Lord's work: here is the main theological statement of chaps 15-20, and a message that was not without relevance for the exilic period readers of the Deuteronomistic history. It is interesting to observe that David's total trust in the Lord does not prevent him from taking a set of far-sighted practical decisions. He arranges for an espionage service in the occupied city of Jerusalem (15:27-28, 34-36), and consolidates Ziba's support by a high-handed grant of Meribbaal's property (16:4). One can note the suggestion of some scholars that the more theological passages here belong to a later redaction of the story.

E. 16:15 — 17:23
A CLASH BETWEEN COUNSELLORS PREPARES ABSALOM'S RUIN

1. *Comment.* The scene changes back to Jerusalem, occupied without a struggle by Absalom's forces. Hushai

presents himself to Absalom, as David had instructed
(15:33-36), and expresses his ostensible change of allegiance
in extravagantly rhetorical terms which include a theological justification for the revolt as deriving from the Lord's
choice of Absalom (16:16-19). Ahithophel, the rival counsellor, then urges Absalom to finalize the break with his
father by publicly taking the latter's concubines (cf. 15:16)
as a symbol of his taking over David's kingship (cf. 3:7 with
the comment), and Absalom complies with this advice
(16:20-23). Read in the light of 12:11-12, this incident can be
seen as a fitting retribution for David's taking Bathsheba
(though 16:21-22 may not have envisaged this connection
originally).

Ahithophel then volunteers to pursue the fugitive David
that very night with a large force; Absalom and the elders
seem ready to accept this potentially lethal advice (17:1-4).
Hushai is called upon for his advice too, and what follows in
vv 7-13 is a masterpiece of rhetoric that serves a crucial
purpose in Yahweh's guidance of events. Briefly, what
Hushai proposes is that Absalom should wait in order to
gather a huge force from all Israel and then move to crush
David in a spectacular way. Absalom and all his followers
hail this plan as "better" than Ahithophel's (v 14a), but a
theological aside of major importance (v 14b) notes that
Yahweh was at work here to nullify Ahithophel's "good"
(that is, sensible) advice and so prepare the ruin of Absalom.

Having thus gained time for David, Hushai sends him a
message by the priests' sons, Jonathan and Ahimaaz (cf. 15:
27-28, 35-36); these elude their pursuers thanks to the help
of a woman (cf. Josh 2), and reach David who immediately
crosses the Jordan into the safer eastern regions (17:15-22).
The section concludes with a short report on Ahithophel's
suicide (17:23); we are to take it that the far-seeing counsellor realized that Absalom's delay meant David's eventual
victory, and so he commits suicide with the same cold-
blooded efficiency that characterized his every word in the
story.

2. *Significance.* It is fitting that the decisive turning-
point of a narrative where direct speech plays such an

important part should be in a duel of words between two counsellors. Absalom's cause is lost in this clash, before ever his troops face David's professional forces. But the real decision has been made elsewhere. At 15:31 David had prayed that Ahithophel's counsel be made vain; at 17:14b the readers learn that the prayer has been answered. Absalom's doom and David's safety are Yahweh's work amid the noisy words and confused movements of history.

F.   17:24 — 19:8a (HEBREW: 17:24 — 19:9a)
A CLASH BETWEEN ARMIES COMPLETES ABSALOM'S RUIN

1. *Comment.* Some preliminary notices are given in 17:24-29. The familial dimension of the revolt is shown once more in the fact that Absalom's commander-in-chief, Amasa, is a relative of Joab (and of David and Absalom too), as the genealogy of v 25 shows. The two armies gather in northern Transjordan where David receives support from local notables (vv 27-29), one of whom, Barzillai, will reappear in the story (19:31ff). The immediate preparations for the battle are recounted in 18:1-5; David explicitly orders his commanders, Joab, Abishai, and Ittai, to "deal gently ... with the young man Absalom" (v 5). A short notice describes the actual battle (vv 6-8); such brevity is usual in OT battle-descriptions. David's experienced soldiers win a decisive victory over Absalom's militia forces, and the ensuing slaughter was facilitated by the heavily wooded countryside which hindered the flight of the defeated.

Two longer narrative units follow. The first (vv 9-17) tells in vivid detail of Absalom's death — against David's explicit orders recalled here in v 12 — at the hands of Joab and his attendants. Absalom dies ingloriously with his head caught fast in the branches of a tree (v 9), that same head whose abundant growth of hair had earlier been noted as one of his most striking features (14:25-26); he receives a hasty and dishonourable burial (v 17: contrast Ahithophel's burial at

17:23). A notice is inserted here (v 18) with information about a funeral monument near Jerusalem which was later associated with Absalom's name; the statement that Absalom had no son clashes with 14:27 and probably indicates that 18:18 is the work of a later glossator.

The following unit (18:19 — 19:8a) tells how the news of Absalom's death was brought to David and how he reacted; in these verses the text reaches a rare level of emotional intensity. Strong narrative suspense is created by the race between the two messengers and by Ahimaaz's concealment of the truth (v 29). When the Cushite (a foreigner, possibly a Nubian) lets it be clearly understood that Absalom is dead (v 32), the anguish of the bereaved father breaks out in despairing cries (18:33 — 19:4). It takes an extremely blunt speech by Joab (19:5-7) to bring David back to an awareness of his responsibilities as king. He resumes his royal role in muted grief (v 8a).

2.   *Significance.*   The theological meaning of the victory is expressed in the words of the two messengers (18:28, 31): it is Yahweh who has thwarted the plans of the rebels and vindicated his chosen king. All this, however, offers little immediate consolation to David, in whose reaction we see the father's anguish rather than the king's triumph: the familial dimension comes to expression once again.

On the political level Absalom's *coup d'état* has collapsed; the mopping-up operations will be recounted in the next section. Joab's role is worth notice. His utter lack of scruple was already shown at 3:22-30, and his ability to manoeuvre the king was seen in chap. 14. Both traits recur here: he disobeys David's solemn order and kills Absalom, and then rebukes the king with brutal frankness, not hesitating to express a threat of desertion. Joab can be seen as the embodiment of autonomous political calculation; reasons of state take precedence over all else — sentiments, the king's orders, ethical principles. Ahithophel represents the same type, and it is significant that both men come to a violent end (17:23; 1 Kgs 2:28-35).

G. 19:8b — 20:26 (HEBREW: 19:9b — 20:26) DAVID RETURNS TO JERUSALEM AND THE LAST STIRRINGS OF REVOLT ARE PUT DOWN

1. *Comment*. The opening unit (vv 8b-15) shows the northern tribes arguing about David's restoration, while David himself plays on the old rivalry between Judah and Israel in order to encourage the Judaean elders to support his return; in a shrewd political gesture of generosity towards the defeated party he offers to appoint Amasa, Absalom's general, as commander in place of Joab whose behaviour in the matter of Absalom's death and afterwards has not been forgotten by the king.

Three encounters are then narrated, reminding the reader of the five encounters earlier (15:19 — 16:13). This time, however, the order is reversed: the king is met first by the personage who had been most hostile to him (Shimei), then come men of dubious loyalty (Ziba and Meribbaal), and finally his faithful supporter Barzillai. In the Shimei scene (19:16-23) one can note Abishai's hot-headed reaction to Shimei's frank admission of guilt and plea for forgiveness (v 21: cf. 16:9 in the first meeting with Shimei) and David's magnanimous reply which betrays no note of duplicity (vv 22-23: contrast 1 Kgs 2:8-9). The David of the present text does not seem to be impressed by the common notion of the quasi-objective efficacy of a curse (cf. 16:5ff); he renounces personal vengeance and forgives sincerely. It must be added, of course, that this attitude had good political reasons in its favour too: Shimei was an influential Benjaminite (cf. v 17a), and reconciliation with Benjamin was essential for David's return.

Meribbaal's meeting with the king (vv 24-30) is told in such a way as to suggest that his explanations may possibly be sincere and hence that Ziba's assertion at 16:3 was untrue (Ziba is mentioned here at 19:17-18 but no words of his are given). However the reader remains in doubt, and the net result seems to be that both men are depicted in a bad light: the house of Saul is thus discredited, and Meribbaal's future depends wholly on David's graciousness (cf. 1 Sam 20:42;

24:20-21). In conclusion David modifies the decision he had made earlier about the property of Saul's family (vv 29-30: cf. 16:4; 9:7-11).

The Barzillai scene (19:31-40a) has none of the shadows of the two previous encounters. It shows David as still capable of attracting spontaneous and generous support, which he repays with equal generosity. Chimham (v 37), apparently Barzillai's son, is not mentioned by name again in Sam and Kgs; there is a reference to Barzillai's sons in 1 Kgs 2:7.

The next unit (19:40b — 20:2) deals with a dispute between the Israelites and the Judaeans; it seems a trivial matter, but the outcome is that a Benjaminite named Sheba leads the Israelites away from David who returns to Jerusalem accompanied by the Judaeans alone. The verbal similarities between 20:1 and 1 Kgs 12:16 suggest that the separation of the two kingdoms, recounted in the latter chapter, was but the final episode in a long history of northern disaffection with the rule of David and then Solomon.

A parenthesis (20:3) tells of the king's treatment of the concubines who had been appropriated by Absalom (cf. 15:16; 16:21-22). The main narrative resumes at 20:4 where David orders his new commander, Amasa, to gather the Judaean militia and to crush Sheba's revolt. Amasa delays beyond the appointed time (v 5), so David sends out Abishai with the mercenaries. Joab (officially in disgrace) joins his brother, treacherously murders Amasa when the latter eventually arrives (vv 8-10: note the several similarities to the account of Joab's murder of Abner at 3:26-27), and calmly resumes his former post as commander. The pursuit of Sheba continues right through northern Israel and finally the rebel is run to earth in the northern city of Abel of Beth-maacah. In the process Sheba appears to have been abandoned by all his Israelite supporters except for the Bichrites (v 14), his own clan. As Joab begins the siege of Abel, a "wise woman" intervenes (compare chap. 14), reminds Joab of the city's reputation as a centre of wisdom, peace, and loyalty (vv 18-19), and negotiates a settlement with the besiegers. Sheba is unceremoniously decapitated by the townsfolk and his head is tossed out to Joab who then returns with the army to Jerusalem (v 22).

The section concludes with an archival list of David's officials. Comparing it with the similar list of 8:16-18, one can note the significant addition of a director of forced labour, Adoram (v 24); royal building projects, civil and military, would have necessitated a regular supply of labour. Adoram must have been a young man towards the end of David's reign, since his violent death came about after Solomon's death (1 Kgs 12:18).

2. *Significance.* David rules as unopposed king in Jerusalem again, but his return is not depicted as an unqualified triumph. He has to renegotiate his position with the Judaeans, and the loyalty of the Israelites seems a fragile thing. It is the autumn season of David's rule, and the winter is soon to come (1 Kgs 1-2). For the moment, however, peace and order have been restored, and the Lord's favour has once again been shown to David (cf. 15:25).

VII. 2 Sam 21:1 — 24:25
Miscellaneous Narratives and Poems about David

These chapters interrupt the main account of David's reign which continues in 1 Kgs 1; the interruption is chronological as well as literary, since most (if not all) of the narrative material here refers to events that are set prior to Absalom's revolt. Though there are old traditions at the basis of most of the accounts, their insertion is probably the work of Deuteronomistic redactors, though some hold that the chapters were inserted even later into the already completed Deuteronomistic history.

The arrangement of the material is worth noting:

A. 21:1-14 Narrative with strong archaic religious colouring
B. 21:15-22 Military traditions in the form of brief notices

C. 22:1-51   A poem: David's song of thanksgiving
D. 23:1-7   A poem: David's last words
E. 23:8-39   Military traditions in the form of brief anec-
              dotes, notices and lists
F. 24:1-25   Narrative with strong archaic religious
              colouring

The correspondences (A/F, B/E, C/D) have given rise to the hypothesis that sections A and F were first inserted between 2 Sam 20 and 1 Kgs 1; then at a later stage sections B and E (which could well have formed a unit in earlier tradition) were put between A and F; finally the two poems (C, D) were placed at the centre.

A.   21:1-14
FAMINE IS AVERTED BY THE SACRIFICE OF
SEVEN SAULIDES

1.   *Comment.*   A cultic oracle reveals to David that the severe famine afflicting Israel for the third successive year is a divine punishment for the blood-guilt incurred by Saul and his family when he broke the ancient treaty-oath that guaranteed immunity to the non-Israelite enclave of Gibeon, a short distance north of Jerusalem (vv 1, 2b: cf. Josh 9). David's reaction (vv 2a, 3-6) is to call the Gibeonites and agree to their request to hand over to them seven members of Saul's family to be ritually executed at Gibeon. The term "hang" at vv 6ff seems to refer to the breaking of the limbs or the dismemberment of the executed persons and their public exposure for violation of a solemn agreement or covenant. The victims are named and the deed is done (vv 7-9): the text distinguishes two persons named Mephibosheth (that is, Meribbaal) — Saul's son (v 8) and grandson (v 7: cf. 4:4; 9:1-13; 16:1-4; 19:24-30), the latter reference probably being a redactional addition.

Two acts of kindness introduce a faint note of humanity into the grim narrative. Rizpah, mother of two of the victims (cf. 3:7), stations herself day and night near the bodies until the time of their ritual exposure terminates with the first rainfall, in order to ward off the birds and wild beasts (v 10). David orders the remains of Saul and Jonathan to be brought from Jabesh-gilead (cf. 1 Sam 31:11-13) and buried in their ancestral grave (vv 11-14); the seven executed Saulides, it would seem (v 13b), are buried with them. The narrative concludes by noting that God then heeded the people's supplications, which implies that the famine ended (v 14b).

The outlines of the story, at least, must have been known to the authors of 2 Sam 9 (cf. vv 1, 3: see the comment there) and 16 (cf. vv 7-8), but as it stands the narrative probably contains several layers of tradition; the allusion to Josh 9 in v 2 points to the work of a Deuteronomistic redactor.

2. *Significance.* David's innocence and piety are stressed throughout the story. One can understand why: the death of seven Saulides removed seven possible rivals to David's throne, and this at a critical moment (probably early in David's reign) when the persistent famine could have been interpreted as a sign that David was not equal to his newly acquired royal office. It was expected, in fact, both in the surrounding cultures and in Israel (cf. Ps 72[71]:6, 16), that among the divine blessings mediated by a good king to his people would be the fertility and abundance of natural products. The present form of the story, however, carefully avoids stressing the fertility aspect with its overtones of human sacrifice, and attributes the active role in the gruesome killing to the Gibeonites. The insistence on David's care for the bones of Saul and Jonathan and the seven Saulides is meant to show that his acceding to the request of the Gibeonites was not motivated, even partially, by an anti-Saulide attitude but solely by concern for the desperate plight of his famine-stricken people. David listened to the Lord's oracle, took the necessary steps, and the people were delivered from their straits — a pattern of behaviour that could have served as a model for David's successors, who all too often refused to listen to the Lord's words communi-

cated by his prophets and so brought upon themselves and their people the disasters of ruin and exile.

B. 21:15-22
HEROIC DEEDS AGAINST PHILISTINE CHAMPIONS

The short notices that make up this section breathe an atmosphere of archaic heroism that is quite alien to the courtly narrative style of chaps 10-20. The Philistine war setting links the section chronologically with 5:17-25, though there is no proof that the two passages ever formed a literary unity.

The anecdote of vv 15-17 describes a critical moment for David who was in danger of being overpowered by a Philistine warrior, a member of an elite corps whom folk tradition apparently saw as descended from giants (thus according to the RSV rendering at vv 16, 18, 20, 22). The king's life was saved by Abishai, Joab's brother, which may help to explain the influence that the two brothers later had over David, their uncle (cf. chaps 16, 19, 20). David's men opposed his taking part in military actions after that (cf. the variant tradition at 18:2b-4), since the prosperity of his people depended on his wellbeing (v 17b); the "lamp of Israel" metaphor there reflects the royal ideology, various aspects of which are rather strongly expressed in chaps 21-24.

The relation between v 19 and the Goliath narratives has been discussed in the commentary on 1 Sam 17.

C. 22:1-51
THE SONG OF DAVID

Since this chapter is identical with Ps 18(17), apart from minor textual variants, the reader is referred to OTM 21 for a more detailed commentary on the text. Here it will suffice to note briefly how the royal psalm can be read in the literary context of Samuel and Kings.

(1) David's experiences: The title (v 1) invites the reader to apply the psalm to David's own life-situation (which was probably not intended specifically at first). The themes of opposition and persecution, of trust in Yahweh, of deliverance from difficulties, of subjugation of enemies at home and abroad — all these have been amply illustrated in the preceding narratives of 1 and 2 Sam. Remembrance now becomes prayer.

(2) The Davidic dynasty: The explicit reference to David's "descendants for ever" (v 51) suggests that the psalm has a dynastic bearing too (cf. 2 Sam 7). David's experience of the Lord's deliverance also holds good for his successors, provided they share his attitudes of humble prayer, unshaken trust, and firm commitment to the Lord's law (vv 21-25). Unhappily most of the Davidic kings fell short of these ideals, and so from the hindsight of the Exile the psalm can be read as an act of accusation against the unworthy Davidic kings. But the last word is not one of accusation: v 51 speaks of "steadfast love ... for ever". The future remains open for the house of David.

(3) The humble people of the Lord: The Lord's deliverance is for "a humble people" (v 28); the Davidic king experiences the Lord's favour in so far as he is one in attitude with Yahweh's faithful ones (vv 21-31). So even when no king sits on the throne of David (during and after the Exile), there is still hope for the Lord's marvellous deliverance if the people remain humbly faithful to his laws and statutes and call out to him trustfully from the depth of their suffering.

D. 23:1-7
DAVID'S LAST WORDS: A POEM

1. *Comment.* It should be noted that, while the main theological message of the poem is reasonably clear, many of its details present philological problems, as can be seen if one compares the RSV translation with that of other English versions. The following notes refer simply to the RSV rendering.

Great solemnity is given to the poem by its prose heading, "the last words of David" (v 1a: cf. Deut 33:1); the expression is to be taken in a broad sense, especially in view of 1 Kgs 2:1ff. A four-line introduction (v 1b) presents David in the third person; one can note the "oracle" vocabulary as in the discourses of Balaam the seer (Num 24:3-4, 15-16). The next four-line unit (vv 2-3a) presents David in prophetic terms; the gift of the Spirit is associated with speech here, which distinguishes this text from others where the king is endowed permanently with the Spirit for his ruling functions (cf. 1 Sam 16: 13; Isa 11:2). The divine words are then quoted (vv 3b-4), and one can notice the conditional formulation. The Lord's blessings, expressed in nature imagery (v 4), will come upon king and people only when the king rules justly and in the fear of God (v 3b); the insistence on these two qualities recalls the presentation of the ideal Davidic king in Isa 11:1-5. Justice was a royal ideal all over the ancient Near East, and the stress on the fear of God is developed in the so-called "law of the king" in Deut 17:14-20 (espec. vv 18-19).

The final unit (vv 5-7) contrasts the favoured situation of David's house with the total ruin that awaits the wicked. The covenant granted by the Lord to the house of David (v 5: cf. 2 Sam 7) is termed "everlasting" (cf. Gen 9:16; 17:7; Isa 55:3; Ezek 16:60; 37:26); this refers to its legal stability ("ordered in all things and secure": v 5) but not to the absence of conditions. It is only when the Davidic king rules justly and in the fear of God that he can hope that the Lord will come to his aid and fulfil his desires (v 5b: using ancient treaty terminology that can now be traced back to a third millennium text from Ebla).

2. *Significance.*   Besides presenting an idealized image of David himself, the poem puts forward a standard against which all the Davidic kings can be measured. The Book of Kings will show how often they failed to live up to what is here solemnly enjoined on them by their ancestor. Even if they seem to come to ruin, however, hope remains, for the Davidic covenant is an everlasting one.

Some scholars have attributed the poem to the period of David's reign, arguing from the undoubted presence of archaic features of style and vocabulary. Others, however, noting several thematic and verbal contacts with texts of the exilic and post-exilic periods, prefer to see in the poem a late idealization of the Davidic monarchy as an expression of Israel's future hope.

E. 23:8-39
ANECDOTES AND LISTS

The ancient material contained in these verses resembles that of 21:15-22, with the addition of a long list of David's foremost warriors (vv 24-39). One can note especially the anecdote of vv 13-17 about David's request for water from the well at Philistine-occupied Bethlehem: the incident shows how David was able to win the hearts of his soldiers and thus build up his power on the strong foundations of personal loyalty.

F. 24:1-25
A SINFUL CENSUS AND ITS PUNISHMENT; DAVID BUILDS AN ALTAR IN JERUSALEM

1. *Comment.* Three parts can be distinguished, dealing mainly with the census (vv 1-9), the plague (vv 10-17), and the altar (vv 18-25). As the text stands, the three parts are linked to form one narrative, but this is probably the end product of several stages of redactional work.

The opening statement about the Lord's anger (v 1a) clearly connects the story with 21:1-14, which also told of a calamity in Israel (compare also 24:25 with 21:14). The census is regarded as sinful, because the king's desire to calculate Israel's military strength (vv 2, 9) betrays a practical lack of trust in Yahweh's ability to save his people "by many or by few" (1 Sam 14:6: cf. Judg 7:2-8). The statement that the Lord incited David to commit this sinful action (v 1b) already caused difficulty in OT times, as can be seen from the parallel passage in 1 Chr 21:1 where the incitement is attributed to Satan and not to Yahweh! 2 Sam 24:1 can be taken as an imperfect way of expressing the conviction that all events, good or bad, are ultimately subject to the Lord's control. The pious protest of Joab (v 3), who has not been remarkable for his religious scruples in the preceding narratives, serves to underline the enormity of David's offence. But the king is not moved and the census is duly carried out (vv 4-9).

The second unit (vv 10-17) begins with David's conscience-stricken reaction (v 10a: cf. 1 Sam 24:5) and his confession of guilt and plea for pardon (v 10b). The prophet Gad (cf. 1 Sam 22:5) is sent by the Lord with a choice of three punishments (vv 11-13). David chooses a punishment affecting the whole people, not himself directly; one can ask whether this is meant to be read as an act of selfishness, atoned for only by his subsequent prayer in v 17. In any case, a plague rages in Israel for three days causing many deaths (v 15). Jerusalem escapes only by a special divine decree (v 16), while David is praying that the people be spared and the Lord's punishment fall on the royal house (v 17).

The climax of the narrative (vv 18-25) is introduced by another divine communication brought to David by the prophet Gad (v 18): the king must build an altar for Yahweh at Jerusalem on the threshing floor of a Jebusite notable named Araunah. The latter's name appears to be of Hittite origin, and it has been conjectured that he was in fact the Jebusite king of Jerusalem. The suggestion remains very hypothetical. The site of Araunah's threshing floor is identified in 1 Chr 21:28 — 22:1 and 2 Chr 3:1 with the hill where the Temple would be built by Solomon; though this identification is not made explicitly in Sam or Kgs, it may well have contributed to the location of the present chapter immediately before the account of Solomon's succession to the throne. After polite exchanges between David and Araunah (vv 20-23), a price is agreed upon (v 24), the altar is built and sacrifices are offered (v 25). The Lord listens to the prayer and the people are delivered from the plague (v 25b).

It has been argued recently that what David actually did was to take over the cultic place of the Jebusites and convert it to the worship of Yahweh; consequently Solomon's building activity (1 Kgs 6-7) would really have been more the extension and embellishment of an already existing sanctuary than the construction of a wholly new one. The suggestion is interesting but it remains rather speculative.

2. *Significance.* This chapter, like chaps 11-12, shows that David's relationship to the Lord included moments of deep repentance after deplorable failings. He was not spared the Lord's punishment, either for himself and his family (chaps 13-20) or for his people (chap. 24), but after the punishment the Lord's favour was renewed. All this is meaningful for David's successors on the throne of Jerusalem, and also for the whole people undergoing the punishment of defeat and exile after the fall of Jerusalem. For it is Jerusalem, and its place of worship, that is the privileged recipient of the Lord's mercy here in chap. 24. Exilic period readers of the text might hope that a new act of divine mercy would lead to a newly rebuilt place of worship in Jerusalem and to the removal of the Lord's punishment from his afflicted people.

THE BOOK OF KINGS: COMMENTARY

I.   1 Kgs 1:1 — 2:46
Solomon's Accession

The first eleven chapters of Kings which present the account of Solomon's reign are best divided into two parts: chaps 1-2 dealing with Solomon's accession and his elimination of various possible rivals and opponents, and chaps 3-11 telling of the king's wisdom, wealth, building activities, and eventual decline. The division is justified also on the grounds of the literary origin of the texts: while chaps 3-11 contain a variety of materials taken from several annalistic, narrative, and Deuteronomistic sources, chaps 1-2 make a much more unified impression and refer back in several ways to the narratives in Samuel. Many scholars, in fact, see 1 Kgs 1-2 as the original continuation and climax of the so-called Succession Narrative (see the discussion before the commentary on 2 Sam 9 above).

The events connected with Solomon's accession are seen in chaps 1-2 as a fulfilment of the Lord's promise to David that a descendant of his would always be ruler of God's people (2:4, 24: cf. 2 Sam 7). On the other hand, the way in which the events are narrated appears at times (especially in chap. 2) to insinuate disapproval of Solomon's unscrupulous elimination of his opponents, real or imagined. No open criticism is voiced, but the present form of the text leaves the reader with the impression that the reign of Solomon began rather ambiguously. Some scholars suggest that the positive and negative aspects in the presentation of Solomon here may have originated in different redactional stages before the final form of the text emerged.

A.   1:1-53
ADONIJAH MAKES A BID FOR THE THRONE BUT SOLOMON IS ANOINTED AS DAVID'S SUCCESSOR

1. *Comment.*   The opening scene (vv 1-4) with its depiction of David's age and feebleness shows that the problem of succession to the throne has now become urgent. Adonijah, apparently David's eldest surviving son (nothing is known about Chileab, his elder brother according to 2 Sam 3:3), takes matters in his own hands: gathering an impressive bodyguard (v 5: cf. 2 Sam 15:1), he begins to act as king-designate. David's followers are split into two camps: Joab and the priest Abiathar, who had been David's supporters in the old days of his flight from Saul, side with Adonijah who had been born in the Judaean centre of Hebron (2 Sam 3:2-5); Solomon's supporters (v 8) include Zadok the priest and Nathan the prophet, both associated with Jerusalem where Solomon was born, as well as the professional soliery. One might see here a tension between those whose roots lay more in the old Judaean tribal traditions and the new men associated with Jerusalem and the royal court with its foreign political connections. The crisis comes to a head when Adonijah organizes what amounts to a coronation feast, inviting all his supporters and excluding the opposition (vv 9-10).

At this point the focus shifts to the other side. Nathan, the grey eminence of the affair, urges Bathsheba to draw David's attention to what is happening and to ensure that he officially names Solomon as his successor before it is too late (vv 11-14). Mention is made of an oath alleged to have been taken by David, which serves as Solomon's title to the throne (vv 13, 17, 30); the problem is that this oath has never been referred to in the preceding narratives. It has been suggested that the text wishes to insinuate that the oath was an invention of Nathan, which the elderly king accepted only because of his failing memory and general senility; if so, then the text presents the succession of Solomon as based on a fraudulent title. Though this explanation cannot be excluded, it is by no means the only possible one. In the first place, the precision and the decisive tone that mark David's instructions in vv 28-35 do not suggest a state of advanced senility such as must be presupposed for the fore-going explanation. Secondly, the question of sucession to the throne has not been broached explicitly before 1 Kgs 1, so a prior mention of the oath was not called for; besides, the mention of the Lord's love for Solomon (2 Sam 12:24-25) is already very significant. It must be admitted, however, that the reader is left with an uneasy feeling of doubt, which forms part of the ambiguity of 1 Kgs 1-2 noted above.

Bathsheba has her audience with David (vv 15-21) and Nathan follows her, as it were by chance, with the same request (vv 22-27). David makes his decision: he confirms Solomon as his successor (vv 28-31) and orders that he be anointed forthwith and acclaimed as king (vv 32-37); amid great popular rejoicing the king's instructions are carried out (vv 38-40). The anointing takes place at the spring Gihon (vv 33, 38), the source of Jerusalem's water supply and possibly a place of sacral significance already in Jebu-site times. Solomon is appointed "ruler" (*nagid*, v 35: cf. 1 Sam 9:16) over Israel and over Judah; the tribal elders have no say in the matter (contrast 2 Sam 2:4; 5:3; 19:11-12). Though the term "king" is used in his regard from v 39 on, there is no indication that David abdicated at this point; it is more likely that Solomon became co-regent with his father, a practice known in the later history of the kings too.

The story then returns to Adonijah's feast which was taking place about half a mile away down the Kidron valley (cf. v 9). News is brought of Solomon's anointing (vv 41-48). Adonijah's guests hurriedly decamp (v 49) and Adonijah himself seeks sanctuary at the altar of the ark shrine (v 50). The chapter closes with Solomon's decision to spare Adonijah's life provided he gives no further cause for alarm; Adonijah meekly accepts the royal decision and retires to private life (vv 51-53).

2. *Significance.*   One possible reading of the chapter will see it as the account of the fulfilment of the Lord's promise to David: "I will raise up your offspring after you ... and I will establish his kingdom" (2 Sam 7:12). Solomon's succession is based on a solemn oath pronounced by David and not on an autonomous bid for the throne as in Adonijah's case. The tone of religious celebration comes out clearly in David's confirmation of the oath (vv 29-30), in Benaiah's prayer (vv 36-37), and in David's thanksgiving (v 48). Solomon's magnanimous treatment of Adonijah (vv 52-53) is an auspicious beginning to his reign.

An anti-Solomonic reading of the chapter would see here the account of a court intrigue, engineered by Nathan and the ambitious Bathsheba, who succeeded in persuading the elderly and ailing king to pass over the rights of Adonijah, the presumptive successor, in favour of the Jerusalemite Solomon, whose title to the throne is thus shown as dubious to say the least.

As the text stands now, the positive reading seems to predominate, though the shadows of criticism and doubt remain. The account of David's rise to the throne was very different; the reader is made to feel that the monarchy is entering a new phase. It remains to be seen what its characteristics will be.

B.   2:1-46
DAVID'S LAST WORDS TO SOLOMON; THE ELIMINATION OF SOLOMON'S OPPONENTS

1. *Comment.*   Verses 1-9 are presented as David's last testament to Solomon. The insistence on the law of Moses in vv

3-4 points to the hand of a Deuteronomistic redactor there. One can also note that the dynastic promise (v 4) is conditional to the obedience of David's descendants; this contrasts with the unconditional promise of 2 Sam 7 but closely resembles Ps 132(131):12. After the exhortation of vv 2-4, David passes on to more practical matters in vv 5-9: there are debts to be collected and to be paid. Solomon is reminded of the murders committed by Joab (cf. 2 Sam 3; 20) and he is urged to bring him to an untimely end; no reason is given why David himself did not act against Joab. The sons of Barzillai, on the other hand, merit Solomon's gratitude and favour because of their father's support for David (v 7: cf. 2 Sam 17:27-29; 19:31-40). Finally (vv 8-9) Shimei the Benjaminite deserves death for the curses he piled on David (2 Sam 16:5-13); David himself swore to spare his life (2 Sam 19:22-23), but Solomon is not bound by that oath and he should act as his wisdom suggests. The implication here seems to be that the baleful influence of a curse could affect the addressee's descendants too; if Shimei receives his well-merited punishment, the effects of the curse would be neutralized.

Verses 10-12, edited by a Deuteronomistic redactor, report David's death, the length of his reign, and Solomon's establishment on the throne as sole ruler.

The second part of the chapter (vv 13-46) describes the measures taken by Solomon to consolidate his position. First, the king's half-brother Adonijah is disposed of (vv 13-25). He is said to have requested Solomon, through Bathsheba's intercession, to have the beautiful Abishag (cf. 1:1-4) as his wife; Solomon interprets this as practically equivalent to a claim for the throne (v 22: cf. 2 Sam 3:7 with comment). Appealing to the dynastic oracle of 2 Sam 7 (v 24), he orders Adonijah's immediate execution which is carried out by Benaiah (v 25: cf. 2 Sam 20:23). Next to be dealt with is Abiathar the priest (vv 26-27), who had been a supporter of Adonijah (1:7ff). Solomon declares that he too merits death but, in view of Abiathar's service during David's reign (cf. 1 Sam 23:6, 9; 30:7; 2 Sam 15:24-29), the sentence is commuted to deposition from his priestly functions at Jerusalem and banishment to his property at Anathoth, north of Jerusalem (cf. Jer 1:1). A Deuteronomistic redactor notes in v 27 that this is the fulfilment of the Lord's oracle against the house of Eli (cf. 1 Sam 2:27-36).

Now it is Joab's turn (vv 28-34). Realizing what was in store, he seeks asylum in the tent-sanctuary of the ark (v 28) and refuses to come out at the king's bidding. A speech by Solomon insists on the blood-guilt incurred by Joab and affecting David's house too (vv 31-33). The king orders Joab's execution which is carried out by Benaiah. One can note that the execution of a treacherous murderer even after he sought asylum at the altar was permitted by Exod 21:14, but the execution was to take place outside the cultic area. Solomon and Benaiah are not scrupulous about such matters however. Benaiah then replaces Joab as army commander, and Zadok takes over Abiathar's functions as chief priest (v 35).

Finally there is Shimei the Benjaminite (vv 36-46). Solomon orders him to reside in Jerusalem and never to leave the city; Shimei complies (vv 36-38). Three years later, however, he goes to the Philistine city of Gath (probably a vassal-state of the Davidic Empire) to retrieve some runaway slaves, a wholly domestic affair with absolutely no political implications. But Solomon has the pretext he needed: in a solemn speech he rehearses Shimei's crimes (vv 42-45) and orders his execution. The indispensable Benaiah is at hand in his now familiar function as court executioner (v 46a). The concluding note (v 46b) on the consolidation of Solomon's rule re-echoes v 12b.

2. *Significance.* The main point of chap. 2, as it stands, is to argue that the removal of Solomon's opponents was not an act of arbitrary tyranny by a cruel despot but was authorized either by David's last wishes (in the case of Joab and Shimei) or by the unbridled ambition of the victim (in the case of Adonijah). Since the establishment of Solomon's rule meant the fulfilment of the dynastic promise (vv 24, 33, 45), these drastic measures were called for. A theological

justification is thus offered for actions which must have given rise to considerable adverse comment in Solomon's own time. The question arises however: is this the proper use of theology?

On an attentive reading the text itself begins to reveal its ambiguity. While there is no explicit criticism of Solomon, the deadpan manner of narration in vv 13-46 may well insinuate an evaluation at variance with that of the explicit theological comments. Furthermore the suspicion arises that David's "last wishes" (vv 5-9) might have been formulated by a Solomonic propaganda writer intent on justifying by David's authority a series of very questionable measures adopted by Solomon on his own initiative and in his own interests. One might also be inclined to question the interpretation Solomon put on Adonijah's request for Abishag — if the request was ever made (Bathsheba appears to have been the only witness). None of these insinuations and suspicions can be proved, but the reader is left with a distinct feeling of unease. The possibility that theology has been, in part at least, manipulated in the service of power and violence in 1 Kgs 2 provides food for thought in today's world also.

II. 1 Kgs 3:1 — 11:43
Solomon's Reign: Glory and Decline

The present form of these chapters is, in its main lines, a Deuteronomistic composition with some post-Deuteronomistic additions. The editors used older sources, especially the Book of the Acts of Solomon (11:41), which must have contained lists, adaptations of annalistic descriptions of building activities, and perhaps some narratives. Direct Deuteronomistic authorship is clear in Solomon's prayer in chap. 8, and in a number of shorter passages that will be indicated below. The structuring of chaps 3-11 is worth noting. The editors arranged their material in a two-part schema: (1) Solomon's glory and successes (chaps 3-

10); (2) his decline caused by his sins of idolatry, and the subsequent punishment in the form of rebellions against his rule (chap. 11). The reader is given the impression that the darker side came at the end of Solomon's reign; in fact, however, the text itself indicates that Solomon had to confront rebellions by vassals from the beginning of his reign (cf. 11:25).

The Deuteronomistic theology of history is shown clearly here in its schematic simplicity. As long as the king remains faithful to the Lord and refuses to offer worship to other gods, then all will be well in his kingdom. Under the wise and obedient king who puts the Temple at the centre of his concerns (chaps 5-8), the people will experience peace, economic prosperity, and the respect of foreign nations. But as soon as the king moves towards idolatry, things begin to go wrong: revolts break out and the very existence of the kingdom is endangered. Chap. 11 is an ominous anticipation of what was actually to be the case during the later history of the monarchy, as the Deuteronomists could see with the wisdom of hindsight.

Solomon receives from the Lord a conditional promise of success and dynastic permanence, the condition being the faithful observance of the Law (3:14; 6:11-13; 8:25; 9:4-5 with the negative counterpart in 9:6-9). It is interesting to note that the rebel northerner Jeroboam receives a similar conditional dynastic promise (11:38); the Lord in his sovereign freedom is not limited in his action to the house of David. Exilic period readers could well take comfort from this point, for the basic demand of total and exclusive fidelity to the Lord is meant as the source of their hope too.

Archaeological studies suggest that the biblical picture of Israel's extraordinary prosperity during Solomon's reign contains a fair amount of idealization generated by the theological view that fidelity to the Lord brings with it material prosperity. This theology is not wholly adequate (as the Book of Job and texts such as Ps 73[72] pointed out), but when we take it as part of a call to repentance addressed to the despondent exilic generation it is easier to see its function in the merciful dealings of the Lord with his people. In any case, it remains true that Solomon's reign marked a high-point of prosperity in the history of Judah and Israel; his economic achievements, however, were based in part on means such as forced labour and heavy taxation which carried within themselves the seeds of future trouble (see 12:3ff). In that sense, the story of Solomon for all its glory can also be taken as an object-lesson in the long-term folly of economic exploitation.

A. 3:1-28
SOLOMON'S WISDOM

1. *Comment.* The introductory editorial notices of vv 1-3 begin with a reference to Solomon's marriage alliance with the Egyptian Pharaoh (cf. 7:8; 9:16, 24), which is meant to show the international prestige enjoyed by David's son. References to sacrifices at the high places follow (vv 2-3). These "high places", mentioned very often in Kings, were cultic centres found throughout Israel in pre-exilic times. The term probably referred originally to an artificial mound or platform on which an altar and various cultic symbols were placed; in many cases, though not always, the "high places" were located on hills outside the towns. The worship performed by Israelites at these local sanctuaries was undoubtedly Yahwistic in its basic intention and could be regarded as perfectly orthodox in some texts (cf. 1 Sam 9:11-25). Many of the high places, however, went back to Canaanite times, so it is easy to understand that elements of the Canaanite religion (in particular, the attention to seasonal cycles and fertility rites) often mingled syncretistically with the worship of Yahweh. This explains the prophetic polemic against the high places (especially Hos 10:8), which was further developed by the Deuteronomic school. In Kings the Deuteronomistic editors regard sacrifice at the high places as one of the most deplorable acts of religious infidelity, since in their view the Jerusalem Temple was the only legitimate place for sacrifice to Yahweh (cf. Deut 12).

Here in 1 Kgs 3:2-3 the fault of the people and of Solomon is excused, in part at least, because the Temple was not yet built.

The next unit (vv 4-15) tells of a dream-revelation to Solomon at the well-known cultic centre of Gibeon (cf. 2 Sam 21: 1-14), a short distance north of Jerusalem. Solomon asks for wisdom to guide him in his arduous task of ruling God's people (vv 6-9). Pleased with this wise request, God grants the king a superlative degree of wisdom and adds three other gifts: riches, honour, and long life (vv 10-14). The insistence on the condition of fidelity to the Lord's commandments attached to the last promise (v 14) points to the hand of a Deuteronomistic redactor. The cultic climax of the scene, as v 15 carefully notes, takes place at the ark sanctuary of Jerusalem, not at the high place of Gibeon (contrast v 4).

Solomon's divine gift of wisdom is then illustrated in the story of his judgement regarding the two harlots (vv 16-28). The basic outlines of the tale are widely attested in Indian and other Oriental texts, so vv 16-27 are probably to be seen as an Israelite adaptation of an international folktale type. One can note that the king and the women remain anonymous throughout the story — another pointer to its folktale origin. The concluding note (v 28) stresses the amazement of the whole people at the wisdom manifested in the Solomonic judgement.

2. *Significance.*   The main concern of the chapter is to show that Solomon's renowned wisdom was a divine gift, not an innate human quality; the divine gift is set in explicit relationship with the Lord's promise to David in 2 Sam 7 (cf. 1 Kgs 3:6-7, 14), and all will be well for Solomon as long as he continues to respond faithfully to this foundational act of divine grace. These theological statements are meant to guide our reading of the more secular achievements of Solomon recounted at length in the following chapters.

B. 4:1-34 (HEBREW: 4:1-20; 5:1-14)
THE ADMINISTRATION OF SOLOMON'S
KINGDOM; HIS WORLD-RENOWNED WISDOM

1. *Comment.* The opening title leads on to the first unit (vv 2-6), an old archival list of Solomon's chief officials (cf. 2 Sam 8:16-18; 20:23-26). One can note the presence of the officer in charge of forced labour (v 6: cf. 2 Sam 20:24). In the absence of a large body of state employees, the kingdom of Solomon could maintain its prosperity only at the cost of imposing on its citizens annual periods of forced labour at state projects (see 5:13-18; cf. 1 Sam 8:11-17). Solomon appears to have exempted the Judaeans from this hated service, which was one of the causes of the separation of the Israelites from the Judaeans after Solomon's death (cf. 12:3-4, 18).

An account of the economic administration of the kingdom follows in vv 7-28, which consists essentially of an old archival list of twelve officials (vv 8-19a) with various later additions (vv 19b-28). The twelve officials may have been provincial governors in the full sense; it is also possible to understand the list, on the model of Egyptian administrative methods, as referring to taxation districts and officers. In any case, the insistence of the text, as it stands, on the lavish provisioning of Solomon's court (vv 7, 22-23, 27) serves to underline the splendour of Solomon's reign. Some of the more hyperbolical statements (e.g. vv 20, 25) may well be post-exilic idealizations of Solomon's time.

The final unit (vv 29-34) highlights Solomon's perfect degree of wisdom (in the Hebrew text the terms "wisdom, to be wise" occur seven times here). The king enjoyed international renown for his unrivalled wisdom (vv 30-31). The "people of the east" (v 30) were nomadic tribes who roamed the desert and its fringes in southern Syria and northern Transjordan; the biblical Job is said to have been one of these easterners (Job 1:1, 3). Egyptian wisdom (v 30) was famous in the ancient world (cf. Isa 19:11-14). The personages mentioned in v 31 are otherwise unknown (the recurrence of some of the names in 1 Chr 2:6; 6:33, 44 adds no useful information); presumably they were renowned figures in pre-Israelite Canaanite wisdom traditions. One can note that Solomon's wisdom in v 33 is not judicial (as in 3:16-28) or administrative (as in 4:1-28), but has to do with knowledge of natural phenomena. Lists of plants, animals, and other natural phenomena are found in Mesopotamian and Egyptian sources; a similar intellectual achievement, preluding the spirit of scientific observation, is here attributed to Solomon. Biblical reflections of this "nature-wisdom" can be seen in parts of Prov 30 and Job 38-41.

2. *Significance.*   The dry administrative lists of chap. 4, when read in the light of Solomon's prayer at 3:6-9, can be seen as a further manifestation of his divine gift of wisdom in all its aspects; this is said explicitly in 4:29 with regard to his intellectual wisdom. The king's wise administrative measures brought about an ideal situation of prosperity for Judah and Israel, described here in hyperbolical terms. The empire extended from northern Syria to the borders of Egypt (vv 21, 24: cf. Gen 15:18; Deut 11:24; Josh 1:4); the population increased greatly (v 20: cf. the promises to the Patriarchs at Gen 22:17; 32:12); they enjoyed idyllic conditions of peace and security (v 25: cf. the prophetic promises of Mic 4:4 and Zech 3:10). And all this is the Lord's gift (cf. 3:12-13).

C.   5:1 — 7:51 (HEBREW: 5:15 — 7:51)
THE BUILDING OF THE TEMPLE AND THE PALACE

1. *Outline.*   The first part of this section is devoted to the preparations for the great building activity of Solomon (5:1-18). Solomon makes an agreement with Hiram, king of the Phoenician city of Tyre, who will supply him with vast quantities of wood from the forests of Lebanon (vv 1-12), while a levy of forced labour in Israel supplies the workforce (vv 13-18). The building of the Temple is described with many technical details in chap. 6: first the exterior structures (vv 1-10); an oracle on the theme of Yahweh's presence

among his people interrupts the description (vv 11-13); then the interior furnishings and decorations of the Temple are described (vv 14-38).

Chap. 7 continues the technical description: first the building of Solomon's palace complex beside the Temple (vv 1-12); then a long account of various metal furnishings for the Temple (vv 13-50) — two massive bronze pillars at its entrance (vv 15-22), an immense water container (the "molten sea" of vv 23-26), further bronze objects (vv 27-47), and various gold furnishings (vv 48-50). In conclusion it is noted (v 51) that Solomon brought into the Temple treasury all the precious metal objects which David had dedicated to Yahweh (cf. 2 Sam 8:7-12).

2. *General Commentary.*   The following remarks concern only the general significance of the section. A detailed explanation of the technical material would be out of place and also quite difficult, since there are a number of terms here whose precise meaning is far from clear. As well as this, the presence of various glosses (reflecting in part later additions to the buildings after Solomon's time) has made a difficult text still more obscure in places. The main outlines, however, are quite clear.

a)   *The Temple building:* The interest of the text is undoubtedly centred on the Temple (all chaps 5 and 6, and 7:13-51); the palace complex is described much more briefly (7:1-12), even though it contained buildings that surpassed the Temple in size (compare 6:2 with 7:2). The Temple was a relatively small building in fact: about 90 feet long, 30 feet wide, and 45 feet high (6:2, the cubit being equivalent to about 18 inches or 45 cm). It has to be remembered, of course, that it was not meant as an assembly hall for the worshippers; only the priests had access to the Temple building itself, while the rest of the people remained in the great courtyard outside.

Situated on the south-eastern hill of Jerusalem just north of the old Jebusite city, overlooking the Kidron valley and facing eastwards towards the Mount of Olives, the Temple building proper was divided into three parts. (1) The outer porch or vestibule whose entrance was flanked by two imposing bronze pillars (6:3; 7:15-22); it is not clear whether this vestibule was roofed over or not. (2) The main hall or nave of the building extended inwards for about 60 feet (6:17). (3) The "inner sanctuary" or "most holy place" (6:16) was a small cubical structure (6:20); it contained two large images of cherubim (mythological creatures, probably to be visualized as part-animal, part-human in form) whose extended wings touched at the centre and spanned the entire width (30 feet) of the inner sanctuary (6:23-28); beneath the wings of the cherubim was placed the ark of the Lord (6:19; cf. 8:3-9). The cherubim may have been free-standing statues of gold-plated wood, or perhaps high-relief carvings on the wooden back wall of the inner sanctuary.

b) *Significance of the construction of the Temple:* Four points can be noted here. First, the Temple is connected explicitly with the foundational promise of 2 Sam 7 (cf. 5:2-5). An explanation is offered in 5:3 for the fact that it was not David, the founder of the dynasty, but his son who built the Temple (slightly different explanations for this are given at 2 Sam 7: 5-7 and 1 Chr 28:3); in Solomon's time at last (5:4) Israel enjoyed peace and security in the land (see however 2 Sam 7:1, 9) and so 2 Sam 7:13 can be fulfilled (5:5). Secondly, Solomon's decision to build the Temple is seen as yet another manifestation of his extraordinary wisdom (5:7), which moves the foreign king, Hiram, to bless Yahweh the God of Israel (cf. Exod 18:10-11; 2 Kgs 5:15). Thirdly, the solemn chronology in the Deuteronomistic note at 6:1 (480 years after the Exodus) suggests that the building of the Temple is the real climax of all Yahweh's interventions on behalf of Israel, beginning with their deliverance from Egypt (cf. Exod 15:17). A dimension of worship had already been expressed in the older Exodus traditions (cf. Exod 4:23; 5:1, 3, 17), and now the Temple is to be the definitive, and (for the Deuteronomistic editors) the only legitimate, place of worship. The Israelites have been freed from oppression and given peace and rest from their enemies, in order that they may become a worshipping people at the place which the Lord has chosen as the symbolic centre of his active presence in their history. Fourthly, the oracle received by Solomon (6:11-13; probably a Deuteronomistic insertion) makes it clear that the Lord's presence is in no way bound automatically or magically to the mere physical reality of the Temple building. On the contrary, the effective reality of his presence depends on the obedience of Solomon to the Lord's commandments. Obedience takes precedence over sacrifice (cf. 1 Sam 15:22-23; Isa 1:10-17; Am 5:21-24), and it is on the king's obedience (6:12) that the fate of the whole people depends (v 13).

c) *Influence of the Temple:* From now on the Temple becomes a major focus of interest in the Book of Kings. The kings are judged by their fidelity or otherwise to its (Deuteronomic) role as the only legitimate place of sacrificial worship. It must be admitted that this criterion is not really a fair one, historically speaking, since the official centralization of sacrifice in Jerusalem took place only in the time of King Josiah (ca. 622 B.C.), whose predecessors were unaware of the criterion by which the Deuteronomists judge them. Yet, though the centralization took place centuries after the building of the Temple, it is true to say that already from Solomon's time the cultic centre of gravity in Israel had moved decisively to Jerusalem, a movement begun by David when he brought the ark of God to his new capital. The Temple priesthood formed an ever more influential body with their own religious traditions (reflected in many psalms), their own archives (extracts from which can probably be seen in chaps 6 and 7 here), and their own theological interpretation of Israel's laws and history (which would take definitive form much later in the Priestly traditions and final form of the Pentateuch). These cultic traditions drew on foreign as well as native Israelite sources. It is said explicitly in 1 Kgs 5 and 7 that there was Phoenician participation in the construction of the Temple and its furnishings, and a comparative study of the structural and decorative features of the building reveals clear points of contact with temple-types and ritual furnishings found in Syria and Phoenicia.

Nor can the foreign influences be limited to material aspects: the language and motifs of the psalms, in many instances, indicate assimilation of Canaanite literary traditions transformed by the Yahwistic religion. There is a certain irony in the fact that the Jerusalem Temple, whose unique status is the touchstone of Israelite orthodoxy and orthopraxis in the eyes of the Deuteronomists, was historically one of the main channels by which foreign influences entered Israelite religion in its various forms of expression.

D.   8:1-66
THE DEDICATION OF THE TEMPLE; SOLOMON'S PRAYER

8   Solomon assembled the elders of Israel and all the heads of the tribes, the leaders of the fathers' houses of the people of Israel, before King Solomon in Jerusalem, to bring up the ark of the covenant of the Lord out of the city of David, which is Zion. ²And all the men of Israel assembled to King Solomon at the feast in the month Ethanim, which is the seventh month. ³And all the elders of Israel came, and the priests took up the ark. ⁴And they brought up the ark of the Lord, the tent of meeting, and all the holy vessels that were in the tent; the priests and the Levites brought them up. ⁵And King Solomon and all the congregation of Israel, who had assembled before him, were with him before the ark, sacrificing so many sheep and oxen that they could not be counted or numbered. ⁶Then the priests brought the ark of the covenant of the Lord to its place, in the inner sanctuary of the house, in the most holy place, underneath the wings of the cherubim. ⁷For the cherubim spread out their wings over the place of the ark, so that the cherubim made a covering above the ark and its poles. ⁸And the poles were so long that the ends of the poles were seen from the holy place before the inner sanctuary; but they could not be seen from outside; and they are there to this day. ⁹There was nothing in the ark except the two tables of stone which

Moses put there at Horeb, where the Lord made a covenant with the people of Israel, when they came out of the land of Egypt. ¹⁰And when the priests came out of the holy place, a cloud filled the house of the Lord, ¹¹so that the priests could not stand to minister because of the cloud; for the glory of the Lord filled the house of the Lord.

¹²Then Solomon said,

"The Lord has set the sun in the heavens,
       but has said that he would dwell in
          thick darkness.
¹³I have built thee an exalted house,
       a place for thee to dwell in for ever."

¹⁴Then the king faced about, and blessed all the assembly of Israel, while all the assembly of Israel stood. ¹⁵And he said, "Blessed be the Lord, the God of Israel, who with his hand has fulfilled what he promised with his mouth to David my father, saying, ¹⁶'Since the day that I brought my people Israel out of Egypt, I chose no city in all the tribes of Israel in which to build a house, that my name might be there; but I chose David to be over my people Israel.' ¹⁷Now it was in the heart of David my father to build a house for the name of the Lord, the God of Israel. ¹⁸But the Lord said to David my father, 'Whereas it was in your heart to build a house for my name, you did well that it was in your heart; ¹⁹nevertheless you shall not build the house, but your son who shall be born to you shall build the house for my name.' ²⁰Now the Lord has fulfilled his promise which he made; for I have risen in the place of David my father, and sit on the throne of Israel, as the Lord promised, and I have built the house for the name of the Lord, the God of Israel. ²¹And there I have provided a place for the ark, in which is the covenant of the Lord which he made with our fathers, when he brought them out of the land of Egypt."

²²Then Solomon stood before the altar of the Lord in the presence of all the assembly of Israel, and spread forth his hands toward heaven; ²³and said, "O Lord, God of

Israel, there is no god like thee, in heaven above or on earth beneath, keeping covenant and showing steadfast love to thy servants who walk before thee with all their heart; [24]who hast kept with thy servant David my father what thou didst declare to him; yea, thou didst speak with thy mouth, and with thy hand hast fulfilled it this day. [25]Now therefore, O Lord, God of Israel, keep with thy servant David my father what thou hast promised him, saying, 'There shall never fail you a man before me to sit upon the throne of Israel, if only your sons take heed to their way, to walk before me as you have walked before me.' [26]Now therefore, O God of Israel, let thy word be confirmed, which thou hast spoken to thy servant David my father.

[27]"But will God indeed dwell on the earth? Behold, heaven and the highest heaven cannot contain thee; how much less this house which I have built! [28]Yet have regard to the prayer of thy servant and to his supplication, O Lord my God, hearkening to the cry and to the prayer which thy servant prays before thee this day; [29]that thy eyes may be open night and day toward this house, the place of which thou hast said, 'My name shall be there,' that thou mayest hearken to the prayer which thy servant offers toward this place. [30]And hearken thou to the supplication of thy servant and of thy people Israel, when they pray toward this place; yea, hear thou in heaven thy dwelling place; and when thou hearest, forgive.

[31]"If a man sins against his neighbor and is made to take an oath, and comes and swears his oath before thine altar in this house, [32]then hear thou in heaven, and act, and judge thy servants, condemning the guilty by bringing his conduct upon his own head, and vindicating the righteous by rewarding him according to his righteousness.

[33]"When thy people Israel are defeated before the enemy because they have sinned against thee, if they turn again to thee, and acknowledge thy name, and pray and make supplication to thee in this house; [34]then hear thou

in heaven, and forgive the sin of thy people Israel, and bring them again to the land which thou gavest to their fathers.

35"When heaven is shut up and there is no rain because they have sinned against thee, if they pray toward this place, and acknowledge thy name, and turn from their sin, when thou dost afflict them, 36then hear thou in heaven, and forgive the sin of thy servants, thy people Israel, when thou dost teach them the good way in which they should walk; and grant rain upon thy land, which thou has given to thy people as an inheritance.

37"If there is famine in the land, if there is pestilence or blight or mildew or locust or caterpillar; if their enemy besieges them in any of their cities; whatever plague, whatever sickness there is; 38whatever prayer, whatever supplication is made by any man or by all thy people Israel, each knowing the affliction of his own heart and stretching out his hands toward this house; 39then hear thou in heaven thy dwelling place, and forgive, and act, and render to each whose heart thou knowest, according to all his ways (for thou, thou only, knowest the hearts of all the children of men); 40that they may fear thee in all the days that they live in the land which thou gavest to our fathers.

41"Likewise when a foreigner, who is not of thy people Israel, comes from a far country for thy name's sake 42(for they shall hear of thy great name, and thy mighty hand, and of thy outstretched arm), when he comes and prays toward this house, 43hear thou in heaven thy dwelling place, and do according to all for which the foreigner calls to thee; in order that all the peoples of the earth may know thy name and fear thee, as do thy people Israel, and that they may know that this house which I have built is called by thy name.

44"If thy people go out to battle against their enemy, by whatever way thou shalt send them, and they pray to the Lord toward the city which thou has chosen and the house which I have built for thy name, 45then hear thou in heaven their prayer and their supplication, and maintain their cause.

⁴⁶"If they sin against thee — for there is no man who does not sin — and thou art angry with them, and dost give them to an enemy, so that they are carried away captive to the land of the enemy, far off or near; ⁴⁷yet if they lay it to heart in the land to which they have been carried captive, and repent, and make supplication to thee in the land of their captors, saying, 'We have sinned, and have acted perversely and wickedly'; ⁴⁸if they repent with all their mind and with all their heart in the land of their enemies, who carried them captive, and pray to thee toward their land, which thou gavest to their fathers, the city which thou hast chosen, and the house which I have built for thy name; ⁴⁹then hear thou in heaven thy dwelling place their prayer and their supplication, and maintain their cause ⁵⁰and forgive thy people who have sinned against thee, and all their transgressions which they have committed against thee; and grant them compassion in the sight of those who carried them captive that they may have compassion on them ⁵¹(for they are thy people, and thy heritage, which thou didst bring out of Egypt from the midst of the iron furnace). ⁵²Let thy eyes be open to the supplication of thy servant, and to the supplication of thy people Israel, giving ear to them whenever they call to thee. ⁵³For thou didst separate them from among all the peoples of the earth, to be thy heritage, as thou didst declare through Moses, thy servant, when thou didst bring our fathers out of Egypt, O Lord God."

⁵⁴Now as Solomon finished offering all this prayer and supplication to the Lord, he arose from before the altar of the Lord, where he had knelt with hands outstretched toward heaven; ⁵⁵and he stood, and blessed all the assembly of Israel with a loud voice, saying, ⁵⁶"Blessed be the Lord who has given rest to his people Israel, according to all that he promised; not one word has failed of all his good promise, which he uttered by Moses his servant. ⁵⁷The Lord our God be with us, as he was with our

fathers; may he not leave us or forsake us; [58]that he may incline our hearts to him, to walk in all his ways, and to keep his commandments, his statutes, and his ordinances, which he commanded our fathers. [59]Let these words of mine, wherewith I have made supplication before the Lord, be near to the Lord our God day and night, and may he maintain the cause of his servant, and the cause of his people Israel, as each day requires; [60]that all the peoples of the earth may know that the Lord is God; there is no other. [61]Let your heart therefore be wholly true to the Lord our God, walking in his statutes and keeping his commandments, as at this day."

[62]Then the king, and all Israel with him, offered sacrifice before the Lord. [63]Solomon offered as peace offerings to the Lord twenty-two thousand oxen and a hundred and twenty thousand sheep. So the king and all the people of Israel dedicated the house of the Lord. [64]The same day the king consecrated the middle of the court that was before the house of the Lord; for there he offered the burnt offering and the cereal offering and the fat pieces of the peace offerings, because the bronze altar that was before the Lord was too small to receive the burnt offering and the cereal offering and the fat pieces of the peace offerings.

[65]So Solomon held the feast at that time, and all Israel with him, a great assembly, from the entrance of Hamath to the Brook of Egypt, before the Lord our God, seven days. [66]On the eighth day he sent the people away; and they blessed the king, and went to their homes joyful and glad of heart for all the goodness that the Lord had shown to David his servant and to Israel his people.

1. *Comment.* The first unit (vv 1-13) of this important chapter has a pre-Deuteronomistic basis, though the present form of the text is due to Deuteronomistic and later editors. The scene is set in vv 1-2 which present the dedication of the Temple as an event involving the whole people of Israel, not just Solomon and the Jerusalemites. The ceremo-

ny takes place in the seventh month, that is, September/October (reckoning from a Spring New Year), which corresponds to the time of the feast of Booths or Tabernacles (Deut 16:13-17). The transfer of the ark to the Temple from its tent-sanctuary constructed by David (cf. 2 Sam 6:17) is seen as the main act of the dedication rite (vv 3-9). In this way the Temple is set in a line of continuity with Israel's ancient religious and cultic traditions. One can note in v 9 the typically Deuteronomic idea that the ark contained the tables of the covenant decalogue (cf. Deut 10:1-5; see the comment on 1 Sam 3:3); this stresses its association with the great saving acts of the Lord on behalf of his people and their consequent commitment to his service.

The cloud that filled the Temple building (vv 10-11) is an expression of the Lord's acceptance of this place of worship; his glory takes possession of the sanctuary. One can compare the account of the inauguration of the Mosaic tent of meeting and tabernacle (Exod 40:34-35: Priestly tradition), and also Ezekiel's vision of the New Temple (Ezek 43:1-5). Solomon's words in vv 12-13 are a quotation from an ancient poem whose source, according to an addition in the Greek text (not in the RSV), is the "Book of the Song" or (with a slight textual emendation) the "Book of Jashar"(see 2 Sam 1:18 and comment). The sun, created by the Lord, is not his dwelling-place; he manifests his presence rather in the thick darkness of the storm clouds (cf. 2 Sam 22:10-12), powerful and yet mysterious. Now this awe-inspiring God has accepted the Temple as his lasting dwelling-place.

Solomon's blessings and prayers that follow in vv 14-61 are entirely the work of Deuteronomistic and later writers. They insist on a number of themes. (1) The building of the Temple is the fulfilment of David's desire (2 Sam 7) and the seal of divine favour on the Davidic dynasty (vv 15-26). One can note the conditional formulation of the dynastic promise in v 25 (cf. 2:2-4; 6:11-13). (2) The problem of the divine presence emerges explicitly here. While the old v 13 expresses the view that the Temple is the actual place of God's dwelling, v 27 questions this in argumentative form, and in the verses that follow (e.g. vv 30, 39) the Temple is seen rather as the privileged place for making intercession to the Lord whose dwelling remains in heaven. The question of divine transcendence and immanence underlies the debate within the different strata of the text. In this context, one can also note the insistence on the presence of the Lord's "name" in the Temple (vv 16-20, 29, 44, 48), a theme frequent in Deuteronomy and in Deuteronomistic texts and later in Chronicles. It has been suggested that this expression reflects a polemic against an overly material concept of Yahweh's presence in the Temple, the affirmation being that it is not Yahweh himself who is present there but rather his name as a sort of extension of his personality. It is more probable, however, that the basic idea in the "name" phrase is not a polemical one but has to do with the cultic proclamation of Yahweh's name; the Lord has taken possession of the Temple in a particular way so as to make it the privileged place of his real self-manifestation and the focus of his worshippers' invocations and prayers. (3) Finally one can note a strong stress on the problems of sin and forgiveness in vv 31-36 and 46-50. The latter text clearly has the Babylonian Exile in view (cf. v 34), and its hopeful message is that repentance by the exiles can still win the Lord's compassion for his people.

The account of the Temple dedication ends with a brief narrative section (vv 62-66). Further sacrifices are offered (cf. v 5), and after a whole week of celebrations the Israelites are sent back to their homes glad of heart for the fulfilment of the Lord's promises to David (v 66).

2. *Significance.* 1 Kgs 8 is one of the key texts in the structure of the Deuteronomistic history. Looking back, it suggests (cf. v 56) that the building and dedication of the Temple represents the climax of the Lord's saving promises uttered by Moses. The Exodus and occupation of the land were preliminary stages; the goal was that the liberated people should become a worshipping people gathered around the sole focus of true worship, the Jerusalem Temple. Looking forwards, the text shows that the Temple was

henceforth to be the centre of the people's life; the monarchy itself was in its service and would be judged accordingly.

E. 9:1-25
THE LORD'S SECOND APPEARANCE TO SOLOMON; FURTHER DETAILS ABOUT HIS BUILDING ACTIVITIES

1. *Comment.* The first unit (vv 1-9) is cast as a divine speech in answer to Solomon's prayer of chap. 8; it is of notable theological importance and is the work of the Deuteronomistic redactors. The reference in v 2 is to the account given at 3:4-15. One can note how the Lord's manner of presence in the Temple is expressed in v 3: his name (cf. 8:16ff), his eyes (cf. 8:29), and his heart (that is, his concern and involvement) will be there always. The dynastic promise (2 Sam 7) is then renewed in vv 4-5, but in conditional form depending on observance of the Law. The case of disobedience on the part of the Davidic king is envisaged in vv 6-9: it is noteworthy that the subsequent punishment is to fall, not simply on the guilty royal family, but on the whole people and on the Temple. A theological interpretation of the fall of Jerusalem and its aftermath is given here. The Exile, far from being an unintelligible experience, is so clear in its theological causes that even foreigners can render a perfect account of it (vv 8-9: cf. Deut 29:22-28; Jer 22:8-9); here, in contrast to vv 6-7, there is reference to the infidelity of the whole people, not just that of the king.

What follows in vv 10-25 is a miscellaneous series of notices about Solomon's activities, based for the most part on old sources; a mention of the Temple opens and closes the unit (vv 10, 25). The exchanges between Hiram, king of Tyre, and Solomon (vv 10-14) appear to be based on the historical fact that Solomon had to cede twenty Galilean border towns to Hiram in return for the latter's supply of building materials (cf. 5:1-12). Verses 12-13 here, told in popular style, try to camouflage this loss of Israelite territory by suggesting that the wise Solomon outwitted his partner in the transaction: he received an enormous quantity of gold (v 13: 120 talents would weigh close to 10,000 lbs!) and in return gave away only twenty insignificant towns (the name Cabul in v 13 could be given a popular etymology meaning "as nothing").

Solomon also set up garrison cities and supply centres at strategic points throughout his realm (vv 15ff). Forced labour was necessary for all this, but vv 20-22 insist that it was only the Canaanite elements in the population, not the Israelites, who were subject to this service. This can only be an attempt (probably by a late redactor) to save Solomon's reputation, for it is clear from other texts (5:13-17; 12:3-4, 18) that the northern Israelites at least were subject to forced labour. The "Millo" referred to in vv 15 and 24 (cf. 2 Sam 5:9) was probably the system of terraces on which part of Jerusalem was built; subject to erosion, it needed constant renovation.

The concluding note (v 25) refers to Solomon's three annual sacrifices, probably at the three great pilgrimage feasts (cf. Exod 23:14-17); in pre-exilic times the kings could perform what would later be seen as exclusively priestly actions (cf. 2 Sam 6:17-18; 2 Kgs 16:12-13).

2. *Significance.*   Verses 1-9 spell out in crystal clear terms the theological truth that Israel's existence and that of the Davidic dynasty depend on their obedience to the Law of Yahweh. This programmatic statement has the effect of relativizing Solomon's splendid achievements; what matters ultimately is religious fidelity, not magnificent constructions (even sacred ones).

F.   9:26 — 10:29
THE VISIT OF THE QUEEN OF SHEBA;
SOLOMON'S WEALTH AND COMMERCIAL
ACTIVITY

1. *Comment.*   A loosely linked collection of notices and anecdotes presents an impressive picture of the prosperity of the Golden Age of Solomon (the term "gold" occurs fifteen

times in this section); the point is underlined by the delightful hyperbole of 10:21 — silver was considered worthless in those days!

The opening unit (9:26-28) mentions the partnership between Solomon and Hiram (cf. 9:11) in maritime gold-import business. The land of Ophir (9:28; cf. 10:11; Ps 45[44]:9), famed for its gold, cannot be identified with precision; it is usually thought to refer to the south-western part of the Arabian peninsula or to the African coast facing it.

The queen of Sheba's visit is told in 10:1-13 (with a parenthesis in vv 11-12 about Hiram's trading fleet). Situated in the Arabian peninsula, Sheba occupied a commanding position on important international trading routes, as indeed did Solomon's Israel. It could well be, then, that the historical basis for the present story was a business visit by the queen with a view to a commercial agreement; some scholars, however, prefer to see the account as a late legendary composition whose purpose is to glorify Solomon and celebrate the prosperity of Israel in the far-off days of the past. Whatever of the historical question, it is clear that the present text is decidedly hyperbolical in its celebration of Solomon's wisdom and wealth through the mouth of a foreign monarch.

Verses 14-27 continue the description of Solomon's wealth by mentioning various costly ornaments and furnishings, with a brief reference to his military power (v 26). The concluding note in vv 28-29 is especially interested in the king's international trade in chariots and horses: Kue (v 28) was probably located in Cilicia, north-west of Syria.

2. *Significance.*   This section records the fulfilment of the Lord's promise of riches, as well as wisdom, to Solomon (3:11-14). The queen of Sheba is moved to bless Yahweh the God of Israel whose delight is in Solomon (10:9; cf. 2 Sam 12:24b-25); Yahweh's love for Israel has been made clear to her now (10:9), and that is why he made Solomon king and granted him such favour. The relationship between Yahweh and his people is shown here to be more fundamental than that between Yahweh and the Davidic king. In a section

where so much gold glitters it is interesting to note that the primordial task of the king is said to be his concern for "justice and righteousness" (10:9). Up to this point Solomon's behaviour has been presented as beyond reproach (at most one could note a slight shadow at 3:3b); this is the basis of his success and prosperity, the description of which has reached its climax here.

G. 11:1-43
SOLOMON'S FINAL YEARS: SIN AND MISFORTUNES

1. *Comment.* The first unit (vv 1-13), largely the work of Deuteronomistic authors, tells how Solomon turned to sin in his old age by supporting idolatrous worship to which he had been led by his foreign wives (whose number is surely somewhat exaggerated in v 3). The wisdom of the Deuteronomic prohibition of marriage with foreigners is thus illustrated (Deut 7:3-4; cf. Exod 34:11-16; Josh 23:6-13). David, on the contrary, is presented as the perfect model of obedient fidelity to Yahweh's commands (vv 4, 6); this motif, which seems to ignore 2 Sam 11-12, will recur several times in Kings. The Lord's anger at Solomon's sin issues in his sentence of punishment (vv 9-13). Solomon would have merited the complete loss of his kingdom (v 11), but a double mitigation is introduced because of the Lord's promise to David (2 Sam 7) and his choice of Jerusalem (cf. vv 12-13, 32, 34-36): it is not all the kingdom but ten of the tribes that will be lost to the house of David, and the loss will not come in Solomon's own reign but in that of his son. One tribe will be left to the Davidic family (v 13: cf. vv 32, 36): this probably refers to Judah itself (cf. 12:20), though it is also possible that Benjamin is meant (the fact that Judah remained with the Davidic dynasty being taken for granted).

Two units follow, dealing with Solomon's external enemies, Hadad of Edom (vv 14-22) and Rezon of Damascus (vv 23-25). In both cases the hostility originated in David's brutal treatment of the peoples in question (vv 15-16, 24; cf. 2 Sam 8:3-8, 13-14; 10:15-19), and it is clear that Solomon experienced the enmity of these kings before his final years. The Davidic Empire was already beginning to lose its grip on some of the subject peoples, and Solomon does not appear to have been of a sufficiently war-like temperament to counteract this tendency. The Aramaean kingdom of Damascus (v 24) emerged as a major rival of Israel in the following century, as will be seen later.

The final unit (vv 26-40) tells of Solomon's most formidable internal enemy, Jeroboam son of Nebat, who was to become the first king of northern Israel after the separation (chap. 12). Jeroboam belonged to the powerful northern tribe of Ephraim and, prior to his revolt against Solomon's authority, had been an important officer in Solomon's forced labour service (v 28). His revolt, of which no details are given here apart from his flight into Egypt (v 40: compare vv 17-22), was one aspect of the Lord's punishment of Solomon for his sin; this is made clear in the words of Ahijah, a northern prophet from the once-prominent sanctuary of Shiloh (cf. 1 Sam 1-4), who is sent as the Lord's messenger to Jeroboam. Ahijah's oracle (vv 29-39) is a Deuteronomistic composition whose main purpose is to give in advance a theological interpretation of the separation of the two kingdoms. As in several prophetic texts, the message is first acted out in a symbolic gesture (tearing the garment into twelve pieces: vv 29-31a; cf. 1 Sam 15:27-28), and then a verbal explanation is given (vv 31b-39). Much of the latter is practically a repetition of vv 11-13; one can note, besides, the conditional dynastic promise offered to Jeroboam (vv 37-38: with echoes of the phraseology of 2 Sam 7).

The chapter closes with Deuteronomistically edited concluding formulas about Solomon's reign (vv 41-43). The "book of the acts of Solomon" (v 41) was probably an account of his reign based on annals and other official documents.

2. *Significance.* The function of chap. 11 as the negative side of the two-part Deuteronomistic presentation of

Solomon's reign has been noted in the special introduction to chaps. 3-11. As well as the points mentioned there, one can note that the present section illustrates another recurrent theme in the Deuteronomistic theology of history: most major events are preceded by a prophetic announcement, so that the course of history is structured as a sequence of prophetic words and their fulfilment. History becomes intelligible in the words of the prophets. Ahijah's oracle performs this function here.

III.   1 Kgs 12:1 — 16:34
The Divided Kingdoms, 1: Before the Appearance of Elijah

The next main division of the Book of Kings (1 Kgs 12 —2 Kgs 17) covers the period from the separation of the two kingdoms of Israel and Judah (ca. 930 B.C.) to the fall of the northern kingdom of Israel and its incorporation into the Assyrian Empire (722 B.C.). Most of the material contained here existed before the Deuteronomists; a large portion of it came from prophetic traditions about Elijah, Elisha, and other prophets, while other parts were taken from annalistic works about the kings of Israel and Judah.

The extensive material will be sub-divided here. The first part is taken as 1 Kgs 12-16, which deals with the first seventy or eighty years of the separate existence of the kingdoms prior to the appearance of Elijah.

A.   12:1-32
THE NORTHERN ISRAELITES SECEDE UNDER JEROBOAM

1. *Comment.*   Verses 1-20 tell of the fateful negotiations at Shechem, a venerable religious centre in northern Israel (cf. Josh 24), between the new Davidic king, Rehoboam, and the representatives of the northern Israelite tribes. Jeroboam's role in the negotiations is not clear: while vv 2-3 and

12 speak of him as present, v 20 shows him being called to the assembly after Rehoboam's departure. The tension here probably results from the presence of different strata within the text. Faced with the demands of the Israelites for a lessening of the burdens (probably of forced labour and taxation) laid on them by Solomon (vv 3-4), King Rehoboam seeks advice from his counsellors (vv 5-11). The older counsellors sensibly propose a mild reply to the Israelites' demands (v 7), but the younger ones urge a policy of arrogant severity (vv 9-11). The "scorpions" mentioned in v 11 probably refer to a particularly cruel type of scourge.

Rehoboam prefers the advice of the younger men, his own contemporaries, and he replies harshly to the Israelites (vv 12-14). This incredible political blunder finds its only explanation, according to the Deuteronomistic note of v 15, in the Lord's hidden guidance of events (cf. 2 Sam 17:14b). Solomon's infidelity receives its due retribution here, as the prophet Ahijah had announced (11:29-39). The Israelites secede, using words in v 16 that are very close to Sheba's cry of secession at 2 Sam 20:1. Rehoboam gives further proof of his ineptitude by sending as his spokesman to the Israelites the elderly Adoram who was the director of the hated forced labour system (v 18: cf. 2 Sam 20:24; 1 Kgs 4:6); the enraged northerners stone the hapless Adoram to death, and Rehoboam himself barely escapes with his life. Jeroboam is chosen as king of Israel, and the break is complete (vv 19-20).

Two units then contrast the religious behaviour of the two kings. In vv 21-24 (a late, perhaps post-Deuteronomistic text) Rehoboam is shown as having planned a military expedition to end the northern secession; Shemaiah, a man of God, intervenes with an oracle forbidding the civil war, and Rehoboam obeys the prophetic instruction. One can note that the tribe of Benjamin is associated with Judah here (vv 21, 23) in contrast to v 20 ("Judah only"); this suggests that vv 21-24 belong to a different source.

Jeroboam, on the other hand, is presented in vv 25-32 (a largely Deuteronomistic text) as committing the crime of setting up his own form of worship in the north to replace the Jerusalem Temple. The Deuteronomists interpret Jeroboam's cultic initiatives in the worst possible light as a blatant transgression of Deuteronomic laws (Deut 12:2-14) and as gross polytheism and idolatry (note v 28 "your gods", and v 32 "sacrificing to the calves"). This judgement is based on later deviations in northern Israelite cult, but it is not at all certain that it reflects Jeroboam's own intention. One can accept that he wished to discourage his subjects from frequenting the Jerusalem Temple (vv 26-27), but he did not create new sanctuaries for that purpose. On the contrary, the sanctuaries he favoured in the north were important cultic centres long before Jeroboam's time: for Bethel, situated in the south of his kingdom only a short distance from Jerusalem, see Gen 12:8; 28:10-22; for Dan, situated in the extreme north, see Judg 18:29-30.

The golden images of calves (or young bulls) were probably intended by Jeroboam, not as idols, but as pedestals for the enthroned Yahweh or as symbols of his invisible divinity; their function, in other words, would have been the same as that of the ark and the cherubim in the Jerusalem Temple. The choice of symbol, however, was a dangerous one. Since the bull image was well known in Canaanite religion (and hence would have been attractive to Jeroboam's many Canaanite subjects), its use in Yahwistic worship constituted a temptation for the Israelites to move towards a syncretism of Yahwism and Canaanite cult. As we know from the northern prophet Hosea, this is what often happened in fact, and the Deuteronomistic judgement here has these later abuses in mind. A further cultic crime, the installation of non-Levitical priests, is laid at Jeroboam's door in v 31 (cf. Deut 18:1-5).

2. *Significance.* The separation of Israel and Judah, which meant the end of the Davidic-Solomonic Empire, is interpreted on two planes here. On the political level, the responsibility for the break is attributed unambiguously to the Davidic king, Rehoboam, and his young counsellors; remoter causes are indicated in Solomon's oppressive

methods of administration. On the religious level, the separation is seen as a great evil, not in itself, but because of the cultic affront to the Jerusalem Temple and to Yahweh's law in its regard; the northern king, Jeroboam, is severely indicted for these offences. Many times in subsequent chapters of Kings reference will be made to "the sin of Jeroboam son of Nebat", meaning his cultic innovations, which are seen by the Deuteronomists as the reason for the later downfall of the northern kingdom.

B.   12:33 — 13:34
PROPHETIC CONFLICT; DOOM FOR BETHEL

1. *Comment.*   An introductory verse (12:33) connects the prophetic traditions of chap. 13 with the account of Jeroboam's cultic transgressions in chap. 12. The story itself can be divided into two parts. Verses 1-10 tell of the prophecy of doom uttered by a man of God from Judah against the northern royal sanctuary of Bethel. The Deuteronomistic v 2 contains a long-range prediction of the cultic reform carried out by King Josiah of Judah about three centuries after Jeroboam's time (2 Kgs 23:15-20); this is a striking example of the prediction-and-fulfilment pattern often used by the Deuteronomists. The dramatic clash between the king and the man of God (vv 4-6) illustrates the ultimate powerlessness of kings in face of the word of Yahweh proclaimed by his authorized messengers. The man of God refuses the king's invitation to take a meal with him, on the grounds that he had been explicitly forbidden by Yahweh to do so (vv 7-9); the point of the prohibition may be to show that northern Israel, and in particular the Bethel sanctuary, had become so defiled by cultic sins that no hospitality could be accepted there.

The second part of the story (vv 11-32) introduces an old prophet of Bethel. (Though the terms "prophet" and "man of God" are equivalent in practice, it will be noticed that the latter expression is used always for the Judaean except at v 23.) The Bethel prophet goes to meet the Judaean and falsely claims to have been instructed by an angel in the Lord's name to invite the man of God to a meal in his home; the Judaean accepts in good faith the truthfulness of this statement and he partakes of the meal as invited (vv 11-19). Two possible explanations can be offered for the deceitful behviour of the old prophet of Bethel. (1) Doubting the authenticity of the Judaean's mission and thinking that he may have been just a political agitator from the rival kingdom (cf. Am 7:10-13), he deliberately tempts him to disobey his alleged mission-instructions. If the Judaean does so and suffers no ill consequences, then it is a sure sign that his oracle of doom against Bethel was not really the word of Yahweh. (2) Or it may be that we are meant to see the prophet of Bethel as acknowledging the genuine prophetic role of the Judaean but hoping to modify the efficacy of the prophetic word. In tempting the man of God to take a meal at Bethel, he would aim at establishing an atmosphere of communion and blessing that would nullify the oracle of doom pronounced against Bethel by the Judaean.

During the meal the old prophet who had earlier lied about his reception of a word of Yahweh becomes the recipient of a genuine word of Yahweh, whose content is an announcement of doom for the Judaean man of God who had earlier uttered a genuine oracle but then disobeyed the divine instructions about his mission (vv 20-22). The story has become rather complicated. Though the Judaean had acted in good faith, he had failed to trust his own experience of having received a divine mission and had accepted without discernment the contrary message of the Bethel prophet. Hence the Judaean's punishment (vv 23-28), which is shown to be an outcome of Yahweh's decision by the quite abnormal behaviour of the lion who killed the man of God but did not devour his body or touch the ass on which he was riding (v 28). The old prophet of Bethel then acknowledges that the Judaean's oracle will certainly come to pass (vv 29-32); the mention of their common grave at Bethel (vv 30-31) is found also at 2 Kgs 23:17-18, and may well point to the locality where the tradition developed in successive retellings from its origin prior to the fall of the northern kingdom.

The section concludes with a Deuteronomistic note (vv 33-34) on Jeroboam's cultic sins which were to bring about the doom of his family.

2. *Significance.*   Besides preparing for 2 Kgs 23 according to the pattern of prediction and fulfilment, this chapter illustrates some conflict situations arising from the prophetic ministry in Israel and Judah: the clash between two oracles each claiming to be prophetic (cf. Jer 27-28); the personal fidelity or otherwise of the prophet; the absolute claim of Yahweh on the prophet's obedience. Several centuries of prophetic activity after Jeroboam's time are reflected in this problem-centred theological narrative. The basic theme is that the word of Yahweh will make its way to its goal, despite the opposition of its antagonists and the shortcomings of its ministers.

C.   14:1-20
AHIJAH'S ORACLE AGAINST THE HOUSE OF JEROBOAM

1. *Comment.*   Though the prophetic story of vv 1-18 may go back to an old local tradition of Shiloh, it now shows clear signs of Deuteronomistic editing. The illness of Jeroboam's young son leads the king to send his wife to the prophet Ahijah of Shiloh who had earlier announced that Jeroboam would be king (cf. 11:29-39). When Jeroboam tells his wife to conceal her identity (v 2), he is shown as well aware that Ahijah could no longer regard him with favour. Neither the queen's dissimulation nor Ahijah's blindness can prevent the word of God from reaching its mark (vv 4-6); the efficacious power of this word is a central theme in the prophetic narratives of Kings.

The message which Ahijah transmits in the Lord's name is one of doom: first for Jeroboam's descendants (vv 7-11: cf. v 14), then for the sick child (vv 12-13), and finally for northern Israel as a whole (vv 15-16). In the Deuteronomistic vv 7-11 one can note the recital of the Lord's gracious acts in Jeroboam's favour (vv 7-8a: compare 2 Sam 12:7-8), which serves to heighten the wickedness of his infidelity. The phraseology of vv 10-11 is very similar to that of 16:3-4 and 21:21-24; not to be buried in the family grave was regarded as a great calamity (contrast v 11 with v 13), for it meant that the deceased person would have no rest in the underworld. The king referred to in v 14 is Baasha (cf. 15:25-30). The end of the northern kingdom, clearly alluded to by the Deuteronomists in vv 15-16, is shown as due ultimately to Jeroboam's sins. The death of the child (vv 17-18) is the first fulfilment of Ahijah's oracle.

The concluding regnal notice in vv 19-20 is, as always in Kings, the work of a Deuteronomistic editor who used material from older sources for the chronological data. The fact that readers are referred to source-material for further information about the reign in question shows that the Deuteronomists were not interested in writing a full history of the various reigns; they selected such material as was most appropriate to illustrate their theological understanding of history. The "Book of the Chronicles of the Kings of Israel" (v 19), and the analogous work for the kings of Judah (v 29), should not be confused with the biblical books of Chronicles. The source-works mentioned here have not been preserved, but one can presume that they narrated the political, military, and administrative deeds of the kings on the basis of official documents available in the archives of the court (and possibly also of the Temple).

2. *Significance.* It was a prophetic word communicated by Ahijah that marked the first stage of Jeroboam's rise to the throne of Israel (11:29-39); this word found its first fulfilment at 12:15. Now, in view of Jeroboam's failure to abide by the conditions laid down at 11:38, the prophetic word becomes active again to announce the doom of his house; the death of the king's son (14:17-18) is the first fulfilment of this word, and the rest will be told in 15:27-30. Kingship in Israel remains subject to Yahweh's word; it is he who makes and unmakes kings and dynasties (as was shown earlier in Saul's case). Absolutism has no place in this understanding of political power.

D. 14:21 — 16:34
REHOBOAM OF JUDAH; THE SUCCEEDING KINGS OF JUDAH AND ISRAEL UP TO ELIJAH'S TIME

1. *Comment.* This section consists of a series of reports about Judaean kings — Rehoboam (14:21-31: reigned approximately from 927 to 910), Abijam (15:1-8: 910-908); Asa (15:9-24: 908-868) — , and Israelite kings — Nadab (15:25-32: 907-906), Baasha (15:33 — 16:7: 906-883), Elah (16:8-14: 883-882), Zimri (16:15-20: a seven-day reign in 882), Omri (16:21-28: 882-871), and finally Ahab (16:29-34: 871-852) who appears prominently in the following chapters too. It should be noted that the regnal dates given here and elsewhere are only approximations (see the Chronological Table at the end of the volume).

The various reigns here, and throughout Kings, are described according to a fairly regular pattern consisting of three parts. (1) An introduction phrased in stereotyped formulas generally contains the following elements: a synchronic note linking the king's reign with that of his contemporary in the other kingdom, the king's age (only for Judaeans), the length of his reign, his capital city, and the name of the queen mother (only in Judah where she had an official and influential role); a religious evaluation of the king follows. (2) The central narrative section contains material selected by the Deuteronomistic redactors according to their theological outlook from older sources or from prophetic traditions. (3) A conclusion phrased in stereotyped formulas begins with a reference to sources of further information about the king in question (cf. 14:19), then mentions the king's death and (in most cases) his burial, and finally indicates the name of his successor. In its final form this pattern is the work of Deuteronomistic redactors, but much of the factual data (names, chronological notes) was available to them in the earlier sources they mention.

The criterion against which the kings are measured, and for the most part found lacking, is the Deuteronomistic ideal of cultic centralization and total opposition to any

form of syncretism in worship. Political successes or failures, on the other hand, are of little importance to the
Deuteronomists. King Asa of Judah, for example, is presented here (15:11-15) in glowing terms for his cultic
reforms, while his treacherous political behaviour towards
Israel and his alliance with the Aramaean kingdom of
Damascus do not appear to have deserved censure (15:16-
22). Another, even more striking, example of the one-
sidedness of the Deuteronomistic presentation is had in the
case of King Omri of Israel (16:23-28). Extra-biblical sources show that he was acknowledged to be one of Israel's
most powerful and successful kings; the Assyrians, in fact,
referred to Israel as "the House of Omri" even after the end
of Omri's own dynasty. In spite of this, the Deuteronomists
ignore all Omri's foreign achievements; they mention only
his construction of the new northern capital, Samaria
(16:24), and add some stereotyped denunciations of his
cultic misdeeds (16:25-26). Facts such as these show clearly
that Kings is not a history book in the modern sense of the
word but rather a definite religious and theological message
based on history.

An important difference between the kingdoms of Israel
and Judah is illustrated in the present section. Judah was
ruled to the end (587/6) by kings descended from David (the
sole exception is recounted in 2 Kgs 11). Israel, on the
contrary, did not experience dynastic stability to anything
like the same degree, and bloody palace revolutions were
quite frequent (see the violent deaths of Kings Nadab, Baasha, and Zimri here). It has been suggested that the decisive
factors in the succession to the throne of Israel were prophetic designation of the future king and the people's acclamation, not the dynastic principle; Israel, according to this
view, had a charismatic concept of kingship at least up to the
time of Omri. A problem is created for this explanation,
however, by the fact that many of the accounts of prophetic
intervention in succession questions in Israel bear clear
signs of later Deuteronomistic composition, which would
tend to suggest that their function is more theological than

historical. If one abandons the theory of a charismatic concept of kingship in Israel, then the northern kingdom's political instability could be explained, in part at least, by the fact that in its early years it possessed no natural centre comparable to the position and status of Jerusalem in the south, and was therefore more exposed to the divisive influence of tribal rivalry. This situation was somewhat remedied by Omri's construction of Samaria (16:24) as his new capital; it is significant that Omri's was the first real dynasty in northern Israel (the next three kings were of his family). It is likely too that the northerners never elaborated a royal theology comparable to that attested in Jerusalem by 2 Sam 7 and the royal psalms, which undoubtedly made for the stability of the Davidic dynasty there.

2. *Significance.* The theological redaction of Kings insists on the efficacious role of Yahweh's word, as communicated by his prophets, within the often far from edifying events of human history. The confusion of history is given form by the prophecy-and-fulfilment pattern: see 15:29-30; 16:1-4, 7, 12-13, 34 (the last text being a striking example of long-range Deuteronomistic compositional activity with its reference back to Josh 6:26). The prophetic word manifests Yahweh's sovereign lordship of history; that statement carried a potentially hopeful message for the readers of Kings during the Babylonian Exile, and the message holds good today too.

IV.   1 Kgs 17:1 — 2 Kgs 1:18
The Divided Kingdoms, 2: Prophetic Narratives about Elijah and the Aramaean Wars

Elijah's time was one of real crisis for Yahwism in the northern kingdom, a crisis all the more insidious in that most of the Israelites appear to have been quite unaware of the gravity of the situation. King Omri and his successor Ahab (cf. 16:23-34) had pursued an ambitious programme of building up Israel's economic and political power.

Friendly relations with the coastal states of Phoenicia, sealed by Ahab's marriage with Princess Jezebel of Sidon (16:31), gave Israel access to Mediterranean trade on a large scale. The internal cohesion of the kingdom, where large numbers of Canaanite subjects lived side-by-side with the Israelites, was fostered by the royal policy of complete impartiality between the two groups. Ahab extended this policy to religious matters by tolerating the public exercise of Canaanite worship on equal terms with Yahwistic worship. It is quite improbable, historically speaking, that Ahab intended to apostatize from Yahwism (as the Deuteronomistic notes at 16:31-33 might appear to suggest); his sons, in fact, were given good Yahwistic names (Ahaziah, meaning "Yahweh has grasped": 1 Kgs 22:51; and Jehoram "Yahweh has exalted": 2 Kgs 3:1). In practice, however, Yahwism was endangered by Ahab's politically motivated policy of religious toleration. Many of the Israelites were attracted to the Canaanite cults by the stress they laid on seasonal cycles and fertility rites, which seemed to answer the needs of an agricultural society, and gradually the two religions began to merge. It took the shock effect of Elijah's uncompromising opposition to open the people's eyes to the dangers of this process.

The Elijah texts (1 Kgs 17-19; 21; 2 Kgs 1) probably existed as a cycle of traditions well before the time of the Deuteronomists, whose editorial interventions are not very extensive here. As it stands, the biblical presentation of Elijah is one that can inspire and challenge today's readers too. His single-minded zeal for Yahweh unmasked the cultic syncretism of his contemporaries and can help unmask the perennial tendencies towards compromise with various more subtle forms of idolatry that menace the life of believers both as individuals and as members of social groupings. Elijah was an uncomfortable personage for the society in which he lived, and he remains so today. Austere and distant though he may seem to be in some of the texts, he appears in others as a man of flesh and blood, experiencing the human weaknesses of fear, depression, and loneliness (cf. 19:1ff).

While the prophet proclaims the word of the Lord, he also stands subject to that word, which is his inner driving force but not his secure personal possession. That too is not without relevance for the life of the prophetic people of God today.

A. 17:1-24
DROUGHT IN ISRAEL; ELIJAH'S MIRACLES

1. *Comment.*   The drought that Elijah solemnly announces to King Ahab (v 1) is not so much a punishment for the king's wickedness (cf. 16:30-33) as rather an occasion for showing that it is Yahweh and not the Canaanite Baal, god of storm and fertility, who is the real giver of rain and lord of nature. This will become clear in chap. 18, which forms a close unity with chap. 17. The account of the miraculous feeding of Elijah by the ravens (vv 2-6) might remind the reader of the Exodus tradition of the manna and the quails (cf. Exod 16); several other allusions to the Exodus and especially to the figure of Moses can be noted in the following Elijah narratives.

The two miracle-narratives that follow in vv 8-24 are set in the Sidonian town of Zarephath (in present-day Lebanon). They show that Yahweh's word is efficacious even beyond the borders of Israel, more precisely, in the native land of Queen Jezebel (16:31) who was to be Elijah's bitterest enemy according to the presentation of chaps 18, 19, and 21. Both stories stress the fundamental Deuteronomistic theme of the power of Yahweh's word (vv 14-16, 24). This word, communicated by a prophet, can restore to life those at death's door (vv 8-16) and even those already dead (vv 17-24), but a response of obedient faith is called for (vv 13-15) and is aroused (v 24). One can also note in v 18 the idea that the presence of the man of God causes a particular exposure to the divine action, in this case a punishment for some unspecified sin committed by the child's mother. Elijah's prayer (v 20) shows him as feeling some responsibility for the woman's distress. His intercession achieves its effect;

the decisive fact is not the seemingly magical action of stretching himself three times upon the child's body (v 21a) but the Lord's gracious hearing of Elijah's prayer (v 22a).

2. *Significance.* While Ahab's kingdom of Israel suffers the deadly effects of a long drought, Elijah becomes the focal point of Yahweh's life-giving benefits. This contrast prepares the reader for the great conflict narrated in chap. 18. That the Lord's word can bring life from death was a message of immediate and hopeful relevance for the exilic period readers of the Deuteronomistic history, and it acquires a further depth of meaning in the light of the NT.

The miracle-stories in the Elijah and Elisha cycles were originally told and handed down among the disciples of the prophets. It could well be that the various stories interacted in the course of transmission; there are remarkable similarities, for instance, between 1 Kgs 17:17-24 and the Elishan story in 2 Kgs 4:8-37, and many scholars hold that the latter text was the model for the former. Be that as it may, the important point to note is that the purpose of the miracle-stories was primarily didactic. Their main concern was to portray in a vivid way the truth that Yahweh was powerfully at work in the word of his prophets; in this way the authority of the prophet is given support against the objections of opponents and unbelievers. The forms that this portrayal took were often coloured by folkloristic motifs capable of making an immediate impact on the unsophisticated hearers for whom these stories were originally intended.

B. 18:1-46
DRAMATIC CONFRONTATION ON MOUNT CARMEL; THE END OF THE DROUGHT

18 After many days the word of the Lord came to Elijah, in the third year, saying, "Go, show yourself to Ahab; and I will send rain upon the earth." ²So Elijah went to show himself to Ahab. Now the famine was severe in Samaria. ³And Ahab called Obadiah, who was over the household.

(Now Obadiah revered the Lord greatly; ⁴and when Jezebel cut off the prophets of the Lord, Obadiah took a hundred prophets and hid them by fifties in a cave, and fed them with bread and water.) ⁵And Ahab said to Obadiah, "Go through the land to all the springs of water and to all the valleys; perhaps we may find grass and save the horses and mules alive, and not lose some of the animals." ⁶So they divided the land between them to pass through it; Ahab went in one direction by himself, and Obadiah went in another direction by himself.

⁷And as Obadiah was on the way, behold, Elijah met him; and Obadiah recognized him, and fell on his face, and said, "Is it you, my lord Elijah?" ⁸And he answered him, "It is I. Go, tell your lord, 'Behold, Elijah is here.'" ⁹And he said, "Wherein have I sinned, that you would give your servant into the hand of Ahab, to kill me? ¹⁰As the Lord your God lives, there is no nation or kingdom whither my lord has not sent to seek you; and when they would say, 'He is not here,' he would take an oath of the kingdom or nation, that they had not found you. ¹¹And now you say, 'Go, tell your lord, "Behold, Elijah is here."' ¹²And as soon as I have gone from you, the Spirit of the Lord will carry you whither I know not; and so, when I come and tell Ahab and he cannot find you, he will kill me, although I your servant have revered the Lord from my youth. ¹³Has it not been told my lord what I did when Jezebel killed the prophets of the Lord, how I hid a hundred men of the Lord's prophets by fifties in a cave and fed them with bread and water? ¹⁴And now you say, 'Go, tell your lord, "Behold, Elijah is here"'; and he will kill me." ¹⁵And Elijah said, "As the Lord of hosts lives, before whom I stand, I will surely show myself to him today.' ¹⁶So Obadiah went to meet Ahab, and told him; and Ahab went to meet Elijah.

¹⁷When Ahab saw Elijah, Ahab said to him, "Is it you, you troubler of Israel?" ¹⁸And he answered, "I have not troubled Israel; but you have, and your father's house, because you have forsaken the commandments of the

Lord and followed the Baals. [19]Now therefore send and gather all Israel to me at Mount Carmel, and the four hundred and fifty prophets of Baal and the four hundred prophets of Asherah, who eat at Jezebel's table."

[20]So Ahab sent to all the people of Israel, and gathered the prophets together at Mount Carmel. [21]And Elijah came near to all the people, and said, "How long will you go limping with two different opinions? If the Lord is God, follow him; but if Baal, then follow him." And the people did not answer him a word. [22]Then Elijah said to the people, "I, even I only, am left a prophet of the Lord; but Baal's prophets are four hundred and fifty men. [23]Let two bulls be given to us; and let them choose one bull for themselves, and cut it in pieces and lay it on the wood, but put no fire to it; and I will prepare the other bull and lay it on the wood, and put no fire to it. [24]And you call on the name of your god and I will call on the name of the Lord; and the God who answers by fire, he is God." And all the people answered, "It is well spoken." [25]Then Elijah said to the prophets of Baal, "Choose for yourselves one bull and prepare it first, for you are many; and call on the name of your god, but put no fire to it." [26]And they took the bull which was given them, and they prepared it, and called on the name of Baal from morning until noon, saying, "O Baal, answer us!" But there was no voice, and no one answered. And they limped about the altar which they had made. [27]And at noon Elijah mocked them, saying, "Cry aloud, for he is a god; either he is musing, or he has gone aside, or he is on a journey, or perhaps he is asleep and must be awakened." [28]And they cried aloud, and cut themselves after their custom with swords and lances, until the blood gushed out upon them. [29]And as midday passed, they raved on until the time of the offering of the oblation, but there was no voice; no one answered, no one heeded.

[30]Then Elijah said to all the people, "Come near to me"; and all the people came near to him. And he repaired the altar of the Lord that had been thrown down; [31]Elijah

took twelve stones, according to the number of the tribes of the sons of Jacob, to whom the word of the Lord came, saying, "Israel shall be your name"; [32]and with the stones he built an altar in the name of the Lord. And he made a trench about the altar, as great as would contain two measures of seed. [33]And he put the wood in order, and cut the bull in pieces and laid it on the wood. And he said, "Fill four jars with water, and pour it on the burnt offering, and on the wood." [34]And he said, "Do it a second time"; and they did it a second time. And he said, "Do it a third time"; and they did it a third time. [35]And the water ran round about the altar, and filled the trench also with water.

[36]And at the time of the offering of the oblation, Elijah the prophet came near and said, "O Lord, God of Abraham, Isaac, and Israel, let it be known this day that thou art God in Israel, and that I am thy servant, and that I have done all these things at thy word. [37]Answer me, O Lord, answer me, that this people may know that thou, O Lord, art God, and that thou has turned their hearts back." [38]Then the fire of the Lord fell, and consumed the burnt offering, and the wood, and the stones, and the dust, and licked up the water that was in the trench. [39]And when all the people saw it, they fell on their faces; and they said, "The Lord, he is God; the Lord, he is God." [40]And Elijah said to them, "Seize the prophets of Baal; let not one of them escape." And they seized them; and Elijah brought them down to the brook Kishon, and killed them there.

[41]And Elijah said to Ahab, "Go up, eat and drink; for there is a sound of the rushing of rain." [42]So Ahab went up to eat and to drink. And Elijah went up to the top of Carmel; and he bowed himself down upon the earth, and put his face between his knees. [43]And he said to his servant, "Go up now, look toward the sea." And he went up and looked, and said, "There is nothing." And he said, "Go again seven times." [44]And at the seventh time he said, " Behold, a little cloud like a man's hand is rising out of

the sea." And he said, "Go up, say to Ahab, 'Prepare your chariot and go down, lest the rain stop you.'" [45]And in a little while the heavens grew black with clouds and wind, and there was great rain. And Ahab rode and went to Jezreel. [46]And the hand of the Lord was on Elijah; and he girded up his loins and ran before Ahab to the entrance of Jezreel.

1. *Comment.* The first unit (vv 1-20) tells of Elijah's meeting with King Ahab to announce that the drought will end and to demand a confrontation with the Baal prophets on Mount Carmel. One can note that it is Jezebel, not Ahab, who is said to have persecuted the prophets of Yahweh (v 4). The king's intensive search for Elijah (v 10) apparently means that he wanted to have the prophet in his power so as to force him to announce the end of the drought (cf. 17:1). Elijah, however, is moved only by the Lord's command (18:1), not by a king's violence; the same idea is expressed by the reference in v 12 to his being transported bodily from place to place by extraordinary manifestations of divine power (cf. v 46 and 2 Kgs 2:16). Again in v 19 the actively anti-Yahwistic role of Jezebel appears; it was she who officially maintained the prophets of Baal and those of Asherah (a Canaanite goddess of fertility).

The second unit (vv 21-40) describes the dramatic clash between Elijah and the prophets of Baal on Mount Carmel, a wooded height whose western extremity overlooks the sea near present-day Haifa. The promontory had been a place of worship even in pre-Israelite times, and it stood now on or near the border between Israel and Phoenicia. One can note that neither the prophets of Asherah (v 19) nor King Ahab takes an active part in the Carmel scene proper. It is clear from v 21 that the real confrontation is between two ways of religion, the Yahwistic and the Baalistic: the people are "limping with two different opinions," that is, making a vain syncretistic attempt to have what they take to be the benefits of both religions. Elijah calls them to make a clear decision for one or the other; the Israelites' silence (v 21b) could be taken as a sign of their unwillingness to do so or as an indication that they simply did not see the need for such a decision.

So the terms of the contest are agreed upon (vv 23-24), and the four hundred and fifty prophets of Baal enter into action (vv 26-29). The scene is one of noisy confusion and fanatical activity, which illustrates the gross nature of Baal-ist worship. Elijah's heavy sarcasm (v 27) helps to raise the temperature, but the only outcome is dead silence on the part of Baal (as v 29b emphasizes). Elijah then takes over; he rebuilds the broken altar of Yahweh with twelve stones (vv 30b-32a: cf. Exod 24:4) that serve to recall Yahweh's saving actions in the past (see also the reference to the Patriarchs in v 36). The twelve jars of water poured over the offering (vv 33-35) will have the effect of heightening the wonder of Yahweh's display of power. What is decisive, however, is Elijah's prayer (vv 36-37 : cf. 17:20-21); in his case there is no need for noisy activity. In answer to the prophet's prayer a bolt of lightning ("the fire of the Lord": v 38) immediately consumes the offering, the altar, and everything around it. The Israelites now acknowledge that Yahweh indeed is God (v 39), and the defeated prophets of Baal are dragged off to suffer the fate that the Deuteronomic law would sanction for their situation (Deut 13:1-5: compare Jehu's action in 2 Kgs 10:18-27).

In the third unit (vv 41-46) the coming of the long-awaited rain is recounted. The emptiness of Baal's claim to be the storm-god and giver of rain has been made clear, and Yahweh's prophet can now announce the end of the drought.

2.   *Significance.*   The main message of the text is that the service of the true God must rest on a clear and uncompromising decision by the people. Half-measures and self-seeking accommodations with idols cannot be tolerated. The message is still needed today, for the choice between God and the Idol (be it called Baal, Mammon, or whatever) has to be made and ratified continually.

The outcome of the Carmel confrontation (v 40) might suggest a total and definitive defeat for Baalism in Israel. This was not the case, however, as can be seen from 2 Kgs 10

and then from Hosea's denunciations about a century after
Elijah's time.

C. 19:1-21
THE THEOPHANY ON MOUNT HOREB; ELISHA
IS CHOSEN AS ELIJAH'S SUCCESSOR

19 He told Jezebel all that Elijah had done, and how he had
slain all the prophets with the sword. ²Then Jezebel sent a
messenger to Elijah, saying, "So may the gods do to me
and more also, if I do not make your life as the life of one
of them by this time tomorrow." ³Then he was afraid, and
he arose and went for his life, and came to Beer-sheba,
which belongs to Judah, and left his servant there.

⁴But he himself went a day's journey into the wilderness, and came and sat down under a broom tree; and he
asked that he might die, saying, "It is enough; now, O
Lord, take away my life; for I am no better than my
fathers." ⁵And he lay down and slept under a broom tree;
and behold, an angel touched him, and said to him,
"Arise and eat." ⁶And he looked, and behold, there was at
his head a cake baked on hot stones and a jar of water.
And he ate and drank, and lay down again. ⁷And the
angel of the Lord came again a second time, and touched
him, and said, "Arise and eat, else the journey will be too
great for you." ⁸And he arose, and ate and drank, and
went in the strength of that food forty days and forty
nights to Horeb the mount of God.

⁹And there he came to a cave, and lodged there; and
behold, the word of the Lord came to him, and he said to
him, "What are you doing here, Elijah?" ¹⁰He said, "I
have been very jealous for the Lord, the God of hosts; for
the people of Israel have forsaken thy covenant, thrown
down thy altars, and slain thy prophets with the sword;
and I, even I only, am left; and they seek my life, to take it
away." ¹¹And he said, "Go forth, and stand upon the
mount before the Lord." And behold, the Lord passed
by, and a great and strong wind rent the mountains, and

broke in pieces the rocks before the Lord, but the Lord was not in the wind; and after the wind an earthquake, but the Lord was not in the earthquake; [12]and after the earthquake a fire, but the Lord was not in the fire; and after the fire a still small voice. [13]And when Elijah heard it, he wrapped his face in his mantle and went out and stood at the entrance of the cave. And behold, there came a voice to him, and said, "What are you doing here, Elijah?" [14]He said, "I have been very jealous for the Lord, the God of hosts; for the people of Israel have forsaken thy covenant, thrown down thy altars, and slain thy prophets with the sword; and I, even I only, am left; and they seek my life, to take it away." [15]And the Lord said to him, "Go, return on your way to the wilderness of Damascus; and when you arrive, you shall anoint Hazael to be king over Syria; [16]and Jehu the son of Nimshi you shall anoint to be king over Israel; and Elisha the son of Shaphat of Abel-meholah you shall anoint to be prophet in your place. [17]And him who escapes from the sword of Hazael shall Jehu slay; and him who escapes from the sword of Jehu shall Elisha slay. [18]Yet I will leave seven thousand in Israel, all the knees that have not bowed to Baal, and every mouth that has not kissed him."

[19]So he departed from there, and found Elisha the son of Shaphat, who was plowing, with twelve yoke of oxen before him, and he was with the twelfth. Elijah passed by him and cast his mantle upon him. [20]And he left the oxen, and ran after Elijah, and said, "Let me kiss my father and my mother, and then I will follow you." And he said to him, "Go back again; for what have I done to you?" [21]And he returned from following him, and took the yoke of oxen, and slew them, and boiled their flesh with the yokes of the oxen, and gave it to the people, and they ate. Then he arose and went after Elijah, and ministered to him.

1. *Comment.*   The first unit (vv 1-18) begins with Jeze-bel's threat to Elijah which forces him to flee south out of the kingdom of Israel (vv 1-3). The prophet's fear and depres-sion (vv 3-4) strikingly contrast with his courage and trust in

Yahweh shown in the Carmel scene: one might explain this of the historical Elijah in terms of a sudden psychological reversal after the exultation of the previous scene (cf. 18:46), but it may be preferable to see 19:1ff simply in narrative terms as forming a necessary transition between the traditions of chap. 18 and the originally separate Horeb tradition that forms the centre of chap. 19. In any case, the image of the prophet presented here is a moving and memorable one in human terms. Memorable too is Yahweh's care for his prophet: he sends an angel (the Hebrew word is the same as that translated "messenger" in v 2!) to bring food and encouragement to the despairing Elijah (vv 5-7) who is thus enabled to journey on for forty days and nights to Mount Horeb (v 8: an alternative name for Sinai).

There is much in the Horeb scene (vv 9-18) that recalls the Moses traditions (cf. Exod 33:18-23; 34:5-8). Just as Moses experienced Yahweh's presence on Sinai amid terrifying natural phenomena (Exod 19), so too — but with significant differences — Elijah is presented as assisting at a theophany in the same place. Moses had been the Lord's instrument in forming his people; Elijah is shown to be the reformer who follows in the footsteps of his unsurpassable predecessor.

Elijah's complaints to the Lord (vv 10, 14) paint a gloomy picture of religious conditions in Israel. The fact that this contrasts with the triumph of Yahwism depicted in the Carmel scene (cf. 18:31-32, 39-40) is another indication that the Horeb theophany originated as a separate tradition. One can also suspect the presence of redactional work within the Horeb pericope from the repetition of vv 9b-10 at vv 13b-14.

The theophany itself is described in an impressive but mysterious way (vv 11-12). There is a triple denial that Yahweh is present in the spectacular phenomena of stormwind, earthquake, and fire. These were traditional motifs in biblical descriptions of theophanies (cf. Exod 19:16, 18; 2 Sam 22:7-16; Isa 29:6; Ps 50[49]:3; 97[96]:2-5), but there is no evidence that the Israelites ever identified the Lord's presence with such phenomena. The polemic here is rather an anti-Canaanite one: Baal was the storm-god, lord of thunder and lightning, before whose mighty voice the earth shook (as Ugaritic mythology recounted). Yahweh's victory over Baal (chap. 18) does not simply mean that he takes Baal's place as storm-god; on the contrary, Yahweh's divinity is of quite a different order, and the text tries to convey this by the unparalleled phrase "a still small voice" (v 12: literally "the sound of a thin silence"). The paradoxical nature of this expression has the effect of suggesting the awesome majesty of Yahweh's presence, which is experienced by the prophet in a communication that has something in common with an audible voice and yet is different. Some have suggested that the point of the description lies in a divine rebuke of Elijah for his violent handling of the prophets of Baal (18:40); this is quite unlikely, however, since the mission that Elijah is about to receive (vv 15-18) is anything but a peaceful one.

Just as the three negations of vv 11b-12a were followed by the affirmative statement about the still small voice (v 12b), so too Elijah's mission has three destructive aspects (vv 15b-17) followed by a constructive statement about the remnant of Israelites who would resist the seduction of Baalism (v 18). Elijah's mission is shown here as influencing the life of Israel for decades to come. Hazael (v 15b), the Aramaean king of Damascus, was to be one of Israel's bitterest enemies (cf. 2 Kgs 8:7-15; 10:32-33). Jehu (v 16a) was to overthrow the dynasty of Omri and Ahab and carry out a bloody purge of Baalist worshippers in Samaria (cf. 2 Kgs 9-10). The curious fact is that Elijah is not said to have carried out any of the three anointings ordered here: it was Elisha who presided over the rise of both Hazael and Jehu, and vv 19-21 here describe the call of Elisha but make no mention of an anointing by Elijah. This seems to be yet another indication of the theological, rather than biographical, orientation of chap. 19. The seven thousand Israelites, whom Yahweh will preserve for himself (v 18), represent the faithful remnant, an important prophetic theme (cf. Isa 10:20-22; Am 5:15; Mic 2:12-13).

The final unit (vv 19-21) describes the investiture of Elisha as Elijah's follower and successor. The relationship here (v 21b) recalls that of Joshua with Moses (cf. Exod 24:13; 33:11).

2. *Significance.* The occasional public success of a prophet (chap. 18) cannot hide the fact that most of his existence is spent in situations of frustration and failure (chap. 19:10, 14). A return to the source is useful and necessary in these circumstances, but the prophet is not allowed to opt out of his uncomfortable situation. The Lord's mysterious voice sends him back to his mission. Yahweh knows best how to further his cause (vv 15-18, 19-21); it is for the prophet to set out again on the way that the Lord indicates.

D. 20:1-43
THE ARAMAEAN WARS: A PROPHETIC NARRATIVE

1. *Comment.* This chapter, which does not mention Elijah, interrupts the sequence of chaps 17-19 and 21. Ahab is mentioned, however, in vv 2, 13, 14 (the RSV "Ahab" in v 34 is not in the Hebrew text), but there are strong reasons for thinking that originally the Israelite king was referred to only by his title in this story. Furthermore, both biblical and extra-biblical data suggest that the war in question did not take place in Ahab's time but some decades later during the reign of King Joash of Israel, a contemporary of Elisha (cf. 2 Kgs 13). In any case, the Deuteronomistic redactors invite us to read the narrative with Ahab as protagonist; knowing that their attitude towards that king was strongly negative (cf. 16:30-33; 21:20-22; 22:38), we can understand more easily the rather surprising shift from a sympathetic presentation of the Israelite king (vv 1-30a at least) to a decidedly antagonistic view in vv 35-43.

The story begins (vv 1-12) by telling how the Aramaeans of Damascus and their allies under King Ben-hadad present the weaker kingdom of Israel (cf. vv 3-4: a situation that hardly obtained in Ahab's time) with deliberately impossible terms (v 6) to avoid an attack on the capital Samaria. The Israelite king has enough spirit to reply bravely by means of a trenchant proverb (v 11), but the situation is critical. At this point an anonymous Israelite prophet pronounces a war-oracle (vv 13-14), and the Israelite forces win the first battle (vv 15-21). It is interesting to note that a regular function of these early prophets was to intervene by oracles in war situations (cf. vv 22, 28); war-oracles of this kind will later leave their mark in the poems of the classical prophets (cf. Isa 34: 63:1-6; Jer 46-51; Ezek 7). The second battle (vv 22-30a) is preceded by two prophetic messages (vv 22, 28) and results in another crushing defeat for the Aramaeans. The idea of Ben-hadad's advisors that Yahweh was only a god of the hills (v 23) — understandable enough in a polytheistic frame of reference, since most of Israel's terrain was hilly country — is flatly rebutted first by the oracle of v 28 and then by the military victory (vv 29-30), which clearly shows that Yahweh's power is not subject to topographical limitations.

It is now the turn of the Israelites to dictate terms to Ben-hadad (vv 30b-34). The mention of the cities which Israel had formerly lost to the Aramaeans (v 34) more probably refers to the situation described in 2 Kgs 13:3-7, 24-25 than to that of 1 Kgs 15:20 (when Samaria did not yet exist). The Israelite king did not kill his defeated enemy but made a covenant with him and sent him home. This leads on to the final unit (vv 35-43), which culminates in an oracle of denunciation and threat against the king of Israel. The incident of vv 35-36 is intended to teach the importance of instant obedience to a prophetic command; the role of the lion as executioner of the disobedient prophet reminds one of 1 Kgs 13:24-28. An important term "sons of the prophets" occurs in v 35: this refers to a prophetic association or guild whose members were disciples of some well-known prophet (cf. 2 Kgs 2; 4; 6). The prophet's piece of acting (vv 37-40) leads the king of Israel to pronounce unwittingly his own condemnation (v 40b: compare 2 Sam 12; 14). In v 42 the Aramaean king is the man whom the Lord had devoted to destruction, that is, whose death was a religious duty for the Israelite king to whom the Lord had granted victory (v 28: cf. 1 Sam 15). The remark that the people of Israel will suffer for the king's negligence (v 42b) assigns to Ahab the blame for all of Israel's future suffering at the hands of the Aramaeans.

2. *Significance.* Besides giving a vivid picture of the military situation, the chapter stresses the important role played by prophets in public life. They encourage the Israelite king, but they can turn against him too. In the last analysis, it is Yahweh's word that must rule Israel's history, not shrewd political calculations such as those of vv 31-34.

E. 21:1-29
NABOTH'S VINEYARD

1. *Comment.* The Elijah story is taken up again after chap. 19. The narrative is set in Jezreel (v 1), a town in the northern plain where King Ahab had a residence (cf. 18:46). Ahab covets the vineyard of Naboth, a respected citizen of Jezreel, and makes him a fair, even generous, offer (v 2), to which Naboth opposes a brusque refusal (v 3). The key term here is "the inheritance of my fathers" (vv 3, 4), which shows that Naboth is holding stubbornly to the ancient concept of patrimonial property: each family was thought to have received its portion of the promised land from Yahweh, which had to remain within the family as a sacred and inalienable trust (cf. Lev 25:23, a text which, though of later composition, reflects much older ideas). King Ahab, on the other hand, though he understood the force of Naboth's reply (vv 4-6), is shown as a representative of a more secularized concept of landed property: for him, and doubtless for others in Israel too, the sale of one's ancestral land was quite legal. Two mentalities clash here, but the biblical text does not take sides in the socio-economic question. Its concern is rather with what followed Naboth's refusal.

The real villain in vv 5-16 is Jezebel. She organizes a rigged trial to eliminate Ahab's obstinate subject. Two witnesses (cf. Deut 17:6; 19:15) are to put forward a (false) charge against Naboth that he cursed God and the king (cf. Exod 22:28). It is not clear whether this accusation has some connection with Naboth's oath of refusal (v 3) or whether it is meant to refer to some other statement of his not mentioned here. In any case, the queen's plan works out perfectly, and Naboth is sentenced to death by stoning. It appears to have been the custom in such cases that the condemned man's property was confiscated by the crown. In v 16, then, we see Ahab preparing to take formal legal possession of the vineyard.

At this point (vv 17ff) Elijah suddenly appears on the scene at Yahweh's bidding and pronounces a tremendous denunciation of Ahab's abuse of power. The prophetic word tears off the mask of legality from the proceedings and reveals the king's responsibility for what it was: murder (the Hebrew term rendered "killed" in v 19 is the same as that used in the Decalogue at Exod 20:13) and, consequently, unjust appropriation of another's property. The punishment announced in vv 20b-22 and 24 is the utter destruction of Ahab's family: the Deuteronomistic language used here is similar to that of 1 Kgs 14:10-11; 16:2-4. An indication of the horrible end of Jezebel was added by a later redactor in v 23 to prepare for 2 Kgs 9:30ff. A later Deuteronomistic parenthesis in vv 25-26 sees the ultimate cause of the disorder in Ahab's favour for Baalism, a heinous offence against the first and fundamental commandment of the Decalogue (Exod 20:2-3).

The final unit (vv 27-29) tells of Ahab's repentance, which wins him a mitigation of the punishment: the threatened doom will fall on his son, not on himself (cf. 2 Kgs 22:18-20), and this corresponds to what actually happened (2 Kgs 9).

2. *Significance.* While the other Elijah narratives are more concerned with the religious crisis caused by the spread of Baalism in Israel, the story of Naboth's vineyard focuses on social themes — abuse of power and greed for

land that does not stop short of murder. This brings the narrative close to the oracles of the great classical prophets (cf. Isa 5:8-23; 10:1-4; Am 2:6-16; 4:1-3; 5:10-12). The God of biblical faith is shown as one who cannot tolerate social injustice and its accompanying crimes. The relevance of this for today's readers needs no further comment.

F. 22:1-53
CONFLICT AMONG PROPHETS; THE DEATH OF THE KING OF ISRAEL

1. *Comment.* The main part of the chapter (vv 1-38) tells of the war undertaken by Israel and Judah against the Aramaeans of Damascus. An old war narrative provides the basis of the text (vv 1-4, 29-37); the story of Micaiah and the other prophets (vv 5-28) was inserted later, possibly in several stages. As it stands, the text is set in the reign of King Ahab of Israel whose name, however, occurs only once in vv 1-38 (at v 20). Historical arguments suggest that the war centered on Ramoth-gilead (v 3) is more likely to have taken place in the reign of one of Ahab's successors, possibly King Joram of Israel (cf. 2 Kgs 8:28 — 9:28); one can compare the remarks made at chap. 20 above. If that is so, then Ahab's presence here is the result of a later redactional decision to use the text to depict the well-merited end of the wicked king. In any case, this is the first time since the separation that Israel and Judah are shown acting as allies (cf. v 44); the military outcome is not successful (vv 29-36), nor is it in the similar situation recounted in 2 Kgs 3. It would seem that the Judaean narrator of the war stories wanted to stress the unwisdom of alliance with Israel, and the Deuteronomistic editors with their religiously motivated negative view of all the Israelite kings were bound to approve this attitude wholeheartedly.

The account of the clash between the prophet Micaiah and the four hundred other Yahwistic prophets (vv 5-28) gives a fascinating insight into the tensions that existed within the prophetic movement in Israel and Judah. The problem of prophetic conflict appears in many texts of the classical prophets (e.g. Jer 23:9-40; 27-29; Ezek 13; Mic 3:5-7), and its basic outlines are presented here in narrative form. The falsity of the four hundred prophets (which is not incompatible with their good-faith: cf. v 24) consists in presenting as Yahweh's word (v 11) what is really only a product of their own wishful thinking or a projection of what their hearers would like to hear. In this case, as in Jeremiah's time, their message is one of encouragement: Yahweh's people will be victorious in the war (vv 6, 11-12). One of the group, Zedekiah, dramatically reinforces the message with the symbolic gesture of the iron horns (v 11: cf. Deut 33:17). Since Micaiah is already well known as a prophet of doom, it is understandable that the king of Israel has little wish to hear from him a message which opposes his plans (v 8); the Judaean king, however, is shown as better disposed towards the genuine prophet (vv 7-8). Though Micaiah initially appears to re-echo the hopeful message of the other prophets (v 15), we are probably meant to detect a heavily ironic tone in his words (as the king's reply in v 16 suggests). The real message, one of doom for the king of Israel, comes in v 17.

Reflections on the origin of false prophetic messages are offered in vv 19-23. Micaiah recounts a vision he had of Yahweh's heavenly court (cf. Jer 23:18, 22; Job 1), where the divine decision to bring the wicked Ahab to his ruin has already been made and all that remains is to determine the means. Eventually a "lying spirit" is sent out to take possession of the king's prophets and lead them to utter false oracles that will bring Ahab to his divinely decreed doom (vv 21-23). False prophecy is daringly presented as part of Yahweh's acts of judgement against the unfaithful king who had refused to listen to genuine prophecy.

Finally Micaiah is arrested and held until the king would return (v 28). The last words of v 28 are a gloss from the Book of Micah (1:2), inserted because it was supposed (incorrectly) that the two prophets were identical. The death of the king of Israel (vv 37-38) is shown by the Deuteronomists as fulfilling Elijah's words of 21:19 (in part at least) as well as Micaiah's oracle of doom (v 17).

The last part of the chapter (vv 39-53) consists of a series of short notices by the Deuteronomistic redactors.

2. *Significance.* The main part of chap. 22 presents a memorable picture of the force of the prophetic word. It moves towards its fulfilment (vv 37-38) in spite of all opposition; neither the king's unbelief and hostility nor the alluring counter-message of deluded prophetic colleagues can withstand the genuine prophetic word. Its force lies in its origin, which is the Lord's decision taken in his heavenly court at which the genuine prophet assists in some mysterious way.

G. 2 Kgs 1:1-18
ELIJAH AND THE ILLNESS OF KING AHAZIAH

1. *Comment.* The prophetic tradition of the Israelite king's fatal recourse to a foreign god (vv 2-17a) is framed by the Deuteronomistic notices of v 1 (cf. 3:5) and vv 17b-18. King Ahaziah's religious infidelity has already been noted at 1 Kgs 22: 52-53 and is illustrated here by his recourse for an oracle to a divinity worshipped in the Philistine city of Ekron (v 2). The name "Baal-zebub" (v 2) probably means "Lord of the flies," which may be a deliberate deformation of the original name "Baal-zebul" (cf. Mt 10:25), meaning "Baal the Prince" (a title also found in the Ugaritic texts). Elijah is sent to meet Ahaziah's messengers and direct them back to their master with Yahweh's message of doom (vv 3-6). The king recognizes Elijah from the description which the messengers give of his unusual austere clothing (vv 7-8: cf. Zech 13:4, and compare the description of John the Baptist at Mt 3:4).

The second part of the story (vv 9-17a) begins with the account, in typical folktale style, of Elijah's three confrontations with Ahaziah's soldiers (vv 9-15). The first two captains arrogantly command the prophet to come down from the hill; the answer is a bolt of lightning which comes down upon them and their soldiers from heaven. The third captain is shown as having learned the lesson; with fear and reverence he pleads for his life from the man of God (vv 13-14), who is then instructed by Yahweh's messenger (the angel: v 15) to go personally to the king. There is nothing new in Elijah's oracle of doom for Ahaziah (v 16: for the third time in the story). The word of the Lord has been pronounced (vv 3-4); it reaches its goal irresistibly (v 16), and then takes effect (v 17a).

2. *Significance.* The main theme of the chapter is that Yahweh's prophetic word cannot be slighted with impunity. Ahaziah first tried to substitute an oracle of a powerless Baal for the powerful word of Yahweh, and then he tried to suppress the word of Yahweh by ordering the arrest of Elijah. But the Lord's word brooks neither substitution nor suppression; it does what it says, sooner or later.

The episode of the arrogant captains and their punishment is not intended as a "moral tale" in the sense of proposing Elijah's behaviour here as worthy of imitation. Already the New Testament criticizes such an understanding of the scene (cf. Lk 9:51-56). What we have in this text (and in many others of the Elijah and Elisha cycles) is rather a popular folkloristic way of expressing the reverence due to the Lord's word and to the person of his prophet. That was, and remains, a deadly serious matter.

V.   2 Kgs 2:1 — 11:20
The Divided Kingdoms, 3: Traditions about Elisha; The Revolt of Jehu and Its Consequences

The central figure in this sub-division is the prophet Elisha (cf. 1 Kgs 19:19-21). 2 Kgs 2 tells how he took over Elijah's role after the latter's assumption, and the following chapters recount his activity in two areas especially: his interventions in the political life of the northern kingdom (3; 6:24 — 9:13) and his miracles (2:19-25; 4:1 — 6:23). The religious struggle against the infiltration of Baalism, which dominated the Elijah stories, is not a prominent feature in the Elisha traditions; it comes to the fore, however, in the second part of the story of Jehu's *coup d'état* (chap. 10) and in the account of the overthrow of Queen Athaliah of Judah (chap. 11).

Two rather distinct images of Elisha emerge from the texts. The miracle-stories present him as leader of a prophetic association, the so-called "sons of the prophets"(cf. 1 Kgs 20:35), and his range of action here is largely restricted to cases of individual need. In the political narratives, on the other hand, he is shown as a prophetic personage of national importance who is well known abroad in Damascus too; his main function here is to announce Yahweh's word concerning kings and wars. These two images are not completely distinct, however, since chap. 5 (for example), though primarily a miracle-story, presupposes Elisha's fame in Damascus. It is hard to say which of the two images corresponds more closely to the Elisha of history; indeed, one cannot exclude the possibility that the historical Elisha was characterized both by paranormal powers and by political interventions, the different emphases in the several accounts being due to the different circles within which the traditions were transmitted. In any case, it is clear enough that there is a fair measure of legendary amplification in the Elisha traditions, particularly in the miracle-stories where the term "hagiography" would often be less misleading than "history writing" as a description of their literary type.

A.   2:1-25
THE ASSUMPTION OF ELIJAH; ELISHA, HIS SUCCESSOR, MANIFESTS HIS AUTHORITY BY MIRACLES

1.   *Comment.*   The carefully constructed narrative of Elisha's succession to Elijah's prophetic ministry (vv 1-18) begins with a stylized three-stage journey towards the Jordan (vv 1-3, 4-5, 6-8). Members of the prophetic groups assist at this last journey of Elijah, but it is Elisha alone who

accompanies him across the river. The parting of the Jordan waters (v 8) recalls the parting of the Sea of Reeds (Exod 14-15); once again Elijah is associated with Moses. Elisha's request to inherit a "double share" of his master's spirit (v 9) does not mean that he wants to have twice as much prophetic power as Elijah; the reference is probably to the custom of giving to the first-born son a share in the father's inheritance double that given to the other sons (cf. Deut 21:17). Elisha, in other words, asks to be acknowledged and endowed as Elijah's authentic heir and successor.

Elijah is swept up to heaven by a whirlwind (v 11). The only other OT reference to an assumption without death is that of Gen 5:24 concerning Enoch; Mesopotamian mythology has similar accounts about heroic kings and semi-divine personages. The departure of Elijah is not an event that can be perceived by ordinary human sight; when Elisha sees it (v 12), he knows that he has been endowed with the prophetic powers that he had asked for (cf. v 10). The title he gives to Elijah here "chariots of Israel and its horsemen" (v 12) is used later, and probably more originally, of Elisha himself (13:14); it refers to his role in the defence of Israel.

Taking up Elijah's mantle (cf. 1 Kgs 19:19), Elisha returns to the Jordan and with his newly acquired power repeats the miracle of separating the waters (vv 13-14): one is reminded of the separation of the Jordan waters in Joshua's time after he had succeeded Moses as Israel's leader (Josh 3-4). The prophetic groups then acknowledge Elisha's status (v 15); they suggest, however, that Elijah may have been swept off in an ecstatic state (cf. 1 Kgs 18:12, 46) and abandoned somewhere in the desert hills (v 16). Elisha knows that their search will be fruitless (v 16b), and his word is proved true (v 18b).

The next episode (vv 19-22) presents a typical miracle-story of the Elisha traditions (compare Exod 15:23-25). The prophet's word is efficacious, and is beneficial for those who approach him with the proper attitude of reverence and trust. The rather shocking anecdote of the boys and the bears (vv 23-24) carries the same message in reverse. The prophet's word, this time a curse, is efficacious and can damage those who treat him with levity and irreverence. One might feel that the forty-two small boys did not deserve such a mauling, but it is good to remember that the story was meant as a cautionary tale and may well be quite fictional in its details. Its anti-Bethel tone, besides, fits well into the Deuteronomistic aversion to that town and its sanctuary (cf. 1 Kgs 13; 2 Kgs 23).

2. *Significance.* The main episode (vv 1-18) focuses on the theme of prophetic succession as one means of legitimating a prophet's authority; another means is the presentation of a vocation account (cf. Isa 6; Jer 1; Ezek 1-3). The mention of Elijah's assumption (or translation) is subordinate to the succession theme; its point is to express Yahweh's absolute dominion even over the forces of death. The theme of life and death has appeared several times in the Elijah traditions (cf. 1 Kgs 17-18; 2 Kgs 1); the last moments of Elijah's earthly life now become a manifestation of Yahweh's life-fostering power and also a privileged acknowledgement of the unique stature of his zealous prophet.

B.   3:1-27
THE WAR AGAINST MOAB AND ELISHA'S ORACLE

1. *Comment.* The Deuteronomistic notice of vv 1-3 presents King Jehoram of Israel (ca. 851-845). He is evaluated negatively (vv 2a, 3), as happens for all the northern kings, but the judgement is mitigated in v 2b (a rare occurrence) by noting that he removed a Baalist cultic pillar set up by Ahab; Elijah's struggle against Baalism is shown to have had at least some effect on the royal house.

The rest of the chapter (vv 4-27) tells of the campaign waged by an allied force of Israelites, Judaeans, and Edomites against Mesha, king of Moab (east of the Dead Sea). Mesha had been a vassal of Israel under obligation to pay a heavy annual tribute (v 4), but had rebelled against his overlord. A Moabite inscription, found in 1868, gives us Mesha's own view of the independence struggle. The allied forces move to invade Moab but find themselves with a severe water shortage (vv 6-9). The Israelite king refuses to believe in Yahweh's assistance (vv 10, 13), but King Jehoshaphat of Judah is more devoted to the Lord and to his prophet Elisha who had accompanied the expedition (vv 11-12: cf. 1 Kgs 22:5ff). With the aid of music (v 15: cf. 1 Sam 10:5) Elisha enters into an ecstatic state and pronounces an oracle from Yahweh (vv 16-19): the water shortage will end as a result of a distant mountain cloudburst which will fill the dry stream-bed with a flash-flood (vv 16-17: a typical occurrence in that region), and after that the Moabites will be defeated (vv 18-19).

Next morning the prophet's word begins to be fulfilled when the flood arrives as announced (v 20). The Moabite forces see the red colour of the water (caused perhaps by the rising sun or by the type of rock in the area); thinking that the allies have fallen to fighting among themselves, they rush to the attack and to their utter defeat (vv 21-24). The land of Moab is then overrun by the invaders who devastate the countryside (v 25: contrast the later law of Deut 20:19-20 which is more sensitive to ecological considerations). Only the capital Kir-hareseth held out (v 25b: where the verb rendered "conquered" by the RSV would better be read as "attacked").

The Moabite king attempted a sally from the besieged city and when this was repulsed he sacrificed his eldest son on the city wall as a desperate last appeal to the Moabite god Chemosh (vv 26-27: cf. 1 Kgs 11:7). The text ends rather enigmatically: "There came great wrath upon Israel" (v 27): this might mean a defeat at the hands of the Moabite defenders, or it might indicate a feeling of dread and panic occasioned by such an unnatural action on the part of the Moabite king; or the wrath in question might be that of Chemosh (thought by the Israelites then to have real power in his own land: cf. 1 Sam 26:19) whose intervention in favour of his people Moab was considered imminent. In any case, the allied forces withdraw (v 27b), and the total subjugation of Moab was not achieved.

2. *Significance.* As minister of Yahweh's word Elisha exercises a real influence on his environment: the prophetic word is efficacious in nature (the flood) and in history (the initial defeat of Moab). The lack of complete success might be attributed to the unbelieving attitude of the Israelite king, which mirrors the general infidelity of the northern kings that would lead to the utter ruin of their state. The Judaean king, however, has more faith, and it is for his sake (v 14) that Elisha utters his oracle.

C. 4:1-44
FOUR MIRACLES OF ELISHA

1. *Comment.* The first anecdote (vv 1-7) describes the distress of a widow whose children were in danger of enslavement to satisfy the debts incurred by their deceased father who had been a member of one of the prophetic groups. Slavery for debt was permitted under Israel's early legislation (Exod 21:7) and, though attempts were made to mitigate it (Deut 15:12-18), the practice continued even in post-exilic times (Neh 5:5). Elisha's intervention brings about an extraordinary flow of oil (vv 3-6), which enables the woman to pay the debts and save her children; one is reminded of the Elijan miracle-story of the flour and oil (1 Kgs 17:12-16).

The main story (vv 8-37) tells of the resuscitation of the Shunammite woman's son. Shunem was situated on the edge of the northern plain some fifteen miles from Mount Carmel; it may have been in his journeys to and from the mountain that Elisha had occasion to accept the generous hospitality of the family (vv 8-10). As a reward the man of God promises the birth of a son to the childless couple (vv 11-17). A similar motif is found in Gen 18:1-16a, and one can also compare the more general theme of conception and birth in seemingly impossible circumstances (Judg 13; 1

Sam 1). The Shunammite woman's incredulity (v 16b) recalls Sarah's laugh (Gen 18:12-15).

The sudden illness of the child and his death (vv 18-20) create the narrative complication. The curious absence of emotion in the mother's reaction (vv 21-23) shows her trust that the situation is not final. Laying the child's body on the prophet's bed, as a way of entering into contact with his holy power (v 21), she hastens to Mount Carmel (vv 24-25). One can note that it was customary for devout folk to visit the prophet on feast-days (v 23). In Elisha's presence the mother's grief comes to expression (vv 27-28). Gehazi, the prophet's attendant, is ordered to go with the utmost speed (v 29b: cf. Lk 10:4) and lay Elisha's staff on the child's face, while Elisha and the mother follow. Gehazi's attempt fails (v 31), which heightens the reader's expectation for Elisha's own intervention.

The account of the resuscitation (vv 33-35) recalls Elijah's miracle at 1 Kgs 17:19-22; in Elisha's case the religious element (v 33b: prayer to Yahweh) is less developed, and the apparently magical gestures are more prominent (vv 34-35). The mother's reaction is wordless (v 37: contrast 1 Kgs 17:24). It seems clear that a literary relationship existed between the present story and the Elijan one; see the comment on 1 Kgs 17.

The anecdote that follows (vv 38-41) is devoid of theological interpretation and simply illustrates Elisha's good sense in practical matters and his care for the prophetic group over which he presides.

The multiplication of the loaves to feed one hundred persons (vv 42-44), on the other hand, is much more theological in tone, and has provided a narrative model for the NT texts about the miraculous feeding of the crowds (Mk 6:30-44; 8:1-10).

2. *Significance.* The Elisha-cycle contains one of the main concentrations of miracle-stories in the OT (the Exodus story is the other main one). These narratives are not interested in miracles as exceptions to the laws of nature (a Greek and Western concept that was not part of the mental

world of the Israelites). Elisha's miracles are, above all, signs that God's marvellous creative power is active and (in the present instance) beneficent. He is a God whose holy servant is used as a means of relieving people's distress and of giving health, nourishment, and life. Our reading of these texts should concentrate on what they say or imply about the Lord and his prophet, not on the material details.

D. 5:1-27
THE HEALING OF NAAMAN THE SYRIAN

1. *Comment.* The first unit (vv 1-14) tells of the cure of Naaman's affliction by Elisha's word. Naaman is an Aramaean military commander, successful and respected; the statement (v 1) that it was Yahweh who granted him his victories (probably including those over Israel: cf. v 2) is a remarkable affirmation of Yahweh's lordship over world history. Naaman's illness (v 1) is hardly to be understood as leprosy in the strict sense (Hansen's disease), since he still takes part in normal social life (vv 2-6); as often in the OT and NT, the reference is rather to some form of disfiguring skin disease.

The Syrian king's letter (v 6) obviously meant that the Israelite king should instruct his famous prophet (cf. v 2) to heal Naaman. The king of Israel, however, is presented as somewhat obtuse and suspicious (v 7). He mistakenly understands the Syrian king's words to contain a request to perform the cure personally; this would constitute an infringement on the sphere of the sacred, an act of impious arrogance, which would then give the Syrians a pretext to intervene and dethrone him. These ridiculous Machiavellian reasonings are cut short by the clear message sent to the king by Elisha (v 8).

Naaman proceeds to Elisha's house accompanied by all his retinue and guards, but he is not admitted to the prophet's presence. Instead a messenger brings him some brief instructions from Elisha (vv 9-10). Naaman, an important personage, had expected a special healing ceremony with ritual gestures and all the rest, and he feels offended by Elisha's brusque behaviour and by the command to bathe in the unimpressive waters of the Jordan (vv 11-12). The sobriety of the word and its appeal for sheer faith are always hard on human nature.

Naaman's servants, however, manage to persuade their irate master to follow the prophet's instructions; their good sense (v 13) recalls the kindly suggestion made by the little servant girl in Naaman's house (vv 2-3). Obedience to the word and immersion in the water then bring about the healing of the foreigner (v 14).

The second unit (vv 15-19a) presents the discussion that took place between Elisha and Naaman who had returned to give thanks. The Aramaean makes a confession of faith in strongly monotheistic terms (v 15: cf. Exod 18:10-11). Elisha, for his part, gives proof of his disinterested service of Yahweh by refusing the rich gifts that Naaman pressed upon him (v 16). Aware that healing has come to him from the land of Israel, Naaman wants to take home two mule-loads of Israelite earth on which to worship Yahweh (v 17). He also asks the prophet to pardon his unavoidable participation in the official worship of the storm-god Rimmon in Damascus (v 18); Elisha's answer (v 19a) is a masterpiece of pastoral tact.

The final unit (vv 19b-27) is a mordantly humorous account of the greed of Gehazi, Elisha's attendant (cf. 4:12ff). Gehazi takes advantage of Naaman's feelings of gratitude to line his own pockets; his avarice and petty cunning (vv 19b-22) are in striking contrast to the disinterested nobility of Elisha's attitude (v 16). At first all goes well for Gehazi (vv 23-24), but he has not reckoned with his master's gift of second sight (v 26: cf. 6:8ff). His lies are pitilessly exposed, and his punishment fits the crime. He had sought to enrich himself at Naaman's expense, but what he gets and bequeaths to his descendants is the affliction from which Naaman had been liberated (v 27).

2. *Significance.* The spirit of openness to non-Israelites is one of the most remarkable features of this splendid

narrative whose lesson has also been underlined in the NT (Lk 4:27-30). The Aramaean Naaman, helped by Yahweh in his battles, is cured by the word of an Israelite prophet, and confesses his Yahwistic faith in admirable terms. The Aramaean king is helpful and considerate, but the king of Israel is depicted much less favourably. Gehazi, the prophet's own Israelite attendant, becomes a model of how a prophetic disciple should not behave. These themes recall the message of the Book of Jonah in several respects, and it is not impossible that post-exilic redaction has left its mark on the Naaman story especially within vv 15-19a.

E. 6:1 — 7:20
ELISHA AS HELPER IN TIMES OF PEACE AND TIMES OF WAR

1. *Comment.* Two miracle-stories (6:1-7, 8-23) are followed by a longer war narrative in which the prophet's word has an important place (6:24 — 7:20). The tale of the floating axe head (6:1-7) shows Elisha as the leader of a prophetic group who live near the Jordan, apparently as a community. Elisha is concerned about the small needs and worries of his followers, and uses his extraordinary powers to aid them in a moment of distress (cf. 4:1-7, 38-41). Little is gained by speculating about the material details here.

The next unit (6:8-23) again stresses Elisha's powers but now in the context of international affairs. His gift of second sight or clairvoyance (cf. 5:26) enables him to warn the king of Israel about an ambush laid for him by the Aramaeans (vv 9-10). The prophet's powers are well known to the Aramaeans who resolve to take him prisoner (vv 11-14). But a prophet is not to be treated in this way (cf. 1:9-15), and it is the Aramaean soldiers who end up as Elisha's prisoners (vv 15-19). One can note the stress on the themes of seeing and not seeing in these verses. Elisha's ability to see the superhuman dimension of reality (v 17: cf. 2:10-12) is shared for a moment by his servant at Elisha's prayer (vv 16-17). Again at Elisha's prayer the Aramaean forces are struck with blindness (v 18: cf. Gen 19: 11) and in this condition are led by Elisha right into Samaria and into the power of the king of Israel, at which point their eyes are opened again in answer to Elisha's third prayer (vv 19-20). The helpless prisoners are not massacred, however, as the Israelite king (thinking perhaps of the old practice of the ban: cf. 1 Sam 15) proposes (v 21). Elisha displays remarkable clemency (vv 22-23), which made good sense politically too as v 23b makes clear.

The third unit (6:24 — 7:20) describes a full-scale invasion of Israel by the Aramaeans, not just a border raid as previously. The tension between vv 23b and 24 shows that the new unit originally belonged to a collection of traditions different to that of the two preceding units. Samaria is besieged and the extreme suffering of the inhabitants is stressed (vv 25-29: cf. Deut 28:53-57). The Israelite king puts the blame on Elisha whose oracles had evidently encouraged the city's resistance by promising divine aid, and he goes so far as to decide to kill the prophet (vv 30-32). Elisha's answer (7:1) is to announce in Yahweh's name that an abundant supply of food, as in times of peace, will be available on the very next day. The king's adjutant scornfully expresses his disbelief (v 2: cf. Gen 7:11; 8:2) but receives an oracle of doom in reply (v 2b).

The Lord's intervention, however, puts the besiegers to flight, and news of their empty camp, packed with provisions, is brought to the Israelite king by four lepers (vv 3-11). The king's initial incredulity is overcome (vv 12-15), and the narrative ends by stressing the fulfilment of the prophet's word, both for the good of the people of Samaria (v 16) and for the doom of the unbelieving royal adjutant (vv 17-20).

2.   *Significance.*   Elisha is shown here as the point of contact between the power of Israel's Lord and the needs of his people. This is conveyed by the stress on Elisha's prayer in the second unit (6:17, 18, 20) and by noting his function in the war story as a messenger who transmits the Lord's powerful word (7:1-2, 16, 20). The mediatory role of the prophet did not always meet with believing acceptance, not

even from those entrusted with leadership over the Lord's people (6:31-33; cf. 7:2), but the Lord's word is victorious in the end.

F. 8:1-29
FURTHER ELISHAN TRADITIONS; NOTICES ABOUT JUDAEAN KINGS

1. *Comment.* The first unit (vv 1-6) tells how the Shunammite woman (cf. 4:8ff), now a widow, was obliged by famine conditions to abandon her ancestral land for seven years; her faith in Elisha's warning was rewarded (vv 1-2). When she returns to Israel, she finds that her property, or its administration, had been transferred to others, perhaps to the crown (the legal situation is not clear). The Israelite king had been listening to Gehazi's account of Elisha's resuscitation of the woman's son (v 5: perhaps this story was originally set after Elisha's death), when the woman appears before him and asks for her land. The king orders that everything due to her should be restored immediately. She has lost nothing by following Elisha's word (v 6). One can note that Gehazi appears here without any sign of his "leprosy" (5:27), an indication that 8:1-6 and chap. 5 were originally quite distinct traditions.

Elisha's international activity is stressed in the second unit (vv 7-15) where he is shown as involved in Hazael's *coup d'état* in Damascus. The respect in which the prophet is held by the Aramaean king is clear (vv 8-9), as is Elisha's power of knowing what is to come (vv 10, 12-13). A perplexing point concerns the answer that Elisha gives to Hazael for the king (vv 10a, 14b); it is a false message, and the prophet knows it to be so (v 10b). Yahweh, the Lord of history, has decreed the death of King Ben-hadad and the accession of Hazael; this decree is brought into effect by the stratagem of Elisha's deceptive oracle, which gives Ben-hadad a false sense of security and enables Hazael to act. In this way Elisha is shown as presiding over the rise to the throne of Damascus of a man who was to cause great suffering to

Israel in the future (vv 12-13: cf. 10:32-33; 13:3). In contrast to 1 Kgs 19:15 it is Elisha, not Elijah, who is shown as having had a hand in the rise of Hazael, and there is no mention of anointing. The factuality of Elisha's participation in Hazael's coup is debated: some scholars see it as historically conceivable, others prefer to read the account as concerned more with the theological affirmation of Yahweh's lordship over history by the prophetic word.

The chapter concludes with Deuteronomistic notices about Kings Jehoram and Ahaziah of Judah (vv 16-29); some older historical material has been used by the editors. Those were dark days for Judah — understandably so (for the Deuteronomists), since there was a marriage alliance between the royal house and the impious Omride dynasty of Israel (vv 18, 26-27). But the Davidic promise still held good (v 19). In Ahaziah's short reign (ca. 845) the alliance was extended to the area of military cooperation (vv 28-29): such folly on the part of the Davidic king would soon receive its fitting retribution (9:27-28).

2. *Significance.*   Elisha's role as the Lord's instrument for weal (vv 1-6) and for woe (vv 7-15) is stressed again here. The Hazael episode tells of one instance of the "strange deed and alien work" (cf. Isa 28:21) that Yahweh can do in the history of his people.

G.   9:1 — 10:36
JEHU'S *COUP D'ÉTAT* IN ISRAEL

1. *Comment.*   This important section tells of the violent overthrow of the Omride dynasty in Israel and builds up to a climax in the description of the anti-Baalist measures adopted with ferocious severity by the new king Jehu (ca. 845-818). Most of the material here comes from an early northern narrative composed during the reign of Jehu himself or shortly after it.

In the first scene (9:1-13) Elisha sends a disciple to anoint secretly as king of Israel the army officer Jehu, thus affording divine authorization for his *coup d'état* that will bring about the downfall of the wicked house of Omri and Ahab (cf. 1 Kgs 19:16, except that it is Elisha, not Elijah, who is responsible for the anointing). The religious motivation and significance of the revolt are stressed in the probably Deuteronomistic vv 7-10a (cf. 1 Kgs 14:10; 16:3-4; 18:4, 13; 21:21-24). The reference to the young prophetic disciple as "this mad fellow" (v 11) shows that the prophetic groups were not regarded with great respect by their more pragmatic fellow-Israelites (cf. 1 Sam 10:11-12; Hos 9:7). Jehu is then acclaimed as king amid the sounding of trumpets (v 13: cf. 2 Sam 15:10).

The next unit (vv 14-26) tells of the assassination of the Israelite king Joram by Jehu. One can note the dramatic suspense with which Jehu's approach to the town of Jezreel is described (vv 17-20: cf. 2 Sam 18:24-27). The fateful meeting with Joram takes place on what had been the property of Naboth (v 21: cf. 1 Kgs 21). In Jehu's denunciation of the religious depravity of Joram's mother, Jezebel, there is a metaphorical use of the term "harlotry" for idolatry (v 22); this will often recur in the oracles of the northern prophet Hosea. Joram's death is explicitly connected with Yahweh's oracle of condemnation against his father Ahab for the wrong done to Naboth (vv 25-26). The reference to the death of Naboth's sons (v 26), not mentioned in 1 Kgs 21, corresponds to the fact that it is Ahab's son who here receives the punishment (cf. 1 Kgs 21:29).

The third scene (vv 27-28) recounts the killing of King Ahaziah of Judah (cf. 8:25-29) who was related to the Israelite Joram through his mother Athaliah (cf. chap. 11). The notice of v 29 seems out of place here (cf. 8:25).

Jezebel's gory but defiant death (vv 30-37) is stated explicitly to be the fulfilment of Elijah's prophecy (vv 36-37), though one can note that v 37 has no correspondence in 1 Kgs 21:23. Jezebel's pointed and scornful designation of Jehu as "you Zimri" (v 31) refers to an earlier *coup d'état* of extremely short duration in the northern kingdom (1 Kgs 16:8-20).

The blood-bath continues in 10:1-11 with the slaughter of

seventy members of the royal house in Samaria carried out
by the terrified leaders of the townsfolk under Jehu's threat
to move against Samaria with his army. Jehu's words to the
people of Jezreel (vv 9-10) seem to invite them to discern
that the death of all these sons of Ahab could not be due
merely to his own initiative but must be seen as the irresisti-
ble working-out of Yahweh's sentence pronounced against
the house of Ahab by Elijah.

The savage butchery of the unwitting kinsmen of Ahaziah
of Judah (vv 12-14) is given no motivation other than their
friendship with the ruling house of Israel.

One of Jehu's chief supporters, Jehonadab son of
Rechab, is mentioned at this point (vv 15-16: cf. v 23). An
intransigent Yahwist, he wholeheartedly approved the violent measures being taken by Jehu against the royal house
and especially against the worshippers of Baal. Over two
centuries later, Jer 35 mentions a group called the Recha-
bites whose refusal to accept sedentary agricultural life
appears to have been an expression of their extremist position of total opposition to Canaanite culture in all its
aspects; they trace their stand to the instructions of the
Jonadab mentioned in 2 Kgs 10.

The massacre of the priests, prophets, and worshippers of
Baal is described with evident relish in vv 18-25a. The cultic
furnishings and the Baal-temple itself are then destroyed (vv
25b-27); in this way Jehu is shown as reversing Ahab's
actions told in 1 Kgs 16:31-33.

There is a curious effect of double vision in the evaluation
of Jehu's reign given in the largely Deuteronomistic vv
28-36. His purge of Baalism is praised (vv 28, 30), but he falls
under the general condemnation of all the northern kings
for having continued to tolerate the schismatic sanctuaries
of Bethel and Dan (v 29) and for his refusal to obey Yahweh's law in this respect (v 31). The loss of Israel's Transjordanian territories to Hazael of Damascus (vv 32-33) is seen
as the Lord's punishment for Jehu's shortcomings (v 32a).

2. *Significance.*   In the final form of the text Jehu is seen
as continuing Elijah's policy of relentless opposition to

Baalism (cf. 1 Kgs 18:40; 19:16-17), and as Yahweh's instrument in carrying out the prophetic sentence already passed on the royal house of Omri and Ahab. This stress on the problem of foreign gods and on the fulfilment of prophecy fits well into the general theological interests of the Deuteronomistic history. Historically, however, it is questionable whether the religious or cultic motivation was quite so central in Jehu's coup. He certainly received support from intransigent Yahwists in the northern kingdom (such as Elisha, the prophetic groups, and Jehonadab), but his thorough-going liquidation of all possible claimants to the throne raises the suspicion that his own basic motivation was the more earthly one of political ambition. It is significant, in this regard, that Jehu's bloody deeds were strongly criticized about a century later by Hosea (1:4).

In any event, the accession of Jehu resulted in a serious political weakening of the northern kingdom; territory was lost to the Aramaeans, and extra-biblical sources show that Jehu soon became a tribute-paying vassal of the Assyrian Empire, presumably to secure some protection against the Aramaean incursions. 2 Kgs 9-10, then, reveal a widening gulf between Yahweh's demands in the religious sphere and the political success and prosperity of the Israelite kingdom. Religion does not exist to prop up the political fabric and its power-holders.

H.   11:1-20
QUEEN ALTHALIAH OF JUDAH

1. *Comment.* This chapter, based on an old Jerusalem tradition, now constitutes a sequel to the events related in chaps 9-10. A brief introduction (vv 1-3) tells of the usurpation of the throne of David by Athaliah, mother of King Ahaziah who had been murdered by Jehu (9:27-28). Athaliah was a granddaughter (or daughter: the Hebrew term is ambiguous) of King Omri of Israel (8:26: cf. 8:18) and therefore of non-Davidic stock. Her seizure of the throne after the slaughter of the Davidic princes (vv 1-2) meant a

break in the Davidic dynasty, which seemed to run counter
to the dynastic promise (2 Sam 7). Though she was to reign
for six years (v 3: ca. 845-840), the Deuteronomists have
omitted all the usual regnal formulas, which suggests that
hers was not considered a legitimate reign at all. One of the
young Davidic princes, Joash, was saved from Athaliah's
executioners by Princess Jehosheba (v 2: cf. Exod 2:1-10)
and hidden away in the Temple outbuildings.

In view of Athaliah's foreign background and Baalist
inclinations (cf. v 18), it is understandable that opposition to
her should have been especially strong among the Temple
priesthood. Six years later this opposition comes to the
surface in a conspiracy organized by the chief priest Jehoiada (according to 2 Chr 22:11 the husband of Princess
Jehosheba). The priest's plan (vv 4-8), though unclear in
details, is based on securing the support of the mercenaries
and elite troops; one can surmise that the Temple treasury
was an important factor in the preliminary arrangements.
Everything then works out perfectly (vv 9ff). Prince Joash is
crowned, anointed, and installed as king in the traditional
manner (details are given in vv 12-14, 17-19), while Athaliah
is brought outside the Temple area for execution (vv 15-16),
since a corpse would profane the sacred precincts (cf. Lev
21:1-3; Num 19:11-16; 31:19).

Two points of detail can be noted. The "testimony" (v 12:
RSV) given to the new king may have been a document
containing the terms of the covenant between Yahweh and
the house of David (cf. Ps 132 [131]:12) or perhaps a list of
the king's rights and duties (cf. 1 Sam 10:25); it is also
possible, however, to translate the Hebrew term as "royal
insignia". Secondly, the mention of covenant-making in v
17 is not altogether clear. As the text stands, two covenants
seem to be indicated. The first is made between Yahweh on
the one side and the king and people on the other; it focuses
on the renewal of the people's fidelity to Yahweh and is the
prelude to the elimination of Baalist cult in v 18 (cf. Josh
24:14-25). The second covenant (v 17b: omitted, however, in
some textual witnesses) is between the king and the people,

and it ratifies the re-establishment of the Davidic dynasty (cf. 2 Sam 5:3).

The Baalist sanctuary, whose destruction (together with the execution of its priest) was a necessary consequence of the renewed covenant with Yahweh, may have been a small cultic centre for Athaliah's own use and that of her immediate retinue. There is no evidence that Baalism had much following among the ordinary Judaean population in this period. It will be noted that the initiative here is taken by "the people of the land" (v 18): the reference is probably to the rural notables of Judah who will appear in several subsequent texts as vigilant guardians of the Davidic succession to the throne of Jerusalem.

2. *Significance.*   The political upheavals in Judah issue in the restoration of the Davidic dynasty, a demonstration of Yahweh's fidelity to the house of David (2 Sam 7). It is fitting that it is Yahweh's priest who presides over these events. At the same time both king and people are called to respond to the Lord with greater fidelity, above all by banishing all traces of idolatry from their midst.

VI.   2 Kgs 11:21 — 17:41
Until the Fall of the Northern Kingdom

The various reigns mentioned in this sub-division cover a period of slightly over a century. The climax comes in chap. 17 which presents a long theological interpretation of the fall of the kingdom of Israel and its capital Samaria in 722 B.C. Deuteronomistic editing is much more evident in these chapters than in the preceding traditions about Elijah and Elisha.

A.   11:21 — 12:21 (HEBREW: 12:1-22)
KING JEHOASH OF JUDAH

1. *Comment.*   The long reign (ca. 840-801) of Jehoash (or Joash) began well, according to the Deuteronomistic redac-

tors, since the young king was strongly influenced by the chief priest Jehoiada who had contrived his accession (chap. 11). Nonetheless the redactors deplore the continuance of worship at the local sanctuaries (v 3).

The central part of the chapter (vv 4-16) is taken up with an account of Jehoash's interventions in the problem of financing the necessary repairs in the Temple. His first proposal, which laid the burden of the work on the priests (vv 4-5), proved to be unworkable (v 6); the priests were not cooperative, it seems. So a second scheme is devised (vv 7-16), this time with the consent of the priests who are relieved of responsibility for the repair work: some of their income is diverted for this purpose (vv 7-8) and a form of entrance tax is instituted in the Temple (v 9); a royal official and the high priest are empowered to administer the funds and deal with the overseers of the workmen (vv 10-12). One can note the use of the term "high priest," found in Kings only here (v 10) and then at 22:4, 8; 23:4. All the other occurrences are in post-exilic texts, which might suggest that the present account has been re-edited in post-exilic priestly circles. In this connection one can also note the reference to "guilt offerings" and "sin offerings" in v 16; these two types of sacrifice (not easy to distinguish in practice: cf. Lev 4-5) became common only in post-exilic times, though it is hardly possible to affirm that they were unknown before the fall of Jerusalem.

A report follows in vv 17-18 about a raid by the Aramaean king Hazael (cf. 8:7-15; 10:32-33); the town of Gath, west of Jerusalem, was taken, and the capital itself was menaced. The Aramaeans had to be bought off with large quantities of gold. Joash was murdered in a palace conspiracy (vv 20-21); we are not told why, but it may be that the losses, in treasures and in prestige, incurred during the Aramaean attack made a change of ruler advisable. The line of David remained unbroken, however, for Joash's son Amaziah succeeded his father in the normal way.

2. *Significance.*   Though Joash reigned for about forty years, the Deuteronomists concentrate almost exclusively

on his dealings with the Temple — yet another indication of their theologically slanted presentation of history. They clearly approve the king's zeal in cultic matters, and the account here serves in fact as a preparation for the great cultic reform under Josiah, the ideal successor of David in the eyes of the Deuteronomists (2 Kgs 22-23).

B. 13:1-25
ARAMAEAN PRESSURE ON ISRAEL; ELISHA'S LAST PROPHETIC SIGNS AND DEATH

1. *Comment.* The first unit (vv 1-9) describes in heavily Deuteronomistic language the reign of King Jehoahaz of Israel (ca. 818-802). Verses 3-5 contain some interesting resemblances (thematic and verbal) to passages in the Book of Judges (2:11-23; 3:7-11, 12-15, 30; 10:6-16); this might suggest the existence of a redactional activity common to the two books. The identity of the "saviour" (v 5) is a matter of dispute. Possibilities include Jehoahaz's son Joash (cf. v 25), Joash's son Jeroboam II (14:27 notes tht he "saved" Israel), the Assyrian King Adadnirari III (who forced Damascus to pay a heavy tribute and thus relieved the pressure on Israel), and finally the prophet Elisha (whose help against the Aramaeans has already been mentioned in chaps 6-7 and is the subject of vv 14-19 here). In any case, the main point is the theological insistence that Israel's successes against the Aramaeans would be due solely to Yahweh's graciousness. For the moment, however, things continued to go badly for Israel (v 7), not surprisingly, for the cultic symbol of a Canaanite goddess (the "Ashera": v 6) continued to be honoured in Samaria. Jehu's purge (chap. 10) had not definitively extirpated Baalism from the capital.

The reign of Jehoash (or Joash) of Israel (ca. 802-787) is mentioned very briefly in vv 10-13. Though his death is noted here, we find various episodes from his reign later in 13:14-25 and 14:8-14 with a repetition of the concluding formulas at 14:15-16.

Two Elishan traditions follow. The first (vv 14-20a) tells of the dying prophet's oracles to King Joash of Israel who acknowledges Elisha to have been Israel's most effective defence (v 14b: cf. 2:12; 6:17). After the symbolic arrow-shot eastwards in the direction of the Aramaean territory in Transjordan (v 17: cf. 10:32-33), the king receives a promise of a decisive victory over the Aramaeans at Aphek in northern Transjordan (cf. 1 Kgs 20 and the comment). Joash, however, does not give proof of unlimited faith in the prophet's word (vv 18-19); hence the concluding oracle limits the number of his victories (v 19b: with the fulfilment in v 25b). The second Elishan tradition (vv 20b-21) is a hagiographical legend, which shows that the life-giving power of the man of God (cf. chap. 4) continues to operate even after his death.

The chapter concludes with notices about Aramaean attacks on Israel and the Israelite resurgence under King Joash (vv 22-25). One can note especially the reference in v 23 to the Lord's compassion, which is connected to his covenant with the Patriarchs; this covenant is mentioned nowhere else in Kings, though it is frequent in Deuteronomy.

2. *Significance.*   The chapter is noteworthy for its strong emphasis on Yahweh's graciousness, even towards a sinful king (v 2) and people (v 6). The divine compassion rests on the Patriarchal covenant, and it is made audible and efficacious in the words and deeds of the prophet Elisha.

C.   14:1-29
JUDAH'S HUMILIATION; ISRAEL'S RESURGENCE

1. *Comment.*   King Amaziah's reign in Judah (ca. 801-773) is introduced by the Deuteronomists in their usual phraseology (vv 1-4). The king's vengeance against the murderers of his father Joash (v 5: cf. 12:20-21) was not extended to their families, and in v 6 the Deuteronomistic

redactor approvingly quotes Deut 24:16 on the legal appli-
cation of the concept of individual responsibility.

The unit that follows in vv 8-14 (probably of northern
provenance) tells of the foolish challenge issued by Amaziah
to the far more powerful king of Israel. Jehoash responds
with a short but pointed fable (v 9: cf. Judg 9:7-15) and some
blunt good advice (v 10), but Amaziah refused to listen. The
disaster that followed for Judah is described in vv 11-14.
The Deuteronomists do not comment explicitly on the episode, but Amaziah's stupid arrogance condemns itself while
Jehoash's seizure of the Temple vessels (v 14) could only
confirm his religious depravity already noted in 13:11.

Amaziah survived for fifteen years after this débâcle and
ended his life the victim of a conspiracy; Lachish, where he
was killed, was an important fortified city south-west of
Jerusalem (vv 17-20: cf. 12:20-21). The people of Judah,
possibly in opposition to the Jerusalemites who had organized the conspiracy (v 19a), installed Amaziah's son, Azariah (also called Uzziah: e.g. 15:13), as king (v 21); the
Davidic line remained unbroken. The new king continued
the expansionist policy of his father (cf. v 7), regaining
control of Elath on the Gulf of Aqabah and refortifying the
town (v 22), which was of strategic importance for the trade
route to Arabia.

The long reign of Jeroboam II of Israel (ca. 787-747),
though characterized by military successes and economic
prosperity (as can be seen from the contemporary oracles of
Amos), is treated by the Deuteronomists with striking brevity (vv 23-29). One can compare their handling of Omri's
reign in 1 Kgs 16. Jeroboam extended Israelite control
almost as far north as in David's time (vv 25, 28: cf. 2 Sam 8
and 10). Though the king's wickedness is noted in stereotyped terms by the Deuteronomists (v 24), the statement
that he was used by the Lord to save Israel from its affliction
(vv 26-27) offers another evaluation of his reign. Furthermore, it is noted in v 25 that Jeroboam's territorial expansion was in accordance with a prophetic oracle delivered by
one Jonah son of Amittai (v 25); this personage, who

appears nowhere else in Kings, will be the protagonist of the Book of Jonah. He appears in v 25 as a typical court-prophet who announces success and victory for his king (cf. 1 Sam 22:5; 1 Kgs 20:13-14, 22, 28). It is interesting to note the almost polemical tone in v 27 which insists that Yahweh did not decree the annihilation of Israel; Amos, on the contrary, proclaimed during the reign of Jeroboam II that "The end has come upon my people Israel" (8:2).

2. *Significance.* As the history of Judah and Israel continues, there are successes and reverses on the political plane, but the decisive factor is the Lord's word, gracious in delivering his people (vv 25-27) and crucial in determining the standards of genuine success (vv 3-4, 6, 24).

D.   15:1-38
THE END OF THE NORTHERN KINGDOM DRAWS NEAR

1. *Comment.* The Deuteronomistic redactors have placed their accounts of five Israelite kings (vv 8-31) between the notices about two Judaean kings (vv 1-7, 32-38). The first of these, Azariah of Judah (ca. 787-736), was afflicted with severe skin disease during his reign (v 5), which obliged him to appoint his son Jotham as regent. The Deuteronomists attribute the king's illness to divine punishment (v 5a), apparently for his laxity in the matter of the local sanctuaries (v 4). A different explanation can be read in the dramatic account of 2 Chr 26:16-21.

The story of the last twenty years of the northern kingdom (vv 8-31) makes bitter reading. Four of the kings were assassinated; the only one who died a natural death, Menahem (vv 14-22), was himself guilty of atrocious violence. Further insights into the political and social chaos of the time can be gathered from the oracles of Hosea, a contemporary of the kings mentioned here. Concerning Zechariah the last member of Jehu's dynasty (vv 8-12), the Deuteronomistic redactor notes the fulfilment of the word of God which had granted Jehu four generations on the throne of

Israel (v 12: cf. 10:30). Zechariah was murdered in his accession year by Shallum who was himself murdered a month later by Menahem (ca. 747-738). The latter's barbarous treatment of the pregnant women in the Israelite town that opposed his *coup* (v 16) can be compared to Hos 13:16 and Am 1:13.

In this period Israel lived under the shadow of the increasingly aggressive Assyrian Empire ruled by Tiglath-pileser III (v 29: the name "Pul" in v 19 represents his throne-name in Babylon) whose reign (ca. 745-727) was marked by a great westward expansion from the Assyrian homeland in Mesopotamia. King Menahem of Israel declared himself an Assyrian vassal and secured his shaky throne with Assyrian support (v 19b); the price was a heavy tribute exacted from all property owners in Israel (vv 19-20). His son Pekahiah (vv 23-26) appears to have continued the pro-Assyrian policy during his brief reign. His murderer and successor, Pekah (v 25), belonged to the anti-Assyrian party, and in his reign a devastating Assyrian invasion took place (v 29: see 16:1-9 for the circumstances). Tiglath-pileser overran the northern and eastern areas of Israel and incorporated them into the Assyrian provincial system of imperial administration; part of the population was deported to Assyria (v 29b: the first occurrence of this fateful verb in Kings). Israel's territory was thus reduced to a small area around the capital Samaria, and it is understandable that Pekah, the king responsible for such losses, should have been replaced by one more in favour with the Assyrians. Verse 30 notes this without comment; an Assyrian text specifies that it was Tiglath-pileser who placed Hoshea on the throne of Israel, that is, ratified his *coup d'état.*

In Judah, meanwhile, Jotham was the effective ruler (v 31: cf. v 5). The Deuteronomists give him a moderately favourable assessment (v 34) but note that the local sanctuaries remained in function (v 35). This is presumably seen as the reason why Yahweh gathered a coalition of Aramaeans and Israelites against Judah (v 37); this conflict, the so-called Syro-Ephraimite war, will be described in 16:1-9.

2.   *Significance.*   Israel's "original sin" in the time of Jeroboam I (vv 9, 18, 24, 28) is shown as bringing the kingdom nearer and nearer to its doom. Judah, on the other hand, is ruled by good, though imperfect, kings, but things will soon change for the worse there. The Lord's sovereign will presides over all these happenings, even over the deeds of a mighty conqueror such as Tiglath-pileser. The exilic period readers of Kings are invited to understand their own situation as under the dominion of the same Lord of history and not as the outcome of blind historical forces.

E.   16:1-20
KING AHAZ OF JUDAH BECOMES AN ASSYRIAN VASSAL

1.   *Comment.*   The reign of Ahaz (ca 741-725) is judged quite negatively by the Deuteronomists (vv 2b-4). To say that his behaviour followed the pattern of the northern kings (v 3a) is a severe condemnation for a descendant of David (cf. 8:18, 27). Ahaz is said to have burned his son in sacrifice (v 3b: RSV); this abominable practice is also attested at 17:17 (for Israel) and 21:6; 23:10 (for Judah: cf. Jer 19:5), and was most severely forbidden by the Law (e.g. Deut 12:31). Some scholars, it must be added, prefer to render the Hebrew phrase here as "he made his son to pass through the fire" (cf. the RSV note at 16:3), which would refer to a symbolic rite of dedication to some pagan divinity, but this explanation seems less probable.

The crisis caused by the alliance of Syria (the Aramaeans) and Israel against Judah (vv 5-9: cf. 15:37) is described in further detail in Isa 7. The Syro-Ephraimite war (ca. 733) was caused by Ahaz's refusal to join Damascus and Samaria in an anti-Assyrian coalition; the allies then decided to dethrone Ahaz and replace him with a ruler more amenable to their policies. While Isaiah urged Ahaz to put his whole trust in Yahweh's goodwill towards Jerusalem and the Davidic dynasty (Isa 7:3-9), the king fell back on human means of deliverance (2 Kgs 16:7-8). Professing himself the "servant and son" of Tiglath-pileser (terms found in the formal diplomatic language of the ancient Near East), Ahaz brings Judah (for the first time) into a state of vassalage to Assyria. A financial contribution to the Assyrians gave concrete form to the new relationship (v 8: cf. 1 Kgs 15:18-19), and the Assyrian king then fulfilled his commitment as overlord by coming to the aid of his beleaguered vassal (v 9: cf. 15:29) — which was conveniently in accord with his own expansionist policies anyway.

Ahaz then journeyed north to the Assyrian-held Damascus to make his formal act of submission to Tiglath-pileser (vv 10-11), and one consequence of this was that he had to remove from the Jerusalem Temple a number of architectural features that symbolized the sovereignty of the Judaean king (v 18). It is not clear whether the new altar (vv 10-16) was another sign of submission, dictated or at least counselled by his status as vassal. In any case, it was used for orthodox Yahwistic worship, not for the worship of Assyrian gods.

2. *Significance.* While Isaiah stresses the political dimension of Ahaz's sin (Isa 7), the Deuteronomists are more interested in underlining his cultic shortcomings. The political reverses (v 6) and errors (vv 5, 7-9) are seen as fitting punishment for the basic religious sin of the king. There is no evidence that Ahaz apostatized from Yahwism, but it remains true (and Isaiah confirms this) that his reign was a dark moment in the history of Yahweh's chosen Davidic line.

F. 17:1-41
THE DOWNFALL OF THE NORTHERN
KINGDOM; THEOLOGICAL REFLECTIONS

17   In the twelfth year of Ahaz king of Judah Hoshea the son of Elah began to reign in Samaria over Israel, and he reigned nine years. [2]And he did what was evil in the sight of the Lord, yet not as the kings of Israel who were before him. [3]Against him came up Shalmaneser king of Assyria;

and Hoshea became his vassal, and paid him tribute. [4]But the king of Assyria found treachery in Hoshea; for he had sent messengers to So, king of Egypt, and offered no tribute to the king of Assyria, as he had done year by year; therefore the king of Assyria shut him up, and bound him in prison. [5]Then the king of Assyria invaded all the land and came to Samaria, and for three years he besieged it. [6]In the ninth year of Hoshea the king of Assyria captured Samaria, and he carried the Israelites away to Assyria, and placed them in Halah, and on the Habor, the river of Gozan, and in the cities of the Medes.

[7]And this was so, because the people of Israel had sinned against the Lord their God, who had brought them up out of the land of Egypt from under the hand of Pharaoh king of Egypt, and had feared other gods [8]and walked in the customs of the nations whom the Lord drove out before the people of Israel, and in the customs which the kings of Israel had introduced. [9]And the people of Israel did secretly against the Lord their God things that were not right. They built for themselves high places at all their towns, from watchtower to fortified city; [10]they set up for themselves pillars and Asherim on every high hill and under every green tree; [11]and there they burned incense on all the high places, as the nations did whom the Lord carried away before them. And they did wicked things, provoking the Lord to anger, [12]and they served idols, of which the Lord had said to them, "You shall not do this." [13]Yet the Lord warned Israel and Judah by every prophet and every seer, saying, "Turn from your evil ways and keep my commandments and my statutes, in accordance with all the law which I commanded your fathers, and which I sent to you by my servants the prophets." [14]But they would not listen, but were stubborn, as their fathers had been, who did not believe in the Lord their God. [15]They despised his statutes, and his covenant that he made with their fathers, and the warnings which he gave them. They went after false idols, and became false, and they followed the nations that were

round about them, concerning whom the Lord had commanded them that they should not do like them. ¹⁶And they forsook all the commandments of the Lord their God, and made for themselves molten images of two calves; and they made an Asherah, and worshiped all the host of heaven, and served Baal. ¹⁷And they burned their sons and their daughters as offerings, and used divination and sorcery, and sold themselves to do evil in the sight of the Lord, provoking him to anger. ¹⁸Therefore the Lord was very angry with Israel, and removed them out of his sight; none was left but the tribe of Judah only.

¹⁹Judah also did not keep the commandments of the Lord their God, but walked in the customs which Israel had introduced. ²⁰And the Lord rejected all the descendants of Israel, and afflicted them, and gave them into the hand of spoilers, until he had cast them out of his sight.

²¹When he had torn Israel from the house of David they made Jeroboam the son of Nebat king. And Jeroboam drove Israel from following the Lord and made them commit great sin. ²²The people of Israel walked in all the sins which Jeroboam did; they did not depart from them, ²³until the Lord removed Israel out of his sight, as he had spoken by all his servants the prophets. So Israel was exiled from their own land to Assyria until this day.

²⁴And the king of Assyria brought people from Babylon, Cuthah, Avva, Hamath, and Sepharvaim, and placed them in the cities of Samaria instead of the people of Israel; and they took possession of Samaria, and dwelt in its cities. ²⁵And at the beginning of their dwelling there, they did not fear the Lord; therefore the Lord sent lions among them, which killed some of them. ²⁶So the king of Assyria was told, "The nations which you have carried away and placed in the cities of Samaria do not know the law of the god of the land; therefore he has sent lions among them, and behold, they are killing them, because they do not know the law of the god of the land."²⁷Then the king of Assyria commanded, "Send there one of the priests whom you carried away thence; and let him go and

dwell there, and teach them the law of the god of the land." ²⁸So one of the priests whom they had carried away from Samaria came and dwelt in Bethel, and taught them how they should fear the Lord.

²⁹But every nation still made gods of its own, and put them in the shrines of the high places which the Samaritans had made, every nation in the cities in which they dwelt; ³⁰the men of Babylon made Succoth-benoth, the men of Cuth made Nergal, the men of Hamath made Ashima, ³¹and the Avvites made Nibhaz and Tartak; and the Sepharvites burned their children in the fire to Adrammelech and Anammelech, the gods of Sepharvaim. ³²They also feared the Lord, and appointed from among themselves all sorts of people as priests of the high places, who sacrificed for them in the shrines of the high places. ³³So they feared the Lord but also served their own gods, after the manner of the nations from among whom they had been carried away. ³⁴To this day they do according to the former manner.

They do not fear the Lord, and they do not follow the statutes or the ordinances or the law or the commandment which the Lord commanded the children of Jacob, whom he named Israel. ³⁵The Lord made a covenant with them, and commanded them, "You shall not fear other gods or bow yourselves to them or serve them or sacrifice to them; ³⁶but you shall fear the Lord, who brought you out of the land of Egypt with great power and with an outstretched arm; you shall bow yourselves to him, and to him you shall sacrifice. ³⁷And the statutes and the ordinances and the law and the commandment which he wrote for you, you shall always be careful to do. You shall not fear other gods, ³⁸and you shall not forget the covenant that I have made with you. You shall not fear other gods, ³⁹but you shall fear the Lord your God, and he will deliver you out of the hand of all your enemies." ⁴⁰However they would not listen, but they did according to their former manner.

⁴¹So these nations feared the Lord, and also served

their graven images; their children likewise, and their children's children — as their fathers did, so they do to this day.

1. *Comment.* The first unit (vv 1-6) consists of a brief report on the fall of Samaria and the end of the northern kingdom. Hoshea (cf. 15:30) is one of the few northern kings whose condemnation by the Deuteronomists is somewhat mitigated (v 2: cf. 3:2; 10:28-31), though the reason is not given. Some years after his accession (ca. 731), he reversed his previously pro-Assyrian stance, withheld the tribute due to his Assyrian overlord, and entered into secret negotiations with the Egyptians who were Assyria's rivals (vv 3-4). In punishment for this act of disloyalty Hoshea was arrested and imprisoned in Assyria (v 4b), and was heard of no more. The anti-Assyrian movement, however, continued in Samaria and an Assyrian reaction was inevitable. The city was besieged and taken by King Shalmaneser V, probably in the autumn of 722 B.C., a few months before the king's death (vv 5-6a).

Samaria's territory became an Assyrian province, and large numbers of its inhabitants (an Assyrian text speaks of 27, 290) were deported under the direction of Shalmaneser's successor, Sargon II, in 720 and the following years. Deportation of conquered or rebel populations was a regular practice in the Assyrian Empire and was accompanied by the settlement of colonists (themselves often deportees) in the depopulated areas (cf. v 24); it has been calculated that the various Assyrian kings forcibly transferred populations amounting to more than four million people.

The account of Samaria's fall provided the Deuteronomists with the opportunity to synthesize their theological comments on the northern kingdom (vv 7-41). Assyria is seen merely as the instrument of Yahweh's great wrath (vv 18, 23), which was provoked by Israel's sins of idolatry and cultic perversion (v 7 and passim). The stereotyped phraseology of these denunciations is familiar by now to readers of Kings, so it will suffice to note a few points of special interest.

The role of the prophets in Yahweh's relations with his people is stressed. No prophet is singled out by name; all are called "the servants of Yahweh" (vv 13, 23). In the Deuteronomistic view (which does not coincide entirely with the image of the pre-exilic prophets that emerges from the prophetic books) the main task of the prophets was to warn the people to turn from sin and obey the whole law of Yahweh as transmitted by a succession of prophets (v 13: cf. Deut 18:15ff); the prophets also threatened disaster if the people did not change their ways, and these threats have now been fulfilled (v 23). It can be noted that this composite picture of the prophetic function makes no mention of any message of hope or eschatological expectation.

Judah too was disobedient to the Lord's commandments, just as Israel had been (v 19), and the outcome was the same for both kingdoms (v 20). The perspective of these two verses is clearly that of the Deuteronomists' own time after the fall of Jerusalem, which shows that the long denunciation of Israel's sins in chap. 17 is meant to be applied in large mesure to Judah as well — all the more so, since there is no comparable piece of lengthy theological reflection in Kings on the fall of Jerusalem.

The religious situation of the new inhabitants of Samaria is described in vv 24-33. The worship of Yahweh continued there (that is the point of the lion-anecdote of vv 25-28), but it was mingled with all sorts of pagan abominations (vv 29-31). Future centuries of Jewish contempt for the Samaritans would be based in part on this description. It is not clear whether vv 34b-40 refer to the exiled Israelites or to those left behind in Samaria with the pagan colonists. In any case, the text stresses that even after the fall of Samaria the Israelites did not return wholeheartedly to Yahweh, as they could and should have done (cf. the repentance theme in Deut 30:1-10; 1 Kgs 8:46-53). Instead they persisted in their infidelity and lost all claim to be regarded as truly "children of Jacob" (v 34).

2. *Significance.* The present chapter is one of the key texts in the Deuteronomistic history. Though several layers

of Deuteronomistic theological interpretation have probably gone into its making, the main point is clear. Reflection on the disaster of 722 B.C. and its causes is meant to summon the readers to a decision of faith. It is not power politics that determine the destiny of God's people, it is how that people respond to the revealed will of their gracious Lord who has manifested himself to them as their liberator (vv 7, 36, 39).

VII.   2 Kgs 18:1 — 25:30
Judah from the Reign of Hezekiah to the Fall of Jerusalem

The final division of Kings covers the last period of Judah's existence as a kingdom, with a concluding note about the fate of her exiled king. Two of the kings, Hezekiah (chaps 18-20) and Josiah (chaps 22-23), are praised highly by the Deuteronomists. Even in these hopeful sections, however, shadows appear (cf. 20:12-19; 22:15-20; 23:26-30), and the darkness thickens in the reigns of the other kings especially the impious Manasseh (chap. 21). Judah slides inexorably to her ruin at the hands of the Babylonians who have succeeded the Assyrians as the major power of the area. But is disaster the last word? The concluding verses (25:27-30) tell of the release of the exiled Judaean king from his Babylonian prison but offer no comment on this event. The enigmatic ending of the Deuteronomistic history constitutes an invitation to the readers to reflect and (more importantly) to act on its message of wholehearted service of Yahweh according to his law.

A.   18:1 — 19:37
KING HEZEKIAH AND THE DELIVERANCE OF JERUSALEM

18 In the third year of Hoshea son of Elah, king of Israel, Hezekiah the son of Ahaz, king of Judah, began to reign.

²He was twenty-five years old when he began to reign, and he reigned twenty-nine years in Jerusalem. His mother's name was Abi the daughter of Zechariah. ³And he did what was right in the eyes of the Lord, according to all that David his father had done. ⁴He removed the high places, and broke the pillars, and cut down the Asherah. And he broke in pieces the bronze serpent that Moses had made, for until those days the people of Israel had burned incense to it; it was called Nehushtan. ⁵He trusted in the Lord the God of Israel; so that there was none like him among all the kings of Judah after him, nor among those who were before him. ⁶For he held fast to the Lord; he did not depart from following him, but kept the commandments which the Lord commanded Moses. ⁷And the Lord was with him; wherever he went forth, he prospered. He rebelled against the king of Assyria, and would not serve him. ⁸He smote the Philistines as far as Gaza and its territory, from watchtower to fortified city.

⁹In the fourth year of King Hezekiah, which was the seventh year of Hoshea son of Elah, king of Israel, Shalmaneser king of Assyria came up against Samaria and besieged it ¹⁰and at the end of three years he took it. In the sixth year of Hezekiah, which was the ninth year of Hoshea king of Israel, Samaria was taken. ¹¹The king of Assyria carried the Israelites away to Assyria, and put them in Halah, and on the Habor, the river of Gozan, and in the cities of the Medes, ¹²because they did not obey the voice of the Lord their God but transgressed his covenant, even all that Moses the servant of the Lord commanded; they neither listened nor obeyed.

¹³In the fourteenth year of King Hezekiah Sennacherib king of Assyria came up against all the fortified cities of Judah and took them. ¹⁴And Hezekiah king of Judah sent to the king of Assyria at Lachish, saying, "I have done wrong; withdraw from me; whatever you impose on me I will bear." And the king of Assyria required of Hezekiah king of Judah three hundred talents of silver and thirty talents of gold. ¹⁵And Hezekiah gave him all the silver

that was found in the house of the Lord, and in the treasuries of the king's house. ¹⁶At that time Hezekiah stripped the gold from the doors of the temple of the Lord, and from the doorposts which Hezekiah king of Judah had overlaid and gave it to the king of Assyria. ¹⁷And the king of Assyria sent the Tartan, the Rabsaris, and the Rabshakeh with a great army from Lachish to King Hezekiah at Jerusalem. And they went up and came to Jerusalem. When they arrived, they came and stood by the conduit of the upper pool, which is on the highway to the Fuller's Field. ¹⁸And when they called for the king, there came out to them Eliakim the son of Hilkiah, who was over the household, and Shebnah the secretary, and Joah the son of Asaph, the recorder.

¹⁹And the Rabshakeh said to them, "Say to Hezekiah, 'Thus says the great king, the king of Assyria: On what do you rest this confidence of yours? ²⁰Do you think that mere words are strategy and power for war? On whom do you now rely, that you have rebelled against me? ²¹Behold, you are relying now on Egypt, that broken reed of a staff, which will pierce the hand of any man who leans on it. Such is Pharaoh king of Egypt to all who rely on him. ²²But if you say to me, "We rely on the Lord our God," is it not he whose high places and altars Hezekiah has removed, saying to Judah and to Jerusalem, "You shall worship before this altar in Jerusalem"? ²³Come now, make a wager with my master the king of Assyria: I will give you two thousand horses, if you are able on your part to set riders upon them. ²⁴How then can you repulse a single captain among the least of my master's servants, when you rely on Egypt for chariots and for horsemen? ²⁵Moreover, is it without the Lord that I have come up against this place to destroy it? The Lord said to me, Go up against this land, and destroy it.' "

²⁶Then Eliakim the son of Hilkiah, and Shebnah, and Joah, said to the Rabshakeh, "Pray, speak to your servants in the Aramaic language, for we understand it; do not speak to us in the language of Judah within the

hearing of the people who are on the wall." ²⁷But the Rabshakeh said to them, "Has my master sent me to speak these words to your master and to you, and not to the men sitting on the wall, who are doomed with you to eat their own dung and to drink their own urine?"

²⁸Then the Rabshakeh stood and called out in a loud voice in the language of Judah: "Hear the word of the great king, the king of Assyria! ²⁹Thus says the king: 'Do not let Hezekiah deceive you, for he will not be able to deliver you out of my hand. ³⁰Do not let Hezekiah make you to rely on the Lord by saying, The Lord will surely deliver us, and this city will not be given into the hand of the king of Assyria.' ³¹Do not listen to Hezekiah; for thus says the king of Assyria: 'Make your peace with me and come out to me; then every one of you will eat of his own vine, and every one of his own fig tree, and every one of you will drink the water of his own cistern; ³²until I come and take you away to a land like your own land, a land of grain and wine, a land of bread and vineyards, a land of olive trees and honey, that you may live, and not die. And do not listen to Hezekiah when he misleads you by saying, The Lord will deliver us. ³³Has any of the gods of the nations ever delivered his land out of the hand of the king of Assyria? ³⁴Where are the gods of Hamath and Arpad? Where are the gods of Sepharvaim, Hena, and Ivvah? Have they delivered Samaria out of my hand? ³⁵Who among all the gods of the countries have delivered their countries out of my hand, that the Lord should deliver Jerusalem out of my hand?' "

³⁶But the people were silent and answered him not a word, for the king's command was, "Do not answer him." ³⁷Then Eliakim the son of Hilkiah, who was over the household, and Shebna the secretary, and Joah the son of Asaph, the recorder, came to Hezekiah with their clothes rent, and told him the words of the Rabshakeh.

19   When King Hezekiah heard it, he rent his clothes, and covered himself with sackcloth, and went into the house of the Lord. ²And he sent Eliakim, who was over the household, and Shebna the secretary, and the senior priests, covered with sackcloth, to the prophet Isaiah the son of Amoz. ³They said to him, "Thus says Hezekiah, This day is a day of distress, of rebuke, and of disgrace; children have come to the birth, and there is no strength to bring them forth. ⁴It may be that the Lord your God heard all the words of the Rabshakeh, whom his master the king of Assyria has sent to mock the living God, and will rebuke the words which the Lord your God has heard; therefore lift up your prayer for the remnant that is left." ⁵When the servants of King Hezekiah came to Isaiah, ⁶Isaiah said to them, "Say to your master, 'Thus says the Lord: Do not be afraid because of the words that you have heard, with which the servants of the king of Assyria have reviled me. ⁷Behold, I will put a spirit in him, so that he shall hear a rumor and return to his own land; and I will cause him to fall by the sword in his own land.' "

⁸The Rabshakeh returned, and found the king of Assyria fighting against Libnah; for he heard that the king had left Lachish. ⁹And when the king heard concerning Tirhakah king of Ethiopia, "Behold, he has set out to fight against you," he sent messengers again to Hezekiah, saying, ¹⁰"Thus shall you speak to Hezekiah king of Judah: 'Do not let your God on whom you rely deceive you by promising that Jerusalem will not be given into the hand of the king of Assyria. ¹¹Behold, you have heard what the kings of Assyria have done to all lands, destroying them utterly. And shall you be delivered? ¹²Have the gods of the nations delivered them, the nations which my fathers destroyed, Gozan, Haran, Rezeph, and the people of Eden who were in Telassar? ¹³Where is the king of Hamath, the king of Arpad, the king of the city of Sepharvaim, the king of Hena, or the king of Ivvah?' "

¹⁴Hezekiah received the letter from the hand of the messengers, and read it; and Hezekiah went up to the house of the Lord, and spread it before the Lord. ¹⁵And Hezekiah prayed before the Lord, and said: "O Lord the

God of Israel, who art enthroned above the cherubim, thou art the God, thou alone, of all the kingdoms of the earth; thou hast made heaven and earth. [16]Incline thy ear, O Lord, and hear; open thy eyes, O Lord, and see; and hear the words of Sennacherib, which he has sent to mock the living God. [17]Of a truth, O Lord, the kings of Assyria have laid waste the nations and their lands, [18]and have cast their gods into the fire; for they were no gods, but the work of men's hands, wood and stone; therefore they were destroyed. [19]So now, O Lord our God, save us, I beseech thee, from his hand, that all the kingdoms of the earth may know that thou, O Lord, art God alone."

[20]Then Isaiah the son of Amoz sent to Hezekiah saying, "Thus says the Lord, the God of Israel: Your prayer to me about Sennacherib king of Assyria I have heard. [21]This is the word that the Lord has spoken concerning him:

"She despises you, she scorns you —
  the virgin daughter of Zion;
she wags her head behind you —
  the daughter of Jerusalem.

[22]"Whom have you mocked and reviled?
  Against whom have you raised your voice
  and haughtily lifted your eyes?
  Against the Holy One of Israel!
[23]By your messengers you have mocked the Lord,
  and you have said, 'With my many chariots
  I have gone up the heights of the mountains,
    to the far recesses of Lebanon;
  I felled its tallest cedars,
    its choicest cypresses;
  I entered its farthest retreat,
    its densest forest.
[24]I dug wells
    and drank foreign waters,
  and I dried up with the sole of my foot
    all the streams of Egypt.'

²⁵"Have you not heard
 that I determined it long ago?
 I planned from days of old
  what now I bring to pass,
 that you should turn fortified cities
  into heaps of ruins,
²⁶while their inhabitants, shorn of strength
 are dismayed and confounded,
 and have become like plants of the field,
 and like tender grass.
 like grass on the housetops;
  blighted before it is grown?

²⁷"But I know your sitting down
  and your going out and coming in,
  and your raging against me.
²⁸Because you have raged against me
  and your arrogance has come into my ears
 I will put my hook in your nose
  and my bit in your mouth,
 and I will turn you back on the way by which you
  came.

²⁹"And this shall be the sign for you: this year you shall eat what grows of itself, and in the second year what springs of the same; then in the third year sow, and reap, and plant vineyards, and eat their fruit. ³⁰And the surviving remnant of the house of Judah shall again take root downward, and bear fruit upward; ³¹ for out of Jerusalem shall go forth a remnant, and out of Mount Zion a band of survivors. The zeal of the Lord will do this.

³²"Therefore thus says the Lord concerning the king of Assyria, He shall not come into this city or shoot an arrow there, or come before it with a shield or cast up a siege mound against it. ³³By the way that he came, by the same he shall return, and he shall not come into this city, says the Lord. ³⁴For I will defend this city to save it, for my own sake and for the sake of my servant David."

³⁵And that night the angel of the Lord went forth, and slew a hundred and eighty-five thousand in the camp of the Assyrians; and when men arose early in the morning, behold, these were all dead bodies. ³⁶Then Sennacherib king of Assyria departed, and went home, and dwelt at Nineveh. ³⁷And as he was worshiping in the house of Nisroch his god, Adrammelech and Sharezer, his sons, slew him with the sword, and escaped into the land of Ararat. And Esarhaddon his son reigned in his stead.

1. *Comment.* Hezekiah's reign is described in chaps 18-20. Much of this material (18:13; 18:17-20:19) is found also (with small textual variants at times) in Isa 36:1 — 39:8. It probably came from a separate collection of traditions and legends about Hezekiah and Isaiah that grew up in the circles interested in the transmission and development of Isaian material after the prophet's death. The Deuteronomists inserted these traditions into their presentation of Hezekiah's reign, with some editorial adjustments. Later on, the material was inserted as an appendix to the first part of the Book of Isaiah, with further adjustments and some additions by the Isaian editors.

The opening Deuteronomistic presentation of Hezekiah's reign (ca. 725-697) is very favourable indeed (vv 1-8); v 5b in fact says that he was the best of all the Judaean kings (see however the comment on Josiah's reign at 23:25). The reason for this praise is the Deuteronomists' view of the king's cultic measures (v 4). His abolition of the local sanctuaries and destruction of the cultic symbols of Canaanite religion (the "pillars" and the "Asherah": v 4a) are seen as an anticipation of the great cultic centralization carried out by King Josiah in accordance with the Deuteronomic law (cf. chaps 22-23). A particular, and curious, detail is given in v 4b: Hezekiah destroyed a much venerated bronze serpent image which popular piety had associated with Moses (cf. Num 21:4-9); in reality this cultic symbol probably had its origins in pre-Israelite religion. These measures are seen as expressions of the king's admirable religious dispositions: his trust in Yahweh (v 5: "trust" is a key term in chaps 18-19 where the root occurs ten times in various forms), and his fidelity to the law of Moses (v 6). In consequence the king's policy of national resurgence was favoured by the Lord (vv 7-8).

Though the Deuteronomists do not mention Hezekiah's nationalistic policy until the end of their introduction (vv 7b-8), it seems historically likely that his religious measures had a political dimension from the start. His attempts to shake off the yoke of Assyrian vassalage, which his father Ahaz had accepted, probably found ready support from groups of faithful Yahwists who had fled south after the fall of Samaria (722), bringing with them to Jerusalem early forms of Deuteronomic theology which had originated in northern Israel. The national independence movement and the religious ideals expressed in the Deuteronomic theology went hand in hand. It is difficult, however, to determine what exactly Hezekiah's religious measures consisted in and how extensively they were imposed, since vv 3-6 (except for v 4b) are phrased in largely stereotyped Deuteronomistic terms. One can at least say that it is hardly correct to limit Hezekiah's "reform" to the removal of Assyrian cultic symbols from the Jerusalem Temple where they would have functioned as signs of political overlordship, for it is doubtful whether the Assyrians ever officially imposed elements of their religion in this way on vassal states such as Judah.

The deliverance of Jerusalem from Assyrian attack in 701 B.C. is the subject of a series of traditions now linked together in 18:13 — 19:37. A brief account of Samaria's fall (18:9-12) forms a contrasting preface to the Jerusalem story. The moral is clear: Samaria fell because its kings and people were unfaithful to the Lord's commands, Jerusalem was saved in 701 because it had a pious king who allowed himself to be guided by the words of a prophet (Isaiah) and who trusted with his whole heart in Yahweh whose laws he faithfully observed. Hezekiah's rebellion which led to the crisis of 701 began four years previously, when the accession of the new Assyrian king, Sennacherib, was greeted by an almost general revolt of the Assyrian vassal-states both in Mesopotamia and in the Syro-Palestinian area. Sennacherib dealt first with the eastern rebels, then moved west, and by 701 was ready to subdue the Judaeans. Jerusalem's situation seemed hopeless, but the city emerged unscathed from the crisis. Our text contains three accounts of this momentous historical fact, which must already have seemed extraordinary in its being so much at variance with the normal Assyrian practice of savage repression.

The first account (henceforth Account A) is found in 18:13-16. This unit, based on an annalistic source, tells in sober non-theological language, how Hezekiah recognized the hopelessness of his situation and sent a message of abject submission to Sennacherib (v 14), who imposed a heavy punitive tribute which Hezekiah duly forwarded to the Assyrian king (vv 14b-16). Account A, then, sees the deliverance of Jerusalem as effected by submission and payment, not by a spectacular divine intervention. Assyrian sources are essentially in agreement with this presentation, which has every likelihood of reflecting the actual course of events.

A very different picture is given in 18:17 — 19:37. These verses are now presented as the continuation of the preceding unit but this is quite unlikely; 18:17ff, in fact, tell of two attempts made by the Assyrians to persuade the Jerusalemites to surrender — which they have already done at 18:14. What we have in 18:17ff is a collection, edited and expanded, of prophetic traditions whose markedly theological character is quite distinct from the annalistic report of Account A. Closer analysis, whose details cannot be given here, suggests that two separate traditions have been combined in 18:17ff; these can be approximately identified as 18:17 — 19:9a + 19:36-37 (Account B/1) and 19:9b-35 (Account B/2).

Account B/1 tells of an Assyrian embassy sent to Jerusalem under the leadership of a high official entitled the Rabshakeh, to demand the surrender of the city. The Rabshakeh in his two speeches (18:19-25, 28-35) uses a series of rhetorical and pseudo-theological arguments to show that Hezekiah and the Jerusalemites have no grounds for trust, neither in Egyptian military aid nor in Yahweh's benevolence. One can note especially the twisted theological statements of vv 22, 25, 30, 32b-35. "In whom can you trust?", says the voice of Assyrian might. The answer is shown by Hezekiah's humble recourse to the Lord (19:1), by his message to the prophet Isaiah (19:2-4), and by the latter's brief oracle (vv 5-7) which foretells the violent death of the Assyrian king (but does not mention the defeat of his army). The Rabshakeh returns to his king (vv 8-9a), and Account B/1 ends with the fufilment of Isaiah's words concerning Sennacherib's death (vv 36-37). (Assyrian sources show that Sennacherib was murdered in 681, twenty years after his confrontation with Jerusalem.)

Account B/2 (19:9b-35) follows roughly the same schema as B/1 but with significant differences. The Assyrian claims are presented more concisely (vv 10-13) and by anonymous messengers (the Rabshakeh is not mentioned here at all). Hezekiah's prayer is now quoted (vv 15-19: contrast v 1); Isaiah's oracles (vv 20-28, 29-31, 32-34) are much longer than in the preceding account (though some of them may be secondary insertions), and their focus is on the deliverance of the city rather than on the death of Sennacherib (cf. vv 32-34 especially). The deliverance comes about in the extraordinary divine intervention told in v 35: an angel of Yahweh slays 185,000 of the Assyrian army in their camp. (The readers are not told how; perhaps one is to think of a plague as in 2 Sam 24:15-17.) It is likely that Account B/2 originally ended by noting the departure of the Assyrian remnant and their king, but this ending has been omitted in favour of the ending of Account B/1 (vv 36-37). One can note, then, that Account B/2 lays greater stress on Hezekiah's piety, gives greater prominence to Isaiah, and has a more spectacular climax than Account B/1.

It is difficult to determine the relations between Accounts B/1 and B/2 on the one hand, and Account A (together with the Assyrian sources) on the other. Some scholars have tried to find a historical setting for B/1 and B/2 in the context of an alleged second invasion by Sennacherib, either a short time after the first one or some years later; the problem here, however, is that the extra-biblical sources say nothing of a second campaign and the biblical material too presents several internal difficulties for this hypothesis. It may be better to see Accounts B/1 and B/2 as essentially theological in nature, confessions of faith rather than historical reports (this is not to exclude the presence of isolated historical data within these accounts). Their authors were familiar with Isaian themes (both those originating with the prophet himself and those developed by later redactors especially during the time of King Josiah): see especially Isa 14:24-27; 17:12-14; 29:5-8. In this hypothesis, then, a historical account of the events of 701 is found only in 2 Kgs 18:13-16; all that follows is primarily a theological meditation in narrative form on the historical fact that Jerusalem escaped assault and devastation, a meditation that magnified the event in the context of Yahweh's promises to his chosen House of David and the chosen city of Jerusalem-Zion.

2. *Significance.*   Where the Lord of history finds true fidelity, trust, prayer, and respect for his word announced by his prophets, he can effortlessly overthrow the most powerful of assailants, and grant deliverance to his king, his city, and his people. The implication is — and readers of the Deuteronomistic history during the Exile could not fail to note this — that if Jerusalem ever fell, then it would not be due to lack of power on Yahweh's part but rather to the absence of sincere obedience and deep trust on the part of king and people.

B.   20:1-21
HEZEKIAH'S ILLNESS: THE BABYLONIAN
EMBASSY

1. *Comment.*   The chapter presents two further accounts of meetings between Isaiah and King Hezekiah: first on the occasion of the king's illness (vv 1-11), then during the visit of a Babylonian embassy (vv 12-19). The Deuteronomistic closing formulas for Hezekiah's reign follow in vv 20-21.

In the first unit one can note how the king's prayer (v 3)

stresses his blameless conduct in terms close to Deuterono-mistic language. The prayer of a blameless king is answered by an act of gracious favour on Yahweh's part; Hezekiah will recover from his illness and live for another fifteen years (cf. 18:2 with 18:13), and Jerusalem will be delivered from the Assyrians (vv 5-6). The remedy which Isaiah proposes for Hezekiah's boil in v 7 seems somewhat in tension with the sign recounted in vv 8-11, all the more so if the verbs in v 7b (rendered by the RSV as imperatives) are translated in accordance with the Hebrew as past tenses ("they took and laid it on the boil and he recovered"). Either v 7 is out of place, or the sign originally belonged in another context.

The sign-action consists basically in the shortening of a shadow which would otherwise lengthen as the hours pass (vv 9-11). There is some doubt as to where the shadow is said to have been observed: the RSV speaks of a sun-dial (v 11), but the Hebrew term could also be understood of an exter-nal stairway leading to an upper building whose shadow was cast on the steps (cf. 23:12).

The story about the Babylonian embassy (vv 12-19) is presented as an immediate sequel of the preceding account, which itself is set in the time of the Assyrian threat to Jerusalem in 701 (v 6). But the presence of a Babylonian embassy in the west around 701 is historically most unlikely, since the Babylonians had been reduced to subjection by the Assyrians before that year. If there is any historical basis to the episode, it must refer to a period when the Babylonian king was in revolt against Assyria (around 711, or more probably in 703) and was seeking allies in the west. In any case, the point of the story is to criticize Hezekiah for the enthusiastic welcome he is pictured as giving to the embassy (v 13). Reliance on foreign aid had been condemned many times by Isaiah (e.g. Isa 30:1-7, 15-17; 31:1-3), so the prophet's intervention here is no surprise. Having question-ed Hezekiah about his actions in authoritative tones (vv 14-15), he then delivers an oracle of doom about the looting of Jerusalem's treasures by the Babylonians (v 17) and the captivity of Hezekiah's descendants (v 18). This received its first fulfilment in the deportation of 597 B.C. (cf. 24:10-17). Hezekiah's reaction (v 19) seems rather selfish; the king is shown in a less favourable light here than in the preceding episodes.

2.   *Significance.*   The main concern of chap. 20 is with the theological message. As in chaps 18-19 the focus is on the destiny of the Davidic king and the city of Jerusalem, but the tone is less optimistic now. The need for total religious fidelity on the part of the king is stressed (v 3), and the lack of trust in Yahweh that he showed by turning to foreign powers will bring its own fitting punishment at the hands of those same powers. Deliverance by Yahweh is not an automatic process, nor does the fact that he chose king and city constitute a guarantee of their survival; the response of trustful obedience is indispensable.

C.   21:1-26
THE WICKED KING MANASSEH AND HIS SON AMON

1.   *Comment.*   The Deuteronomistic editors leave their readers in no doubt as to the disastrous state of religion in Judah during the reign of Hezekiah's son, Manasseh. The local sanctuaries, whose suppression by Hezekiah had been mentioned at 18:4, flourished again (v 3a). Canaanite cults had royal approval and even found a place within the Jerusalem Temple (vv 4, 7). Astral worship ("the host of heaven": vv 3b, 5) was practised as well; here we may see the influence of Assyrian religion, though it is not necessary to think that it was imposed by the imperial power. Small wonder then that the Deuteronomists compare Manasseh with the wicked king Ahab of Israel (vv 3, 13: cf. 1 Kgs 16: 30-33; 21:20-26), in whose reign Canaanite worship seriously threatened the religion of Yahweh.

The Lord's sentence is pronounced (in Deuteronomistic terms) by "his servants the prophets" (v 10). Though Manasseh is blamed as the arch-sinner (v 11), he is not singled out for punishment. The fact was that he died peacefully (v 18) after the longest reign of any of the Judaean kings (ca. 696-642) — surely one of those cases where the common belief in direct retribution during the person's life must have created problems (as the treatment of Manasseh in 2 Chr 33:10-20 confirms). The Lord's drastic sentence is for Judah and Jerusalem as a whole (vv 12-15); one can note that v 14 appears to deny the validity of any form of "remnant" theology as providing hope for a new beginning after the catastrophe, and the image of v 13b is in line with this.

Though the Deuteronomists say nothing at all about political conditions during Manasseh's reign, it is these that can help us to understand in some measure the religious deterioration of Judah. The Assyrian Empire was at its most powerful during this period; Egypt itself had fallen in 663 B.C. Nationalistic resistance in Judah was simply unthinkable and one can well imagine that Hezekiah's religious policies were seen by many as a calamitous mistake, since their outcome was an even greater degree of political subservience to Assyria. The resurgence of Canaanite religion and the practice of Assyrian astral cults could well have been favoured not only by the personal intervention of Manasseh (as chap. 21 presents it) but also by some measure of popular inclination too.

Manasseh's successor, Amon (vv 19ff), had a short reign (ca. 641-640). He continued the religious policies of his father (vv 20-22) and was assassinated in a palace conspiracy (v 23), perhaps the work of an anti-Assyrian party. The rural notables of Judah ("the people of the land": v 24) saw to it, however, that he was succeeded by a Davidic prince, his son Josiah (compare 11:17-20; 14:19-21).

2. *Significance.* The closing years of Judah's independent existence are depicted by the Deuteronomists as an alternation of good and bad reigns. Hezekiah's was one of light (for the most part), Manasseh's is one of deepest darkness whose baneful effects will outlast their originator (cf. 23:26; 24:3-4). The mention of Josiah's name at the end of the chapter (v 26) serves to dispel the gloom momentarily.

D.   22:1 — 23:30
JOSIAH'S RELIGIOUS REFORM AND HIS TRAGIC END

22 Josiah was eight years old when he began to reign, and he reigned thirty-one years in Jerusalem. His mother's name was Jedidah the daughter of Adiah of Bozkath. [2]And he did what was right in the eyes of the Lord, and walked in all the way of David his father, and he did not turn aside to the right hand or to the left.

[3]In the eighteenth year of King Josiah, the king sent Shaphan the son of Azaliah, son of Meshullam, the secretary, to the house of the Lord, saying, [4]"Go up to Hilkiah the high priest, that he may reckon the amount of the money which has been brought into the house of the Lord, which the keepers of the threshold have collected from the people; [5]and let it be given into the hand of the workmen who have the oversight of the house of the Lord; and let them give it to the workmen who are at the house of the Lord, repairing the house, [6]that is, to the carpenters, and to the builders, and to the masons, as well as for buying timber and quarried stone to repair the house. [7]But no accounting shall be asked from them for the money which is delivered into their hand, for they deal honestly."

[8]And Hilkiah the high priest said to Shaphan the secretary, "I have found the book of the law in the house of the Lord." And Hilkiah gave the book to Shaphan, and he read it. [9]And Shaphan the secretary came to the king, and reported to the king, "Your servants have emptied out the money that was found in the house, and have delivered it into the hand of the workmen who have the oversight of the house of the Lord." [10]Then Shaphan the secretary told the king, "Hilkiah the priest has given me a book." And Shaphan read it before the king.

[11]And when the king heard the words of the book of the law, he rent his clothes. [12]And the king commanded Hilkiah the priest, and Ahikam the son of Shaphan, and Achbor the son of Micaiah, and Shaphan the secretary,

and Asaiah the king's servant, saying, [13]"Go, inquire of the Lord for me, and for the people, and for all Judah, concerning the words of this book that has been found; for great is the wrath of the Lord that is kindled against us, because our fathers have not obeyed the words of this book, to do according to all that is written concerning us."

[14]So Hilkiah the priest, and Ahikam, and Achbor, and Shaphan, and Asaiah went to Huldah the prophetess, the wife of Shallum the son of Tikvah, son of Harhas, keeper of the wardrobe (now she dwelt in Jerusalem in the Second Quarter); and they talked with her. [15]And she said to them, "Thus says the Lord, the God of Israel: 'Tell the man who sent you to me, [16]Thus says the Lord, Behold, I will bring evil upon this place and upon its inhabitants, all the words of the book which the king of Judah has read. [17]Because they have forsaken me and have burned incense to other gods, that they might provoke me to anger with all the work of their hands, therefore my wrath will be kindled against this place, and it will not be quenched. [18]But as to the king of Judah, who sent you to inquire of the Lord, thus shall you say to him, Thus says the Lord, the God of Israel: Regarding the words which you have heard, [19]because your heart was penitent, and you humbled yourself before the Lord, when you heard how I spoke against this place, and against its inhabitants, that they should become a desolation and a curse, and you have rent your clothes and wept before me, I also have heard you, says the Lord. [20]Therefore, behold, I will gather you to your fathers, and you shall be gathered to your grave in peace, and your eyes shall not see all the evil which I will bring upon this place.'" And they brought back word to the king.

23 Then the king sent, and all the elders of Judah and Jerusalem were gathered to him. [2]And the king went up to the house of the Lord, and with him all the men of Judah and all the inhabitants of Jerusalem, and the priests and the prophets, all the people, both small and great; and he read in their hearing all the words of the book of the covenant which had been found in the house of the Lord. ³And the king stood by the pillar and made a covenant before the Lord, to walk after the Lord and to keep his commandments and his testimonies and his statutes, with all his heart and all his soul, to perform the words of this covenant that were written in this book; and all the people joined in the covenant.

⁴And the king commanded Hilkiah, the high priest, and the priests of the second order, and the keepers of the threshold, to bring out of the temple of the Lord all the vessels made for Baal, for Asherah, and for all the host of heaven; he burned them outside Jerusalem in the fields of the Kidron, and carried their ashes to Bethel. ⁵And he deposed the idolatrous priests whom the kings of Judah had ordained to burn incense in the high places at the cities of Judah and round about Jerusalem; those also who burned incense to Baal, to the sun, and the moon, and the constellations, and all the host of the heavens. ⁶And he brought out the Asherah from the house of the Lord, outside Jerusalem, to the brook Kidron, and burned it at the brook Kidron, and beat it to dust and cast the dust of it upon the graves of the common people. ⁷And he broke down the houses of the male cult prostitutes which were in the house of the Lord, where the women wove hangings for the Asherah. ⁸And he brought all the priests out of the cities of Judah, and defiled the high places where the priests had burned incense, from Geba to Beersheba; and he broke down the high places of the gates that were at the entrance of the gate of Joshua the governor of the city, which were on one's left at the gate of the city. ⁹However, the priests of the high places did not come up to the altar of the Lord in Jerusalem, but they ate unleavened bread among their brethren. ¹⁰And he defiled Topheth, which is in the valley of the sons of Hinnom, that no one might burn his son or his daughter as an offering to Molech. ¹¹And he removed the horses that the kings of Judah had dedicated to the sun, at the

entrance to the house of the Lord, by the chamber of Nathan-melech the chamberlain, which was in the precincts; and he burned the chariots of the sun with fire. [12]And the altars on the roof of the upper chamber of Ahaz, which the kings of Judah had made, and the altars which Manasseh had made in the two courts of the house of the Lord, he pulled down and broke in pieces, and cast the dust of them into the brook Kidron. [13]And the king defiled the high places that were east of Jerusalem, to the south of the mount of corruption, which Solomon the king of Israel had built for Ashtoreth the abomination of the Sidonians, and for Chemosh the abomination of Moab, and for Milcom the abomination of the Ammonites. [14]And he broke in pieces the pillars, and cut down the Asherim, and filled their places with the bones of men.

[15]Moreover the altar at Bethel, the high place erected by Jeroboam the son of Nebat, who made Israel to sin, that altar with the high place he pulled down and he broke in pieces its stones, crushing them to dust; also he burned the Asherah. [16]And as Josiah turned, he saw the tombs there on the mount; and he sent and took the bones out of the tombs, and burned them upon the altar, and defiled it, according to the word of the Lord which the man of God proclaimed, who had predicted these things. [17]Then he said, "What is yonder monument that I see?" And the men of the city told him, "It is the tomb of the man of God who came from Judah and predicted these things which you have done against the altar at Bethel." [18]And he said, "Let him be; let no man move his bones." So they let his bones alone, with the bones of the prophet who came out of Samaria. [19]And all the shrines also of the high places that were in the cities of Samaria, which kings of Israel had made, provoking the Lord to anger, Josiah removed; he did to them according to all that he had done at Bethel. [20]And he slew all the priests of the high places who were there, upon the altars, and burned the bones of men upon them. Then he returned to Jerusalem.

²¹And the king commanded all the people, "Keep the passover to the Lord your God, as it is written in this book of the covenant." ²²For no such passover had been kept since the days of the judges who judged Israel, or during all the days of the kings of Israel or of the kings of Judah; ²³but in the eighteenth year of King Josiah this passover was kept to the Lord in Jerusalem.

²⁴Moreover Josiah put away the mediums and the wizards and the teraphim and the idols and all the abominations that were seen in the land of Judah and in Jerusalem, that he might establish the words of the law which were written in the book that Hilkiah the priest found in the house of the Lord. ²⁵Before him there was no king like him, who turned to the Lord with all his heart and with all his soul and with all his might, according to all the law of Moses; nor did any like him arise after him.

²⁶Still the Lord did not turn from the fierceness of his great wrath, by which his anger was kindled against Judah, because of all the provocations with which Manasseh had provoked him. ²⁷And the Lord said, "I will remove Judah also out of my sight, as I have removed Israel, and I will cast off this city which I have chosen, Jerusalem, and the house of which I said, My name shall be there."

²⁸Now the rest of the acts of Josiah, and all that he did, are they not written in the Book of the Chronicles of the Kings of Judah? ²⁹In his days Pharaoh Neco king of Egypt went up to the king of Assyria to the river Euphrates. King Josiah went to meet him; and Pharaoh Neco slew him at Megiddo, when he saw him. ³⁰And his servants carried him dead in a chariot from Megiddo, and brought him to Jerusalem, and buried him in his own tomb. And the people of the land took Jehoahaz the son of Josiah, and anointed him, and made him king in his father's stead.

1.   *Comment.*   The importance of Josiah's reign is shown by the superlative terms of approval (22:2; 23:25) with which

the Deuteronomists comment on the king's actions, and by the way in which Josiah's reforms are shown to synthesize and bring to perfection the partial cultic reforms of his predecessors, notably Jehoash (2 Kgs 12) and Hezekiah (18:3-6). The positive climax of the Deuteronomistic history is found in chaps 22-23; what comes afterwards is a tragic epilogue.

a)   *Historical setting:* The religious themes stressed by the text can be understood more concretely when one notes that Josiah's reign (ca. 639-609) coincided with the downfall of the Assyrian Empire. Torn by internal dissension and under pressure from outside by various northern and eastern peoples, the Assyrians were forced on the defensive (ca. 630) and their hold on the outlying provinces and vassal-states weakened. Josiah thus found himself in the position to act with ever greater autonomy. A movement of national revival gathered impetus, one of whose components (for the Deuteronomists, the decisive one) was the restoration and purification of the traditional religion. It is interesting to note that similar revival movements, also with religious aspects, were taking place about this time in Babylon and Egypt, both of which had been subject to Assyria.

b)   *The finding of the book of the law:* After the Deuteronomistic introduction (22:1-2), the first main part of the account of Josiah's reign (22:3 — 23:3) deals with the discovery of a book of religious law in the Jerusalem Temple in Josiah's eighteenth year (ca. 622) and the effect that this had on the king. The circumstances of the finding are described in 22:4-7; one can note how closely these directives about Temple repair-work resemble those mentioned in King Jehoash's time (2 Kgs 12:4-16). The theological point is that Josiah's zeal for the Temple of Yahweh was the occasion for the discovery of the book of the law. The book is read to the king who, shocked to discover the distance between the Lord's commands and the present state of the people, realizes that a major reform is needed to avert Yahweh's wrath (22:10-13).

In this critical situation Josiah seeks prophetical guidance, and his high officials go to ask an oracle from Huldah the prophetess, wife of a Temple functionary (vv 13-14). Her connection with the Temple establishment may explain why the officials went to her, rather than to Jeremiah who (according to most scholars) had already begun his ministry by this time. Huldah's oracle has two parts: vv 15-17 proclaim (in typically Deuteronomistic language) the doom of Jerusalem for its infidelity to the book of the law, no account being taken of any attempts at reform; vv 18-20 are addressed to Josiah personally, acknowledging his right response to the reading of the book and exempting him from being involved in the disasters soon to fall upon Jerusalem. If there is a pre-Deuteronomistic basis in Huldah's oracle, it can only be found within vv 18-20 where it appears to be said that the king will die a peaceful death (v 20a), which was not in fact the case (23:29-30); as they stand, however, vv 18-20 have been re-edited by the Deuteronomists.

The first unit concludes in 23:1-3 with the account of a solemn renewal of the covenant with Yahweh on the basis of the words of the book of the law, entered into by the king and all the people of Judah and Jerusalem (cf. 11:14, 17a).

For the Deuteronomists the book of the law discovered in the Temple during Josiah's reign undoubtedly corresponded to what we call the Book of Deuteronomy (or at least its nucleus). This is clear from important correspondences between 2 Kgs 22-23 and Deuteronomy: (1) the centralization of the cult in the place that Yahweh has chosen is a fundamental Deuteronomic requirement (Deut 12), and is the reason for Josiah's measures described in 23:4ff, many of which correspond to specific Deuteronomic laws; (2) Deut 28 contains fearful threats for the disobedient (cf. 2 Kgs 22:13, 16); (3) covenant is a basic theological category throughout Deuteronomy (cf. 2 Kgs 23:1-3). The Deuteronomists, then, see Josiah's actions as ruled by the Law of Moses presented by the Deuteronomic school, and this fits their concept of the ideal king (cf. Deut 17:18-20).

If one raises the question of the historical origins of

Deuteronomy (and this is not the main point of 2 Kgs 22), various hypotheses can be put forward. One of these would trace the origins of the Deuteronomic movement to northern Israel; after the fall of Samaria in 722 B.C. refugees from the north brought the proto-Deuteronomic traditions to Jerusalem where they were reworked over a period of time and deposited in the Temple archives. King Hezekiah, as noted above, may well have been influenced by aspects of the Deuteronomic theology, but in the long reign of his successor Manasseh, who was quite out of sympathy with those ideals, the Deuteronomic traditions would have been relegated to obscurity and, as far as public life was concerned, altogether forgotten. When the changed political situation made a national revival possible in Josiah's reign, the Temple priesthood could have judged the moment opportune to publicize the strongly nationalistic Deuteronomic tradition again. Hence the "finding" of the book of the law in the Temple (22:8).

c) *Religious reforms:* The account of Josiah's cultic reforms (23:4-20) is probably the work of several hands. Only a general picture can be given here. The reform probably began in Jerusalem where it was mainly concerned with those features of astral worship that had been admitted during the period of Assyrian domination (vv 5b, 11-12); then as Josiah extended his activity to those areas of Judah that had been seized by the Assyrians in Hezekiah's time, his reform was directed especially against the local sanctuaries where Canaanite fertility cults were an ever-present menace to Yahwism. Finally, as Assyrian power collapsed altogether, Josiah was able to extend his rule and his reforms over some areas of the former northern kingdom, especially the sanctuary of Bethel (vv 15-20); one can note here the theological anecdote about the bones of the Judaean man of God (vv 16-18) which links back to 1 Kgs 13 in the familiar Deuteronomistic pattern of prophecy and fulfilment.

The constructive side of the cultic reform consists in the establishment of Jerusalem as the sole legitimate centre for sacrificial worship in Judah and Israel; the new order of things is expressed by the great Passover celebration held at Jerusalem in the same year as the finding of the book (23:21-23; cf. 22:3). In its origins the Passover was a family celebration which did not involve pilgrimage to a central sanctuary (cf. Exod 12; 23:14-17). The Deuteronomic tradition, however, "nationalized" the feast by ordering its celebration only "at the place which the Lord will choose" (Deut 16:1-8); the Passover of the whole people of God can only be celebrated in Jerusalem. Josiah's Passover, the first fulfilment of this requirement, was a demonstration of religious and national unity that is hailed by the Deuteronomists (v 22) as a return to the founding ideals of Israel, expressed in Deuteronomy.

d)   *Josiah's death:* In 609 Pharaoh Neco moved north to aid the remnants of the Assyrian forces against the victorious Babylonians and Medes who had captured the Assyrian capital of Nineveh in 612. Josiah apparently tried to bar the Pharaoh's way at Megiddo in northern Israel and was killed there (23:29-30). The king's death in such circumstances must have caused widespread dismay: how could such an exemplary king have come to such a tragic end? One attempt to answer that question is found in vv 26-27: Manasseh's sins (cf. chap. 21) were so appalling that they outweighed, so to speak, Josiah's good actions; the wrath of Yahweh remained, and Josiah's death was the beginning of the end for Judah. From now on the path went straight downhill to the ruin of kingdom and city. Huldah's oracles in their present form (22:15-20) also reflect the debate about Josiah's death.

2.   *Significance.*   The king's tragic end does not take from the fact that the Deuteronomists look back on his reign as the ideal moment in the chequered course of monarchy in Israel and Judah after the time of David. But it can also constitute an inspiration for the future. It is by living their covenant commitment based on the book of the law (23:1-3) and rejecting all temptations to syncretism (23:4ff) that the exilic-period Judaeans can preserve and foster their identity

as Yahweh's chosen people and special possession. Jerusalem has fallen but the book of the law remains.

E. 23:31 — 24:17
FROM JOSIAH'S DEATH TO THE FIRST
DEPORTATION FROM JERUSALEM

1. *Comment.* Josiah's successor, Jehoahaz, had been installed by the rural notables of Judah (23:30); his sympathies must have been strongly nationalist and anti-Egyptian, as his father's had been. But he was deposed by Pharaoh Neco, who now controlled most of the Syro-Palestinian area, and led off to imprisonment and death in Egypt (vv 33-34). The Deuteronomists make a stereotyped comment on his wickedness (v 32); what is meant, presumably, is that Josiah's religious policies were allowed to lapse.

The Pharaoh then chose the deposed king's elder brother as Judah's new ruler, changing his name from Eliakim to Jehoiakim as an act of overlordship (v 34). The tribute imposed by the Egyptians was exacted by Jehoiakim from the Judaean rural nobility who had supported his predecessor (vv 33b, 35). The negative evaluation expressed by the Deuteronomists (v 37) is confirmed by the denunciations uttered by the prophet Jeremiah during this reign. Meanwhile the international context had changed: the Babylonians routed the Egyptians at the Battle of Carchemish in northern Syria in 605 B.C. and Judah now fell under Babylonian sway. Jehoiakim became a tribute-paying vassal of Nebuchadnezzar of Babylon (24:1), probably in 603. Some three years later, on the occasion of a reverse experienced by the Babylonians when they attempted to invade Egypt, the Judaean king threw off the yoke and rebelled (24:1). Initially the Babylonians themselves could not intervene in force, but they sent auxiliary troops and their loyal vassals to harass Judah (v 2). The Deuteronomists see this as the expression of the Lord's decision to destroy Judah for the sins of Manasseh (vv 2-4: v 2b probably refers back to 21:10-15); the terrible statement that the Lord refused to pardon Judah (v 4b) can be compared to Deut 29:20.

At this critical moment King Jehoiakim died (598 B.C.) and was succeeded by his son Jehoiachin (vv 6, 8ff). The Babylonian army laid siege to Jerusalem and shortly after Nebuchadnezzar's own arrival the city surrendered; a Babylonian chronicle gives the date, corresponding in our calendar to 16 March 597. The treasures of palace and Temple were carried off and the sacred vessels desecrated (v 13: cf. 20:17 and Jer 27:16). What is usually termed the First Deportation from Jerusalem then took place (vv 14-16): Jehoiachin and his family, the royal officials, the military officers and the elite troops, together with some groups of skilled artisans (armourers and the like) were carried off to exile in Babylon (perhaps in several stages). The deportees included some priests and prophets (cf. Jer 29:21ff), among them a member of a priestly family named Ezekiel who would be called to the prophetic ministry a few years later in Babylon (Ezek 1:1-3). The Babylonians installed as king in Jerusalem a third son of Josiah, changing his name from Mattaniah to Zedekiah (v 17: cf. 23:34). He was to be Judah's last king.

2. *Significance.* Josiah's admirable obedience to the book of the law is a thing of the past. His successors allowed the reform to lapse; the disasters that followed were the Lord's answer to this infidelity.

F. 24:18 — 25:30
THE FALL OF JERUSALEM AND DESTRUCTION OF THE TEMPLE; THE KING IN EXILE

1. *Comment.* Though installed as puppet king by the Babylonians, Zedekiah was unable to resist the pressure of the anti-Babylonian party in Jerusalem (cf. Jer 37:16 — 38:28) and after several years of vacillation he rebelled openly against Nebuchadnezzar (ca. 589 B.C.), hoping (vainly, as things turned out) for Egyptian aid. In the circumstances the revolt was an act of blind and suicidal folly without the slightest chance of success; the Deuteronomistic

reference to Yahweh's anger at 24:20 (cf. 23:26-27) says this in theological terms. The siege of Jerusalem was directed by Nebuchadnezzar in person (25:1). Though the inhabitants were reduced to dire straits by famine (v 3), the city did not surrender (as it had done ten years earlier) but had to be taken by storm in the summer of 587 or 586 (the date is disputed).

Zedekiah tried to escape eastwards, probably towards the Ammonites (cf. Ezek 21:19-20), but was captured near Jericho and taken to Nebuchadnezzar's western headquarters at Riblah in northern Syria (vv 4-6). There he paid the penalty for his violation of the oath of vassalage — an oath taken in Yahweh's name as well as that of the Babylonian gods (Ezek 17:13-21): his sons were executed before his eyes, he was then blinded and led off in chains to Babylon (v 7) where he disappears from history. Meanwhile back in Jerusalem the Babylonians set fire to the Temple, the royal palace, and the houses of the nobility, and razed the city walls to the ground (vv 8-10). A certain number of leading personages were executed (vv 18-21); others were deported to Babylon (v 11: the Second Deportation). The plundering of the Temple furnishings (vv 13-17) is described in technical language that recalls 1 Kgs 6-7 and points perhaps to the hand of a priestly chronicler. The period of the Exile had begun (v 21b).

The governor installed by the Babylonians, Gedaliah (a member of the influential but non-Davidic family of Shaphan: cf. 22:3ff), was murdered by a Davidic prince named Ishmael in his residence of Mizpah a short distance north of Jerusalem (vv 22-25). Fearing Babylonian reprisals, the Judaeans gathered at Mizpah fled to Egypt (v 26); Jeremiah the prophet (whose name is not mentioned in Kings) was taken with them against his will (cf. Jer 41-43). In this way the last of the maledictions threatened by Deut 28 for breach of Yahweh's covenant has come to pass, the return to Egypt (Deut 28:68); it is as if the Exodus has been undone.

The final verses of the Deuteronomistic history (2 Kgs 25:27-30) tell how the Davidic king, Jehoiachin, exiled in the first deportation (24:15), was rehabilitated in 561 B.C.

by the new king of Babylon, Evil-Merodach. Jehoiachin's release from prison and change of prison garments may signify that he was recognized once again as of effective royal standing; the "kindly" words of the Babylonian king in his regard (v 28a) may mean the re-establishment of official vassal-king status. If that is so, then Jehoiachin's new situation could be seen as a hint that the old promise to David had not been cancelled (cf. 2 Sam 7:14-16; 1 Kgs 11:39). Other interpretations, it is true, have been proposed for these last verses of Kings which lack explicit editorial comment. Some, for instance, would see them merely as a fading grace-note, telling of an act of personal favour for Jehoiachin without dynastic implications or future hope of any kind; others would see the insertion of these verses simply as a literary device to avoid ending the book inauspiciously on a totally negative note.

2. *Significance.* The warnings of disaster often proclaimed by Yahweh's prophets have become a reality; the unfaithful people and their king have been cast out from the Lord's presence (24:20). Now that the word of doom has been proved true, what of the word of eternal favour for the house of David (2 Sam 7)? The Deuteronomists do not dare, or do not feel able, to express hope in this regard here, but the account of Jehoiachin's release at least does not close the door on a Davidic future. In the meantime the call to sincere repentance remains (Deut 30:1-10; 1 Kgs 8:46-53) in accordance with the words of the book of the law; after that, the future is in the Lord's hands. The open ending of the Deuteronomistic history is above all a call to communitarian and personal re-commitment, in the light of a theological understanding of the lessons of history.

EXCURSUS:
THE DAVIDIC DYNASTY AND
THE HOLY CITY ZION

The taking of Jerusalem by David about 1000 B.C. brought the city into the mainstream of biblical and world history. The city was already old then: second millennium texts from Egypt mention Urusalim ("the foundation of the god Shalem") as an important town, and archaeologists have found traces of human settlement there that go back to the fourth millennium. Our concern, however, is to trace its biblical role, as a city and a symbol, in pre-NT times and to examine its connection with the Davidic dynasty. Several points in the following sketch have been discussed in rather more detail in the commentary above, to which the reader is referred.

I. Jerusalem and the Beginnings of the Davidic Dynasty

Shortly before the capture of Jerusalem David, who had been king of Judah already for almost seven years, was chosen as king of the northern Israelite tribes (2 Sam 5:1-5). The old Judaean centre of Hebron, up to then his royal residence, was too far south to serve as the capital of the united kingdoms. Jerusalem, on the contrary, situated as it was between Judah and Israel and belonging to David by personal title through his conquest of the city, was admirably fitted to become the capital of the new state.

The religious policies adopted by David and Solomon with regard to Jerusalem added to the city's already considerable political significance. David brought to Jerusalem the ark of God, which was the venerable cultic symbol of the northern tribes, and thus made his capital the religious centre for Israel too (2 Sam 6). Solomon completed this process by building there a magnificent Temple (1 Kgs 5-8). From then on, the religious significance of Jerusalem was closely associated with its role in the national life of the people; indeed in some traditions the religious aspects of the city would become autonomous.

In the same period the dynasty of David too received a religious significance through Nathan's oracle (2 Sam 7), which contained a promise of lasting divine favour for the house of David. Though the unconditional nature of this promise would be modified in other texts, as will be seen below, the theological significance of the Davidic dynasty remained a permanent acquisition for the people of God.

II. Jerusalem During the Period of the Monarchy

a) The Davidic kings: The personal union of the kingdoms of Israel and Judah under David and Solomon broke up shortly after the latter's death (1 Kgs 12). In the northern kingdom various royal families succeeded each other, often as a result of a violent *coup d'état*, but in Judah the throne was held by the Davidic dynasty right up to the end of the monarchy. The sole exception, the reign of Queen Athaliah (2 Kgs 11), was not tolerated for long. This dynastic stability rested in part on the dynastic oracle (2 Sam 7), but it is probable that the vital original link between Jerusalem and the house of David was another important factor in guaranteeing the continuance of the dynasty. On several occasions a Davidic king was overthrown and murdered by disaffected parties in Jerusalem, but each time the successor was the murdered king's son (2 Kgs 12:20-21; 14:19-21; 21:23-24) and the line of David remained unbroken.

b) The Temple becomes ever more central: Though the Jerusalem Temple was not the only place where Yahweh was worshipped publicly in Solomon's time (and for some three centuries afterwards), it was undoubtedly the most important cultic centre. The northern sanctuaries of Bethel and Dan, given official royal status by Jeroboam I (1 Kgs 12:26ff), were in no way equal to it in splendour. It was in the Jerusalem Temple that much of Israel's psalmody took shape and developed; the Jerusalem priesthood elaborated a code of ritual and ethical prescriptions whose final post-exilic form we read in the second half of the Book of Exodus, all of Leviticus, and much of Numbers. Ancient narrative traditions too, it would seem, were transmitted in priestly circles, and there is reason to believe that the redactors of Kings drew on priestly chronicles as sources for some of their descriptions (see 1 Kgs 6-7 especially).

A decisive change took place during the reign of King Josiah in the context of his religious reform (ca. 622 B.C.: cf. 2 Kgs 22-23). The Jerusalem Temple, already the most important cultic centre, was now officially declared to be the only legitimate place for sacrificial worship. The Deuteronomic insistence that the Israelites should sacrifice only "at the place which the Lord will choose" (Deut 12:14) was brought into effect by Josiah, when he destroyed various local sanctuaries and brought their priests to Jerusalem where they served as inferior functionaries in the Temple (2 Kgs 23:8-9). The Deuteronomistic theologians urged the principle of Jerusalem's cultic uniqueness with such force (making it one of the keys for their reading of Israel's history during the monarchical period) that after the Exile the people never seriously questioned the claim of the rebuilt Temple to be the sole legitimate place of worship. The priestly legislation in the Pentateuch developed the implications of this position, and centuries later it would provide the basis for the priestly christology of the Epistle to the Hebrews.

c)   The Zion tradition: Up to now our description of the importance of Jerusalem and its Temple has been formulated largely on the basis of historico-theological and legal texts. There are other OT texts, however, that depict the city's role in exalted poetic language, coloured at times by mythological motifs that can be found ou tside the Bible too (especially in the Ugaritic texts). Scholars are accustomed to refer here to the "Zion tradition". The term "Zion" itself originally referred to the old city occupied by David; later on, the word was applied also to the Temple mount north of the original settlement; eventually "Zion" became practically synonymous with Jerusalem in its whole extent, though it almost always had cultic and religious overtones. By "Zion tradition", then, is meant a complex of motifs which recur in various combinations in the so-called Zion psalms (Ps 46[45]; 48[47]; 76[75]) and in some prophetic texts such as Isa 17:12-14; 29:5-8. Among these motifs the following four can be noted in particular: Zion, a lofty and splendid mountain, is God's earthly abode (Ps 48[47]:1-2); the river of paradise flows out of it (Ps 46[45]:4); God has subjugated the unruly forces of cosmic chaos there (Ps 46[45]:1-3); hostile kings and peoples gather to attack the city but are routed by God's power (Ps 46[45]:5-7; 48[47]:4-6).

The main point of all this is to convey Zion's centrality both in cosmic and in historical terms, the city's unique place in God's designs and his special protection of Zion against all assaults. There is some discussion as to the origin of this complex of ideas and imagery. Some scholars see the Zion tradition as having come in large measure from the religious traditions of pre-Israelite Jerusalem; others trace its crystallization to the great imperial age of David and Solomon; others again see the deliverance of Jerusalem from the attack of King Sennacherib of Assyria in 701 B.C. (cf. 2 Kgs 18-19) as the decisive impetus especially for the growth of the invincibility motif; others finally prefer to see the developed form of the Zion tradition (as in Ps 46[45]; 48[47]) as a product of post-exilic eschatological hope.

Whatever of this question, it can be said that the Zion tradition as it stands in the completed OT offers a set of powerful hope-filled images that are open to transposition and reinterpretation in terms of Christian typology.

III. Jerusalem and the Davidic Dynasty as Focal Points of Future Hope

Our discussion of the Zion tradition has already touched on this aspect. Two further themes, of particular significance in the prophetical writings, can be added here.

a) The purification and renewal of Jerusalem: Among the various denunciations uttered by the pre-exilic prophets we find a series of texts directed specifically against the inhabitants of Jerusalem and in particular the ruling class (e.g. Isa 1:21ff; 3:1ff; 28:14ff; Jer 5:1ff); idolatrous worship and a widespread neglect of the demands of social justice are singled out for harsh condemnation. The Lord's response, in many of these texts, consists in announcing the imminent punishment of the wicked city. Isa 1:21ff, however, sees further than the merely punitive aspect, when it speaks of Yahweh's intention to purge out the dross and restore the city to its ideal state of integrity and justice. The same longing for a renewal of Jerusalem according to justice is found in Jer 33:15-16 in connection with the Davidic theme.

Other exilic and post-exilic texts develop further aspects of hope associated with Jerusalem. Second Isaiah, proclaiming his joyful message of liberation to the disheartened exiles, directs their thoughts and imagination to Zion, the goal of their return (Isa 40:9-11); the devastated city remains the privileged object of Yahweh's love (49:14-18) and will be rebuilt with new splendour (54:1-17), as befits its title of "holy city" (48:2; 52:1). When Jerusalem is thus restored, it will stand out like an island of light amid the darkness of the world (Isa 60:1-3); foreign nations will then stream towards Zion, bringing their treasures as homage (Isa 60-62) and seeking from the holy mountain the light of Yahweh's law

(Isa 2:2-5; Mic 4:1-4) and the benefits of his favour (Zech 8:20-23).

The closing chapters of the Book of Ezekiel (40-48) contain a detailed blueprint for the new living conditions of the people of Israel. The central place is occupied by the new Temple whose furnishings and cultic ministers are described in minute detail (chaps 40-44). This Temple will be filled with the glory of the Lord's presence (43:1-5), and the political life of Israel will be subordinated to its pre-eminent cultic function (45:7-17). In Ezek 47 we find a reflection of the Zion tradition motif of the river of paradise: a wonderful stream issues from the side of the Temple and gives life all along its course towards the eastern desert. The ultimate reason for all this is indicated in the new name which is to be given to Jerusalem: "The Lord is there" (Ezek 48:35). Finally one can note the eschatological poem of Isa 65:17-25 with its highly idealized description of the future Jerusalem as part of Yahweh's new creation.

b)   The ideal Davidic king to come: It was not long after the establishment of the Davidic dynasty that a complex of ideals and hopes began to crystallize about the figure of the king. Nathan's oracle (2 Sam 7) is a basic text in this regard, and a number of pre-exilic royal psalms can be mentioned here too (cf. Ps 2; 45[44]; 72[71]; 89[88]; 110[109]; 132[131]). The seemingly extravagant claims to universal dominion expressed in some of these psalms can probably be taken as traditional royal hyperboles that may have been adapted by the Judaean psalmists from pre-Israelite traditions.

Many of the Davidic kings failed, however, to live up to the high ideals of those texts. So we find several of the pre-exilic prophets sharply criticizing the shortcomings of the Davidic kings of their time (e.g. Isa 7:1-17; Jer 22:13-19), and the Deuteronomistic redactors of the Book of Kings later set out a more systematic critique based on the stance taken by the kings in cultic matters. Some texts in the Deuteronomistic history present the dynastic promise, no longer as an unconditional promise of abiding divine favour (as in 2 Sam 7), but as conditional to the king's obedience to the Law of Yahweh (e.g. 1 Kgs 2:4; 8:25; 9:4-5: cf. also Ps 132[131]:11-12).

Nevertheless the dynasty of David remained one of the sources of hope for the people's future. One can see this in the well-known "Advent" texts of Isa 9:2-7 and 11:1-9, which look forward to a faithful descendant of David whose reign will bring his people the blessings of justice, peace, and paradisiacal prosperity. These messianic passages are echoed in shorter prophetic texts such as Jer 33:14-18; Ezek 34:23-24; 37:24-25; Hos 3:5; Am 9:11-12; Mic 5:2-4. The future king, according to Zech 9:9-10, will be humble and peace-loving in the exercise of his universal dominion.

IV. Beyond the Canonical OT

The themes of Zion and the Davidic dynasty were further developed in various ways in intertestamental literature. Explicit mention is made of a "new Jerusalem" (Test. Dan 5:12), a phrase that does not occur in the OT itself; other texts speak of a heavenly Jerusalem which will descend to earth as the inauguration of Yahweh's definitive reign (2 Apoc. Bar. 4:2-6; 4 Ezra 13:36). The NT Apocalypse draws heavily on that tradition (cf. Rev 21-22) as well as on older prophetic themes.

The ideal Davidic king was seen by some groups within Judaism around the turn of the era as a glorious ruler who would rout his people's oppressors (the Romans) and establish a splendid messianic kingdom. The drastic reinterpretation given to these hopes by Jesus and the NT writers is too well known to need comment. But the OT Davidic ideals of social justice, peace among peoples, and harmony with nature remain as a powerful source of hope and an urgent challenge to Christian readers who see in the enthronement of Jesus, son of David, at the right hand of his heavenly Father the decisive beginning of his universal dominion.

CHRONOLOGICAL TABLE

In the present state of knowledge it is not possible to establish a precise chronology for the monarchical period in Israel that satisfies at once all the biblical data (as given in the Hebrew and Greek texts of the OT) and the extra-biblical synchronisms. The various systems proposed differ by ten or more years for some of the reigns. The following dates, then, must be taken simply as approximations; it will be noted that co-regencies are presumed on a number of occasions.

I.   The Origins of the Monarchy; the United Kingdoms
         Philistine victory at Aphek (ca. 1050)
         Samuel (ca. 1040)
         Saul (1030-1010)
         David (1010-970)
         Solomon (970-927)

II. The Separate Kingdoms of Israel and Judah

Israel	*Judah*
Jeroboam I (927-907)	Rehoboam (927-910)
	Abijam (910-908)
Nadab (907-906)	Asa (908-868)
Baasha (906-883)	
Elah (883-882)	
Zimri (882)	
Omri (882-871)	
Ahab (871-852)	Jehoshaphat (868-847)
Ahaziah (852-851)	
Jehoram (851-845)	Jehoram (847-845)
Jehu (845-818)	Ahaziah (845)
	Athaliah (845-840)
Jehoahaz (818-802)	Jehoash (840-801)
Joash (802-787)	Amaziah (801-773)
Jeroboam II (787-747)	Azariah/Uzziah (787-736)
Zechariah (747)	
Shallum (747)	
Menahem (747-738)	Jotham (756-741)
Pekahiah (737-736)	Ahaz (741-725)
Pekah (735-732)	
Hoshea (731-723)	Hezekiah (725-697)
Fall of Samaria: 722	

III. The Kingdom of Judah from 722 until the Exile

> Hezekiah (725-697)
> Manasseh (696-642)
> Amon (641-640)
> Josiah (639-609)
> Jehoahaz (609)
> Jehoiakim (608-598)
> Jehoiachin (598-597)
> Zedekiah (597-587/6)
> Fall of Jerusalem: 587 or 586
> Exile in Babylon until 538.

FOR FURTHER READING

I. The Deuteronomistic History

Childs, Brevard S., *Introduction to the Old Testament as Scripture* (Philadelphia: Fortress; London: SCM, 1979), espec. chaps XI, XIV, XV.

Kaiser, Otto, *Introduction to the Old Testament* (Oxford: Blackwell; Minneapolis: Augsburg, 1975), espec. chaps 14, 15, 16.

Nelson, Richard D., *The Double Redaction of the Deuteronomistic History* (Journal for the Study of the Old Testament, Supplement Series 18; Sheffield: JSOT Press, 1981).

Noth, Martin, *The Deuteronomistic History* (JSOT Supplement Series 15; Sheffield: JSOT Press, 1981). From the German original of 1943; of fundamental importance.

von Rad, Gerhard, *Old Testament Theology*. Vol. I: *The Theology of Israel's Historical Traditions* (Edinburgh: Oliver and Boyd, 1962), espec. pp. 306-347.

II.   Commentaries on Samuel

Ackroyd, Peter R., *The First Book of Samuel* (The Cambridge Bible Commentary on the New English Bible; Cambridge: University Press, 1971).

Ackroyd, Peter R., *The Second Book of Samuel* (CBCNEB; Cambridge: University Press, 1977).

Hertzberg, Hans Wilhelm, *I and II Samuel. A Commentary* (London: SCM; Philadelphia: Westminster, 1964).

McCarter, P. Kyle, Jr., *I Samuel* (The Anchor Bible, 8; Garden City, NY: Doubleday, 1980).

III.   Commentaries on Kings

Gray, John, *I and II Kings. A Commentary*. Third edition (London: SCM; Philadelphia: Westminster, 1977).

Robinson, J., *The First Book of Kings* (CBCNEB; Cambridge: University Press, 1972).

Robinson, J., *The Second Book of Kings* (CBCNEB; Cambridge: University Press, 1976).

IV.   Histories of Israel

Bright, John, *A History of Israel*. Third edition, completely revised and updated (Philadelphia: Westminster; London: SCM, 1981).

Hayes, John H., and J. Maxwell Miller (eds), *Israelite and Judaean History* (Philadelphia: Westminster; London: SCM, 1977).

Herrmann, Siegfried, *A History of Israel in Old Testament Times.* Second revised and enlarged edition (London: SCM, 1981).

V.   Background Studies

Beyerlin, Walter (ed.), *Near Eastern Religious Texts Relating to the Old Testament* (London: SCM; Philadelphia: Westminster, 1978).

Kenyon, Kathleen M., *Archaeology in the Holy Land.* Fourth edition (London: Benn; New York: Norton, 1979).

Pritchard, James B. (ed.), *Ancient Near Eastern Texts Relating to the Old Testament.* Third edition with Supplement (Princeton, NJ: University Press, 1969).

de Vaux, Roland, *Ancient Israel. Its Life and Institutions.* Second edition (London: Darton, Longman and Todd, 1965).

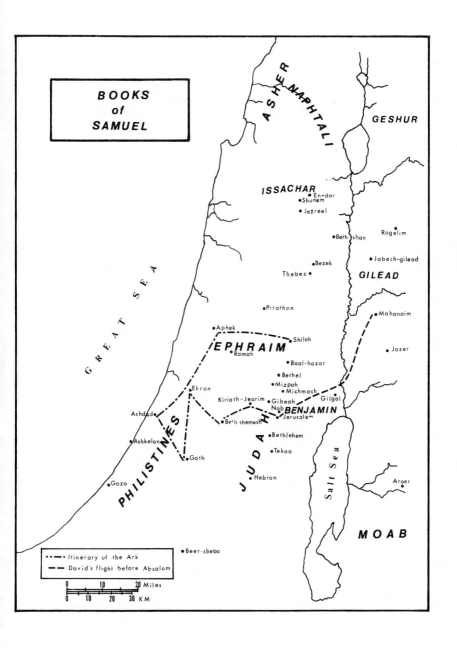

BOOKS
of
SAMUEL

ASHER

NAPHTALI

GESHUR

ISSACHAR
•En-dor
•Shunem
•Jezreel

Rogelim•

•Beth-shan

•Jabesh-gilead

•Bezek

Thebez•

GILEAD

G R E A T   S E A

•Pirathon

•Mahanaim

•Aphek

•Shiloh

EPHRAIM
•Ramah

•Jazer

•Baal-hazor

•Bethel
•Mizpah
•Michmash

Ekron•

Kiriath-Jearim•

•Gibeah
Nob•
•Jerusalem

•Gilgal

BENJAMIN

Ashdod•

•Beth-shemesh

Ashkelon•

•Bethlehem

•Tekoa

Gath•

J U D A H

Salt Sea

Gaza•

•Hebron

Aroer•

P H I L I S T I N E S

M O A B

•••• Itinerary of the Ark
— — David's flight before Absalom

0   10   20 Miles
0   10   20   30 K M

•Beer-sheba

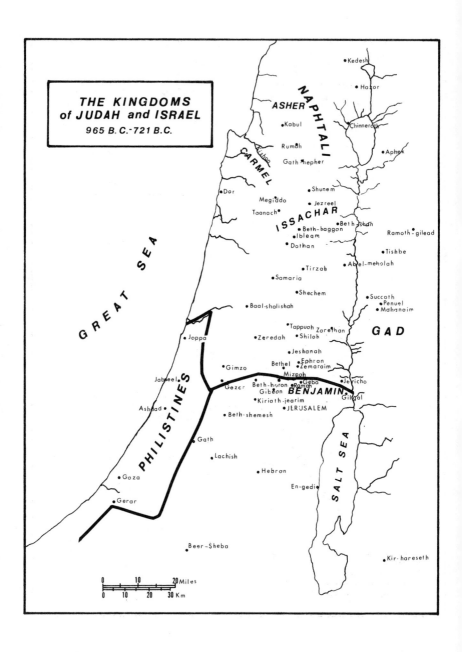

THE KINGDOMS
of JUDAH and ISRAEL
965 B.C.-721 B.C.

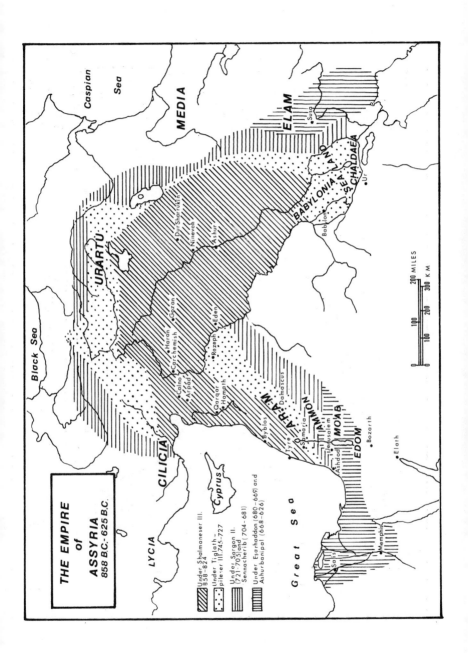

THE EMPIRE
of
ASSYRIA
858 B.C.- 625 B.C.

Under Shalmaneser III.
858-824

Under Tiglath-
pileser III.745-727

Under Sargon II.
(721-705) and
Sennacherib (704-681)

Under Esarhaddon (680-669) and
Ashurbanipal (668-626)

Black Sea

Caspian
Sea

MEDIA

ELAM

URARTU

• Susa

• Dur-Sharūkin
Nineveh
• Ashur

BABYLONIA LAND

SEA
CHALDAEA

Babylon•

• Ur

LYCIA

CILICIA

• Harān
• Gozan

Cyprus

• Carchemish
Calno •
Arpad •

• Eden

• Rezeph

Qarqar •
Hamath •

ARAM

Damascus•

AMMON

Byblos•

Samaria•
Tyre•
Jerusalem •
Ashdod•
Ashkelon

MOAB
EDOM

• Bozrah

• Elath

Great Sea

Sais•
Memphis•

200 MILES
100
0
100   200
300 K M
0
K M

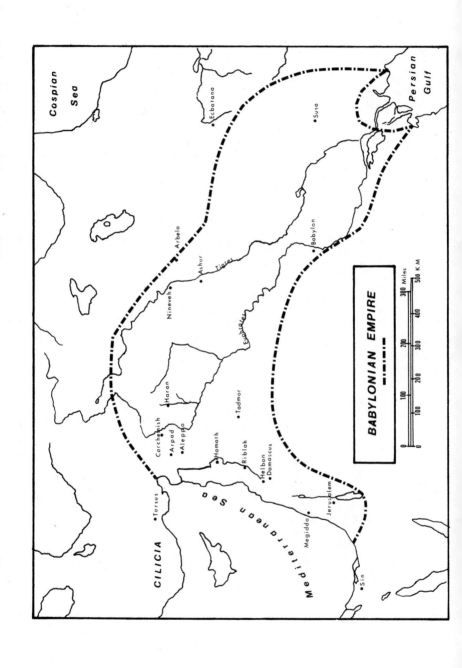